DATE DUE

SEP 2 7 2006		

GAYLORD   #3523PI   Printed in USA

No One Was Turned Away

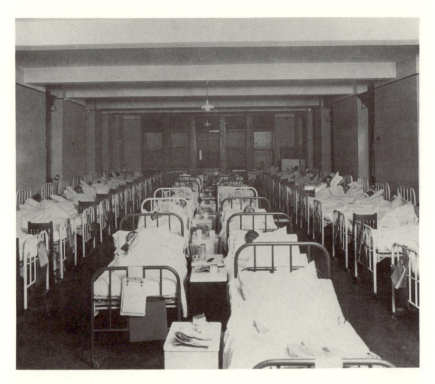

Crowded wards at Bellevue Hospital during the Great Depression of the 1930s. *Courtesy of Chest Collection, Bellevue Hospital Archives.*

No One Was Turned Away

The Role of

Public Hospitals

in New York City

since 1900

SANDRA OPDYCKE

New York   Oxford

Oxford University Press

1999

Oxford University Press

Oxford　New York

Athens　Auckland　Bangkok　Bogotá Buenos Aires　Calcutta
Cape Town　Chennai　Dar es Salaam　Delhi　Florence　Hong Kong　Istanbul
Karachi　Kuala Lumpur　Madrid　Melbourne　Mexico City　Mumbai
Nairobi　Paris　São Paulo　Singapore　Taipei　Tokyo　Toronto　Warsaw

and associated companies in
Berlin　Ibadan

Library of Congress Cataloging-in-Publication Data
Opdycke, Sandra.
No one was turned away : the role of public hospitals in
New York City since 1900 / Sandra Opdycke.
p.　cm.
Includes bibliographical references and index.
ISBN 0-19-511950-9
1. Public hospitals—New York (State)—New York—History—20th
century.　2. Hospital care—New York (State)—New York—
History—20th century.　3. Multihospital systems—New York (State)—
New York—History—20th century.　4. Public Welfare—New York
(State)—New York—History—20th century　I. Title.
RA982.N49063　1999
362.1'1'09747109049—dc21　98-3753

1 3 5 7 9 8 6 4 2

Printed in the United States of America
on acid-free paper

To Leo

Always the beautiful answer
who asks a more beautiful question.

E. E. Cummings

The public hospitals of any country may be fairly taken as a standard of a civilization.

Florence Nightingale

Acknowledgments

My interest in New York City's public hospitals grew out of my work at another kind of public facility: Hudson River Psychiatric Center. It was my experience at this state-run mental hospital that first led me to think seriously about the role of public institutions—their unique obligations and their distinctive contribution to our society. My interest in hospital workers also began during the same period, as I witnessed the hard work and dedication of Hudson River's employees. Thus, two ideas that have helped to shape this book—my belief in the value of public institutions and my regard for the contribution of hospital workers—are legacies from my years at Hudson River.

Academically, my greatest debt is to my friend and mentor, Kenneth Jackson. As my adviser at Columbia University, he played a major role in helping me develop this project from prospectus to dissertation to book. A generation of urban historians have found their inspiration in Ken, and I am proud to be one of them. I also received invaluable assistance from David Rothman, David Rosner, and Joshua Freeman, all of whom gave me valuable comments as my work progressed, while their own writing provided continual reminders of what good social history looks like. I would like to express my appreciation, too, to Herbert Gans, Alan Brinkley, and Eugene Litwack for their ideas and suggestions during the early stages of this project.

The materials for this book came from more than a dozen archives in and around New York City. These repositories are one of the city's treasures, and they deserve more support than most of them receive. Especially valuable to me was the archive at Bellevue Hospital, for which every New Yorker owes a debt of thanks to Lorinda Klein, the woman who began assembling it in the late 1980s. I would also like to express my appreciation to Adele Lerner at New York Hospital, both for her helpfulness to me and for having made her archives one of the best resources anywhere for American hospital history. Other collections that provided me with valuable assistance are the NYC Municipal Archives, the NYC Municipal Library, the libraries of the United Hospital Fund and the New York Academy of Medicine, the New York Public Library, the archives of New York University and its Medical Center as well as NYU's Robert F. Wagner Labor Archives, and Columbia University's many archival resources, including its Oral History Collection.

Because history lives in memory as well as on paper, I am most grateful to the many people who permitted me to interview them about their experiences in the world of New York City hospitals. From administrators and physicians to ward aides and labor organizers, their vivid accounts helped bring the past to life. In particular, I would like to thank Pamela Brier, Dr. Lewis Goldfrank, and Gloria Bailey at Bellevue Hospital; Paul Macielak, Dr. E. William Davis, Jr., and Dr. George Reader at New York Hospital; Dr. Saul Farber and Martin Begun at NYU Medical Center; James Tallon at the United Hospital Fund; Dr. Jeremiah Barondess at the New York Academy of Medicine; Gerard Piel; Victor Gotbaum, Lillian Roberts, and Ella Woodley at District Council 37; Barry Feinstein at the Teamsters; and Moe Foner at Local 1199.

On a more personal note, I would like to express my appreciation to Marc and Marque Miringoff, close friends and colleagues, for their indispensable counsel on the book and for the privilege of sharing in their lifetime project: social science in the interest of social justice. My editor, Thomas LeBien, has been a most valuable adviser in the revision of my manuscript. My heartfelt thanks go also to my family—my father, sister, daughters, and step-daughters—for their continuing support. Above all, I thank my dear husband, who has reviewed more drafts of this work than anyone else; who has sustained me in every possible way; and who has constantly helped me remember that we study the past not only for its own sake but to learn its lessons for today.

Poughkeepsie, New York   S.O.
1998

Contents

No One Was Turned Away

Introduction

This book is about New York City's public hospital system, which has served the city for more than two hundred years. Private hospitals have also been important to the city; indeed, their history is intertwined with that of the public system. Nevertheless, the public hospitals have been New York's true safety net, consistently accepting all who needed care, regardless of their diagnoses, their behavior, their social characteristics, or their financial status. In the 1990s, New York, like many cities, began debating whether its public hospital system should be maintained. This book explores the role that these institutions have played in the city and suggests what might be lost if they were to disappear.

Public Institutions in American Life

Understanding the contribution of the public hospital system is important, because it sheds light on a much larger topic: the role of public institutions in American life. Contemporary discourse puts such emphasis on the values of the marketplace and of individual endeavor that it is easy to forget how many of our proudest national achievements have been accomplished through government action. When there were wars to be fought, highways to be built, rivers to be spanned, diseases to be conquered, or disasters to be overcome, private efforts often lacked the scope and resources to do the job. From the

First Continental Congress to Medicare, we have repeatedly chosen to tackle our biggest challenges by working together through public institutions.

Many of our most important public institutions emerged in times of crisis. The chaos and cruelty of industrial capitalism in the late nineteenth century paved the way for the reforms of the Progressive Era. In the 1930s, the urgent problems engendered by the Great Depression led to the historic expansion of federal programs under the New Deal. Later, during the 1960s, compelling evidence of poverty and discrimination in a wealthy society generated enough political and moral pressure to establish a national structure for enforcing civil rights, as well as the funding of programs such as Head Start, Medicare, and Medicaid.

Born of crisis, these institutions lived on to become part of the political landscape, widely accepted as essential elements in the American way of life. To what do they owe their longevity? What features do they have in common that have made them valuable to our society? Four characteristics stand out: inclusiveness, continuity, responsiveness, and visibility. Public institutions have not always displayed these four characteristics with perfect consistency; nor can it be said that private institutions have never displayed them. The key distinction between the two types of institution is the level of obligation. Public institutions are *expected* to adhere to these standards, and they are routinely criticized when they fail to do so. Private institutions, by contrast, may choose to follow these principles, but they are much freer to ignore them when they find it necessary or appropriate.

The special nature of the public obligation becomes clear as we consider the first of the four characteristics: inclusiveness. Public institutions are inclusive because they are expected to serve all members of the society. Time and again, these institutions have acted as the providers of last resort, the sources of help that could be counted on when all other doors were closed. In this capacity, they have cared for the most marginalized members of society— the destitute, the homeless, the incurable, and the insane. They have also served the community as a whole, offering a range of programs that appealed to a sizable proportion of the general population. From mass transit to federal highways, from public schools to mortgage insurance, from Project Head Start to state universities, Americans have learned to count on the public sector for the most accessible, most affordable services. The hallmark of the public program is the fact that it is intended for the many rather than the few.

Public institutions are also expected to maintain continuity over time. If the need continues, so should the program. Private organizations (both profit-making and charitable) may more easily redefine their priorities according to available funding, market pressure, or institutional preference. If a private corporation finds that running a school, prison, or water system involves more expense or more problems than anticipated, it can choose to end its participation when the contract ends. Even charitable agencies have been known to close programs when the grants behind them ran out. Yet the problems remain, however the funding patterns fluctuate. Public institutions are not immune to change, but they operate under stricter obligations. Year in, year out, they are expected to continue performing their missions, whatever the vicissitudes of social or financial change.

Another important characteristic of public institutions is their responsiveness; they are uniquely obligated to respond to public input. As branches of government, they are expected to be egalitarian and accountable, operating according to the priorities of the people. Their policies are much more likely than those of private agencies to be debated in the press, their finances are a matter of public record, and their leaders must answer to the people's elected representatives. Even the many checks and balances—so often cited as a drawback of government operations—represent the special accountability that is required of public, not private, agencies. The very responsiveness of public institutions can sometimes cause problems by involving them in partisan politics or bureaucratic infighting; but it also ties them more closely to the communities they serve, ensuring that the way they function remains open to public review and debate.

Finally, public institutions offer two important kinds of visibility. First, by offering services that are open to all, they make visible the needs of the whole population. If there were no public hospitals, no public schools, no public housing, who would know how many people were being left unserved by the private sector? With their broad eligibility and low fees, public institutions make more visible the community's overall level of need. They also provide visibility in another sense. As products of the whole society, public institutions give people a concrete example of community solidarity at work. Just as a limousine with darkened windows conveys a message of separateness and exclusivity, so public libraries, buses, and parks convey the opposite idea, demonstrating the feasibility and benefits of building for common purposes. Public institutions let the community see itself functioning as a community.[1]

By providing services that include many different social groups, by pursuing their missions despite changing conditions, by responding to the demands of the community, and by ensuring that the needs of even the least valued groups are made visible, America's public institutions have exemplified a social approach that extends well beyond the provision of specific programs. They have demonstrated the importance of connectedness and a shared community life.

Public Institutions under Fire

Today, America's public institutions are in decline. Fewer people use them; fewer take pride in them; fewer are committed to their preservation. Many of them are struggling to survive. Across the United States, thousands of public institutions face financial distress and the money to resolve their problems seems difficult to find. Meanwhile, the welfare system, begun in the 1930s, is being replaced by fifty state-level experiments whose outcome no one can predict. Proposals to privatize elements of Social Security and Medicare may stabilize their funding, or they may undermine two of the nation's strongest public programs. The entire network of government services and protections built up for nearly a century appears to be in danger. Individual groups have risen to the defense of individual programs, but the overall trend seems to have aroused little focused concern.

The erosion of support for America's public institutions is part of a broader trend—a declining commitment to public life of all kinds. One way of visualizing the change is to consider a time when public life was more active. Look, for example, at a photograph of an urban downtown in 1900. The trolley tracks along Main Street tell you that the residential neighborhoods have already begun to spread outward, but one glance at the crowded downtown streets makes clear that the community still revolves around a single center. Here, people from all over the city come together, sharing the same public space. One need not romanticize the turn-of-the-century city; its social divisions were many and severe. Yet in important ways, its physical arrangements tended to minimize rather than aggravate those divisions. Making common use of the urban center kept the city's various social groups physically aware of each other, promoted at least casual exchanges, and gave the more prosperous citizens a stake in many of the same facilities that served poorer residents. Thus, the shared use of public space reinforced the message conveyed by public institutions: that being a member of the community constituted a significant and valuable identity.

Seek a vantage point for a similar urban picture today and you will find that there is no single location where a cross-section of the community can be captured in a single snapshot. In economic and technological terms, the world has never been so closely connected, but in social terms, Americans are living increasingly separate lives. Today the barriers that have divided us for many years—those of class and status, of race and ethnicity—are powerfully reinforced by spatial separation.

Look at a typical downtown area of the 1990s. The new office towers clustered there provide few services for the community at large, and none at all for the low-income residents whose neighborhoods spread out around the business district. A few core institutions remain—the hospital, the library, and the art museum—but most of their visitors arrive and depart by car, spending as little time as possible in the surrounding city. Now look outward, beyond the city limits. There lies a ring of separate municipalities, each one housing specific income levels and often specific ethnic groups, each maintaining its own government, its own police force, its own schools, its own zoning. Among these towns are landscaped office parks, where many of the suburban residents work, connected only by multilane highways. Here, too, are found the stores, banks, restaurants, and movie theaters that used to bring people downtown; now they are dispersed among dozens of shopping malls. These malls are not a replication of the old Main Street, however; visually, economically, and socially, they are far less diverse. Indeed, mall owners are free to exclude from their property any groups or activities that they deem disruptive or controversial.

Many people do not even use these protected malls as much as they used to. Instead, they take advantage of the growing number of home-based facilities—television, video, and computer, shopping by catalog and banking by mail—that make it less necessary to congregate at all in public places. Insulated within their own houses, cars, and families, Americans have less and less need, and less opportunity, to interact physically with people unlike themselves. The outside world may appear on television but it remains at arm's length, ready to be dispatched with one click of the remote-control button. One's home may indeed become one's castle, in the most literal sense imaginable. It is not that the old urban centers have been replaced by new ones—there are few centers of any kind, few physical spaces where diverse members of a large community can breathe the same air, share the same institutions, and see themselves acting like a community.

Political discourse has reinforced this retreat from public space by promoting a social philosophy that matches and justifies our spatial fragmentation. During some eras in our history, like the Depression and World War II, the importance of solidarity and mutual support was emphasized by our nation's leaders. In more recent years, these values have been overshadowed by a stress on individualism and self-sufficiency. If, as contemporary discourse suggests, each person is solely responsible for his or her own success or failure, then indeed there is little reason to think or act as a member of the larger society. Why pay taxes for public transport if you have your own car? Why worry about the homeless if you live far from where they congregate? Thus, a way of life shaped by such disparate elements as video cassette recorders and shopping malls, reinforced by a political rhetoric that stresses self-sufficiency over social solidarity, has promoted a general turning away from the pleasures and obligations of a shared public life.

If the overall sphere of public experience has been devalued in recent years, public institutions have suffered the harshest criticism of all. President Ronald Reagan used to observe that the biggest lie in the English language was: "Hi, I'm from the Federal Government and I'm here to help you." Although Reagan played an important role in popularizing this view, he was neither the first nor the last politician to seek government office while belittling government performance. Indeed, when pollsters document Americans' distrust of government, it is important to remember how enthusiastically many political leaders have seconded that distrust. Federal programs have been blamed for nearly all our nation's social ills, and many leaders suggest that personal responsibility plus a bit of local voluntarism can accomplish handily all the things that government tried to do in the past.

In such a political environment, one hears little about the many ways in which our country has benefited from public programs. For instance, thanks to the Social Security Act and its various amendments, poverty among elderly Americans is less than half what it was in 1970. Yet in a recent poll, 60 percent of the respondents expressed the opinion that poverty among the elderly had increased during these years, and that federal programs had either had little effect on the situation or had made things worse.[2] These responses suggest the average citizen's lack of information, but they also reflect the tone of the political discourse to which the citizenry has been exposed in recent decades. Few public speakers help us remember what it meant to lose one's job before unemployment insurance was available; few point to the difference that public clinics, mass transit, and subsidized housing have made to millions of working-class families. Nor do they often remind suburban homeowners that benefits like interstate highways and guaranteed mortgages are government initiatives, just like welfare. The difficulties encountered by public programs—especially those that serve the poor—have been widely noted. The historic contributions made by these programs tend to be overlooked.

Budgetary concerns have pushed this argument one step further, helping to legitimate the idea that whether or not our public institutions have been successful in the past, we can no longer afford them. Even the Democratic President William Clinton has declared that "the day of big government is over," and that assertion is echoed daily by leaders across the political spectrum. Even programs like Medicare, with articulate and active constituencies, are facing new limits, while those that serve the politically voiceless, like the welfare program, have been decimated. Since erasing government deficits has become a top priority, along with cutting taxes, the task of maintaining the nation's parks, schools, libraries, and social programs at their former levels has come to seem like a prohibitively expensive luxury.

One justification for cutting back public programs is the often expressed conviction that the private sector can do the same job more efficiently and effectively. Since the 1970s, many communities have turned to private corporations to screen welfare clients, run prisons, operate hospitals, or manage public schools. Certainly there have been examples of mismanagement in the public sector, but privatization itself has a mixed record. The evidence on cost-saving is at least ambiguous, and private entrepreneurs have often proved reluctant to sustain the inclusiveness, continuity, responsiveness, and visibility that public programs provide. Nevertheless, the advantages of privatization have been reiterated so emphatically by so many political and business leaders that they have come to be widely accepted.[3]

At this time, when public institutions are more vulnerable than ever, the fiscal pressures they are experiencing have made it even more difficult for them to prove their worth. Just when they are facing the harshest criticism, these agencies find themselves having to ration services, reduce staff, and let their facilities go unrepaired. To the extent that these changes impair quality, they encourage the idea that public programs are less good than private ones, isolating them still further. Who attends public school even when the buildings are crumbling? Who rides the buses even when service deteriorates? Who uses public clinics even when waiting-times are long and doctors few? Only the people with the fewest options. As dissatisfied clients gravitate toward private services, the public systems become still more vulnerable, having lost their most articulate and politically active constituencies—and often a sizable share of their revenue. On goes the cycle; the more that public institutions are perceived as existing only to provide second-rate service to society's outsiders, the more other citizens abandon them and the stronger that perception becomes.

During the nineteenth and twentieth centuries, generous public investment by cities, states, and the federal government built an array of public institutions in which many Americans took pride. At the end of the twentieth century, many of these same institutions are in decline. As a nation, we need to reflect on the contribution they have made to our society, and to consider whether we can afford to be without them in the future.

The Case of Public Hospitals

It is in this context that we turn to the subject of this book: the public hospital. Public hospitals are among the oldest of America's public institutions, dating back to colonial times, and they provide a vivid illustration of the patterns discussed above. Some public hospitals are administered by county or state governments; others, like New York's, are municipal facilities, run by the city. Like other public institutions, these hospitals have a tradition of serving those who need it most. Particularly in the largest U.S. cities, where the need has been most pronounced, they have played a major part in ensuring that people of all kinds and all classes received the health services they needed.

To understand the role of public medical institutions, it is necessary to consider first the overall pattern of hospital care in the United States. The majority of care is provided in private nonprofit hospitals, also called voluntary hospitals. This country has traditionally acknowledged the charitable role of its voluntary hospitals by according them certain privileges not available to profit-making organizations. For example, voluntary hospitals have benefited from both private philanthropy and public grants; they have been exempted from taxation; and for many years they were legally protected both against being sued and against having to engage in collective bargaining with their workers. At the same time, the voluntaries' charitable status has established an expectation—indeed, a legal requirement—of community service.

Pointing to their community-service tradition, leaders of voluntary hospitals have sometimes suggested that their facilities offered all the social benefits of public institutions without their political drawbacks. In 1904, a trustee of New York's Presbyterian Hospital explained that such institutions were private "only in the sense that they were founded and have been supported by private benevolence" and were directed by "managers recruited by natural selection from our best citizens, and not subject, as is too often the case with municipal hospitals, to political change or popular caprice."[4] Sixty years later, another administrator reiterated the same theme, describing the voluntary hospital as "the most involuntary enterprise in its community." Emphasizing the institution's high-minded service and freedom from politics, he concluded that the voluntary hospital was the best of all possible combinations, "a public agency operating under private auspices."[5]

That view has been repeated over the years; it resonates in contemporary arguments for turning public hospitals over to private management. (It has also been brought to the fore by the fact that voluntary hospitals now face new competition from private facilities organized for profit.) Implicit in the voluntaries' argument is the idea that it does not matter whether an institution operates under public or private auspices, as long as it has charitable goals. But as demonstrated in this book, the reality is more complicated. The history presented here suggests that the type of auspices does indeed make a difference—even among charitable institutions—and that the voluntaries' private status has often set them apart in important ways from public hospitals.

Throughout U.S. history, private hospitals, both profit and nonprofit, have been granted certain freedoms unavailable to public facilities. They have not only enjoyed freedom from political intrusion, but also freedom from certain kinds of accountability, and freedom from some of the heaviest social burdens. For example, public hospitals have been required to provide unlimited access in a way that has rarely been demanded of private institutions. The outcome has often been a segmented pattern of care, with private hospitals handling the more appealing or affordable tasks, while the public hospitals were left to deal with the problems and people that the private sector did not want to tackle. Periodically, critics have condemned the duplication inherent in America's dual system of public and private care, yet its persistence in so many cities over so many years suggests that whatever its drawbacks, many groups in the community have found it useful.

That private hospitals have not met all the nation's needs is indicated by the fact that one still finds public general hospitals operating in twelve of the country's twenty largest cities, including the four largest: New York, Chicago, Los Angeles, and Houston. When the federal government granted Los Angeles $364 million in 1995 to help keep its public hospitals open, it bore testimony to the importance of a system that served almost 3 million poor residents a year and provided the majority of trauma care in its county. Los Angeles is richly provided with private medical institutions—as are New York, Chicago, and Houston—yet each continues to find a role for public as well as private medical care. Like public transportation, public schools, public housing, and a host of other tax-supported institutions, public hospitals have continued to survive because they have met social needs that private providers have been unable or unwilling to address.

If public hospitals exemplify the importance of public institutions in community life, they also provide a dramatic example of these institutions' current endangered state. Nowhere else can one see more vividly illustrated the trends described above. Like other public institutions, public hospitals have been adversely affected by the declining social and political commitment to public services. Fiscal cuts, too, have been particularly aggressive in this field. More recently, the national drive to control health costs has put public hospitals in a two-way bind. First, as more people have lost health insurance coverage, the demand for free care has increased. Second, the country's nonprofit hospitals, facing their own budget pressures, have shown new interest in treating the public's only significant pool of funded patients: those covered by Medicaid. These two intersecting trends have produced rising deficits, which hard-pressed local governments are increasingly less inclined to cover. Furthermore, as other public institutions have found, budget pressures tend to be reflected in service problems, which encourage more funded patients to seek care elsewhere, producing additional budget pressures.

Under such conditions, supporters of privatization have won a friendly hearing when they decried the existence of "two-track medicine," calling on the government to "get out of the hospital business." Appeals of this kind are well-suited to the times. In an era when public initiatives of all types are viewed with skepticism, when privatization is being offered as a panacea in many fields, it may not be difficult to persuade people that hospital care, too, can best be improved by turning it over to private managers. Yet this argument leaves a number of questions unanswered. What will happen if future policy changes make Medicaid patients less fiscally attractive than they are at present? What about patients with no funds at all—can private hospitals be counted on to provide a satisfactory level of care for them? What about the types of patients that private facilities have long excluded—even when there was adequate funding for their care—the homeless, the violent, the chronically ill? Public hospitals have always functioned as their communities' providers of last resort. Will their private successors be willing to do the same?

Learning from New York City

To answer these questions, there is a rich source of information: the example of the past. For more than a century, public and private hospitals have coexisted in many American cities. During those years they developed certain consistent patterns and relationships, making clear what they valued and how they understood their respective missions. Observing how these institutions operated—separately and together—over the course of the twentieth century provides important information about what can be expected in the years ahead.

Any number of large cities could provide the focus for this story: Chicago, New Orleans, Los Angeles, and Washington, D.C., all have public hospital systems, and each has its own history. This study concentrates on New York City, however, for two reasons. First, many of the things that happened in New York reflect, in intensified form, patterns found elsewhere in the country. As in other communities, hospitals in New York grew more elaborate and more technologically sophisticated during the twentieth century; administratively, they developed close relationships with medical schools; financially, they became increasingly dependent on health insurance payments and on Medicare and Medicaid. Moreover, the balance of power and responsibilities between New York's public and private hospitals paralleled, to some extent, the experience of many other large U.S. cities. In those respects, New York is rewarding to study because it displays in high relief the experiences of many other cities. In New York, as Mayor Seth Low observed, "tendencies that exist everywhere are to be found in their most extreme development."[6]

The second and even more important reason for studying New York is that nowhere else in the United States does there exist a public hospital system of such scope and generosity. This huge network is the product of one exceptional community and its openhanded investment in health care for more than two centuries. The history of New York's public hospitals is not simply a story of medicine and health-care financing. These are municipal institutions, part of city government, and their story is the story of the city—of the various social groups who lived there, the rise and fall of the local economy, the shifting patterns of employment, the way various urban neighborhoods developed, the way views on poverty have changed, the succession of mayors in City Hall, how the labor movement evolved, and how New Yorkers' ideas about their public institutions have altered over time.

Each generation of New Yorkers has played its own part in defining the relationship between public and private medical care in the city. The answers that emerged were shaped disproportionately by people with economic, political, or institutional power: mayors and legislators, hospital directors and medical school deans, physicians and bankers, trustees and donors—most of them male, most of them white. But less eminent New Yorkers also helped to influence events: the immigrant woman choosing whether to have her baby delivered in a hospital, the factory worker considering whether to buy health insurance, the hospital aide deciding whether to risk joining a union, the emergency room intern making it easy or difficult for a patient to be admitted, the Medicare recipient weighing whether to go to a public hospital or a private one. The hospital network we see today is the product of a million such choices, conscious and unconscious, by succeeding generations of New Yorkers, each expressing the priorities of its own era yet operating within a framework established by those who went before.

The development of public hospitals in New York recapitulates in many respects the experience of other American cities. The precise pattern of events that unfolded here, however, was the product of a particular social context, and that context was New York. In tracing the development of New York's municipal hospitals, we see the potential for public medical care at its fullest, and the contrast between public care and private at its purest.

To explore this subject as specifically and vividly as possible, this book concentrates on one of the most famous public medical institutions in the country: Bellevue Hospital. This facility, with more than 1,200 beds, is one of the largest hospitals in New York City and the biggest in the municipal system. It is also America's oldest public hospital, tracing its ancestry to the Almshouse infirmary that opened in 1736. Bellevue's history has included landmark innovations, scandalous abuse, superb treatment, corruption and graft, Nobel Prize–winning research, demoralizing shortages, and heroic emergency medicine. For many Americans, Bellevue symbolizes the very best and the very worst that a public hospital can offer.

Bellevue's story, although compelling, cannot be studied in isolation. Only by looking at both public and private hospitals together can we begin to understand how New York's public system functioned in each era, who benefited, and how responsibilities and resources were divided between public and private institutions. Public and private hospitals in the city have often acted separately—and sometimes in opposition to each other—but they have always been part of a single system, whether that fact was acknowledged or not. Each group of hospitals developed the way it did partly because the other group was there, shaping by its very presence the available choices and resources.

To provide a parallel in the private sector that will illuminate Bellevue's history, a leading voluntary institution was selected: New York Hospital. About the same size as Bellevue, New York Hospital faces the same East River in Manhattan, only forty blocks to Bellevue's north. New York Hospital has been the beneficiary of wealthy sponsorship ever since it first opened its doors in 1791. It has achieved recognition as one of the nation's leading teaching hospitals, but it has also sometimes been criticized for failing to respond adequately to the needs of the poor. As a top-rated voluntary teaching hospital, it makes an illuminating contrast to Bellevue, providing a good example of what public and private hospitals have in common and how they differ.

Bellevue and New York Hospital are both distinguished for their size, their eminence, and their histories. They are no more typical hospitals than New York is a typical city, but together they represent two great traditions in urban medical care: the public hospital of last resort and the private academic medical center. Exploring their shared histories provides a useful means of studying the history of hospital care in New York City, of exploring the environment within which the public system operated and, consequently, the distinctive nature of the public contribution.

A century ago, both Bellevue and New York Hospital were much smaller and less complicated institutions than they are today, providing few services that could not have been provided as efficiently (and often more safely) at home. The great majority of their patients were poor, being treated without charge. Most of the attending physicians volunteered their time, and nursing students provided most of the daily patient care in exchange for a tiny monthly stipend. The two hospitals took in relatively little money each year, spent relatively little, and owned very little technical equipment.

Today both hospitals have grown into huge medical complexes, providing highly sophisticated care in buildings filled with large salaried staffs and elaborate machinery, at a cost of hundreds of millions of dollars per year. Despite these similarities, however, Bellevue and New York Hospital stand much farther apart today than they did at the beginning of the century. New York Hospital is famous for its elegant architecture, fashionable private patients, and high-level medical research; Bellevue has become the very symbol of the beleaguered city hospital. They are still two of the city's best-known medical institutions, but the contrast between them is great.

Changes Over Time

Following Bellevue through the years will clarify the extent to which this hospital has exemplified the four characteristics that were identified earlier with public institutions: inclusiveness, continuity, responsiveness, and visibility. Tracing New York Hospital's parallel history will further illuminate the story, by making clear how Bellevue's experience compares to that of a leading private hospital during the same years in the same city. Chapter 1 sets the stage, by describing the considerable common ground that existed between New York's public and private hospitals at the beginning of the twentieth century. At that time, almost all those facilities existed primarily to serve the poor, and they did so with relatively little use of modern medical techniques. Soon, however, as chapter 2 explains, the missions of public and private hospitals began to diverge. Starting around 1910, leading private facilities like New York Hospital began to redefine themselves as scientific institutions, placing new emphasis on research and education, cutting back on their provision of charity care, and reaching out to more prosperous citizens. Bellevue and the other public hospitals were also striving to become more scientific, but both law and tradition compelled them to place their primary emphasis on ensuring that care would remain available to all. The changes in hospital care between 1910 and 1930 gave new force to the idea that inclusiveness was primarily the obligation of the public, not the private, system.

The unequal division of labor that emerged between public and private hospitals is further explored in chapter 3, which focuses on the public hospitals' second unique obligation, to maintain continuity of care in troubled times. Throughout the darkest days of the Depression and in the surge of demand following World War II, New York City's private hospitals served as many charity patients as they felt they could, but only public institutions like Bellevue were expected to take in every New Yorker who applied to them for help. During these years, what had long existed as a tendency became accepted as policy. Private hospitals would serve the community to the extent they felt able, but the primary responsibility for maintaining continuity of care through good times and bad would be borne by the public system.

Chapters 4 and 5, which deal with the 1950s and 1960s, broaden the analysis to explore a third way in which the public system carried an unequal burden: its obligation to respond to pressures from the community. During these years, Bellevue was obliged to balance the competing demands of medical schools, city officials, business interests, labor unions, state investigators, the press, federal agencies, and a host of others. Meanwhile, private hospitals were respected as community institutions yet left relatively free to choose their own priorities. The limitations of this policy can be seen in the city's experience with two initiatives launched between 1965 and 1970: Medicare/Medicaid and the Health & Hospitals Corporation (HHC). Private hospitals were receiving millions of public dollars, yet neither initiative was designed to hold them accountable for these funds by requiring them to tailor their services to public priorities, as the municipal hospitals had always done. Largely because of this fact, neither Medicare/Medicaid nor HHC did as much as had been hoped to achieve a uniform level of health care for all New Yorkers.

Chapter 6 describes the challenges faced by the public system during the final decades of the twentieth century. Until then, the principal agenda of nearly all health-care reform efforts had been to make the unquestioned benefits of medical care available to greater numbers of people. But attitudes began to change in the 1970s, forcing hospital leaders to rethink how they organized, how they financed, and how they conceptualized their institutions. At the same time, a growing skepticism toward social programs further eroded support for charity medicine. In this climate, the fourth characteristic of public hospitals played a vital role: their capacity to make visible the needs that were being left unmet by the private sector—needs that might have disappeared from view if public services were not available. Despite the importance of this contribution, however, fiscal constraints, rising health costs, and a more conservative political atmosphere led city leaders to begin questioning whether New York could still afford—or even needed—its public hospitals. In the mid-1990s a hand-picked mayoral panel recommended that the whole system be dismantled.

Through the years, various observers had suggested that the only way to provide equal care for all New Yorkers was to turn the public system over to private management. Yet until the 1990s, the idea had never won wide support. In truth, for more than a century, the system served many interests just as it was. For private hospitals like New York Hospital, the public institutions represented a set of facilities to which unwanted patients could always be sent; for city employees, the public hospitals meant jobs; for union officials, they meant members; for medical schools, they meant expanded access to teaching patients; for local politicians, they meant economic activity and medical care in underserved neighborhoods. Most important, for the poor and the uninsured, the city hospitals meant that care was available at all times and under all circumstances, no matter how institutional goals or teaching needs or funding policies changed.

These points remain compelling considerations. As the history of the past hundred years is reviewed, it is important to recognize the vital part that such concerns have played in keeping the city's public hospital system alive. It is also important to consider whether any other set of institutions is prepared to do for New York City in the future what its public hospitals have done in the past.

1

New Century, New Start
1900–1910

On an April day in 1904, Dr. John Brannan promised that the greatest hospital in the world would soon be erected in New York City. With those words he unveiled the plans for a majestic rebuilding of Bellevue Hospital, the oldest public hospital in America. Brannan spoke as board president of Bellevue & Allied Hospitals, a city department that had recently been established to oversee the four municipal hospitals in Manhattan and the Bronx. Soon after the new trustees took charge, they had determined that Bellevue, the flagship of the city system, would have to be completely rebuilt. The hospital's patients were nearly all poor or working-class New Yorkers, but Brannan and his colleagues were committed to erecting a first-class facility for their care. The plans were finished in 1904, and Brannan announced them with pride. The new Bellevue would be a vast project. It would take ten years and $11 million to build, it would cover three city blocks when it was completed, and it would house some 3,000 patients.[1]

These plans demonstrated the trustees' confidence in Bellevue's vitality and in the willingness of New Yorkers to support the hospital. At the same time, they expressed the outlook of an era during which public ventures were conceived on a grand scale. As the nineteenth century turned into the twentieth, the residents of American cities had become accustomed to great community institutions that transformed and enhanced the lives of ordinary citizens. New Yorkers were particularly rich in this respect, thanks in part to the city's size, in part to its wealth, and in part to a conviction shared by its leaders that such enterprises would enhance both New York's image and its economy. This expansive philosophy had led in 1898 to the creation of Greater New York, which extended the city's boundaries to incorporate Brooklyn, Queens, and Staten Island. Some of the new institutions established during this period were begun through private initiative, whereas others were municipal projects, but all were characterized by sweeping vision, generous public support, and wide general use. The public libraries, the Brooklyn Bridge, the subways and elevated lines, museums, zoos, Grand Central Terminal, the parks, and the magnificent water system—each of these stood as an expression of urban vitality and resourcefulness, affirming the value of membership in the broad community of New York City.

In this expansive environment, Bellevue Hospital's plans represented more than a construction project. To the trustees the new facility would be living proof—like the waterworks or the parks—that the city was wealthy enough, generous enough, and farsighted enough to care handsomely for its citizens. When Brannan made his announcement, he did not say simply that the new Bellevue would stand out among *public* hospitals; he said flatly that it would be the best hospital in the world.

A few years after Brannan announced the plans for Bellevue, another hospital also made a bold decision about its future. In this case the institution was a private one—New York Hospital. Although the hospital had been administered since its founding by a small circle of wealthy and socially prominent men, it served mainly the poor, just as Bellevue did. In 1877, New York Hospital had erected a new facility on West 15th Street between Fifth and Sixth Avenues. Now its board of governors decided to move again and to construct a new and much larger building. "The City of New York is growing," proclaimed the board president, "and the standards both of medical science and charitable endeavor are higher every day. The New York Hospital cannot stand still."[2]

Bellevue and New York Hospital had different histories and different resources but they served similar patient groups, and their trustees shared similar aspirations: both were convinced that they could build their facilities into top-ranking institutions—hospitals that would provide medical care worthy of the new century, while bringing credit to the men who led them and to New York City itself.

The Nineteenth-Century Legacy

It is appropriate that this story of New York City hospitals should begin with Bellevue and New York Hospital, since the city's hospital care itself began with these two institutions. Supporters of Bellevue and New York Hospital sometimes dispute which is the oldest, but everyone agrees that together they predate all others in the city; indeed, they are among the oldest hospitals in the United States.[3]

Bellevue Hospital's institutional ancestor, the city Almshouse, opened in

1736 where Broadway intersects Park Row, now the site of City Hall. Like most communities of the period, New York used cash allowances to help the poor stay in their own homes whenever possible, so the inmates of the Almshouse tended to be the people least able to care for themselves—orphans, old people, the insane, the blind, the disabled, and the sick. Thus ill health became one important reason for poor people to be admitted, and from the start, a six-bed infirmary was maintained in an upstairs room of the Almshouse. In 1796, to make room for the present City Hall, the whole complex was moved to nearby Chambers Street. In 1816, the Almshouse moved again, to new buildings erected on a site about two miles north in the countryside, where 27th Street meets the East River. (This property, the former Bellevue Farm, had for many years held the municipal fever hospital.) The new Almshouse complex came to be called the Bellevue Establishment. Over the next quarter-century the able-bodied poor, the aging, the disabled, the orphans, and the insane were gradually transferred to other institutions. What remained on 27th Street was the medical facility, by then called Bellevue Hospital.[4]

New York Hospital, like Bellevue, began in the eighteenth century. The original call to establish the facility came in 1769, at the first commencement of the oldest medical school in New York City, then part of King's College (now Columbia University). On this occasion a rising young physician, Samuel Bard, urged that a hospital be founded, both to care for the sick and to help train young doctors. A charter was obtained from King George III in 1771, and the Colonial Assembly promised to fund the project for twenty years. Then numerous delays developed—most notably the Revolutionary War. Finally in 1791, New York Hospital officially opened its doors. The new hospital was a handsome structure set amid shaded lawns on the northern outskirts of town. It stood on Broadway between what are now Duane and Worth Streets, not far from the original site of the Almshouse.[5] The facility remained there nearly eighty years, but it was gradually engulfed by the northward expansion of the city's business district. Seeking a more peaceful location (plus the income to be earned by leasing the now valuable downtown property to a commercial tenant), New York Hospital moved northward in 1877 to a new building on 15th Street, just west of Fifth Avenue.

A Growing Network to Serve the Poor

Dozens more hospitals joined Bellevue and New York Hospital during the nineteenth century, some organized by religious groups, some by ethnic associations, and others by individual philanthropists. This movement was part of a wider effort to improve conditions among the urban poor. As an expanding capitalism transformed the economy, as expanding industrialization transformed the workplace, and as increasing numbers of rural and foreign migrants crowded into the nation's cities, urban slums began to develop that looked uncomfortably like those in industrial Europe. This trend troubled many middle-class Americans, who began to see urban poverty as a moral challenge and, perhaps a social threat as well. Poverty was not new to American society, but class divisions were becoming more visible, especially in cities like New York, where they were reinforced by ethnic differences. A poor and hungry working class could become a dangerous class as well. As the New York reformer Charles Loring Brace observed: "The neglect of the poor, and tempted, and criminal, is fearfully repaid."[6] Partly from humanity, partly from fear, middle-class reformers devoted new attention to urban poverty.

Some reformers focused only on the moral failings of the poor, but many also became interested in improving the conditions of their lives, particularly their health. The city needed a strong and productive working class; furthermore, epidemics could spread from the slums to other neighborhoods. New public health programs were established, and so were hospitals. Many of the new hospitals were tiny—sometimes just ten or twelve beds in a rented house—but larger institutions opened as well, including virtually every leading private hospital of present-day New York. Mount Sinai was founded in 1855 by leaders of the German Jewish community, and was originally called the Jews' Hospital. Saint Luke's Hospital, established by Episcopalians, admitted its first patient in 1858. German doctors organized German Hospital (now Lenox Hill) in 1868, while private philanthropists founded Roosevelt Hospital in 1871 and Presbyterian Hospital in 1872.

Reflecting the Protestantism of the city's dominant class, many of the new hospitals included a strong dose of evangelism with their medical services. Even a public institution like Bellevue was described as making "ample provision . . . for bringing [its patients] under the benign influence of the precepts of Christianity."[7] Since the people who dominated such activities tended to define Christianity as Protestantism, both Jewish and Roman Catholic groups began establishing their own institutions in which their coreligionists could be treated without such evangelistic pressure. These facilities—hospitals like Mount Sinai, Beth Israel, and Saint Vincent's—also provided professional opportunities for Jewish and Roman Catholic physicians, who were generally excluded from the staffs at Protestant-dominated hospitals.

Public hospitals were being erected as well as private ones. In 1847, a city guidebook noted that, while the endowments of New York's private hospitals might not yet equal those in some other cities, the scale of the city's investment in public medical care was "unsurpassed."[8] Kings County Hospital emerged (like Bellevue) from an almshouse infirmary that was orginally supported by the then-independent city of Brooklyn. Harlem Hospital began as a tiny way station on a dock at East 120th Street, built to accommodate patients awaiting ferry transport to the specialized facilities on Blackwell's Island (later Welfare Island, now Roosevelt Island). As neighborhoods grew up nearby, both Kings County Hospital and Harlem Hospital began to serve the general population. The prison infirmary on Blackwell's Island evolved into Charity Hospital (later City Hospital, now relocated as Elmhurst Hospital in Queens); this facility specialized in long-term care—a service offered by few private institutions. Over the course of the nineteenth century, more than a dozen more municipal facilities opened, many of them designed to serve the types of patients that the private hospitals found difficult or unrewarding to treat: alcoholics, the paralyzed, the insane, the retarded, and those with tuberculosis or other contagious diseases.

Besides diagnoses, assumptions about character helped steer some patients toward the public system. Like many charitable managers, trustees of private hospitals preferred patients who were clean, sober, and industrious—the group that contemporaries sometimes described as the "worthy" poor. The trustees were convinced that many people were poor simply because of their disorderly lives; giving free care to dissolute citizens, they reasoned, would only encourage their profligacy. As *Charities Review* explained: "Medical advice is as much a commodity as bread, and to give the one or the other to the unworthy is wrong."[9] To guard against exploitation by the unworthy, some hospital trustees personally reviewed each applicant for admission; others required letters of reference. Solid citizens like disabled artisans and genteel widows were usually accepted, while shady characters like tramps, prostitutes, and unwed mothers were passed on to the public hospitals. These institutions were also used by many respectable poor people, for reasons of convenience or familiarity or because the closest private hospital was full. Public hospitals nevertheless acquired a special responsibility for New Yorkers classed as unworthy.

If the wrong diagnosis or the wrong social characteristics might lead a patient to be excluded from a private hospital, poverty generally did not. Throughout the nineteenth century, both public and private hospitals served mainly the poor. Although Saint Vincent's Hospital (established by the Sisters of Charity in 1850) became one of the first hospitals in the city to open a few rooms for ailing travelers who could pay for their care, private patients remained a minority at nearly all hospitals until the twentieth century. As late as 1899, New York Hospital had only six private rooms. The rest of its 200-odd beds, as in most hospitals, were in large charity wards that accommodated twenty-five to thirty people each.[10]

Being a patient could impose costs other than money—pain, discomfort, shame, and loneliness—but however distasteful hospitalization was, thousands of New Yorkers had no alternative when they were in trouble. Some were destitute; many more fell into the category that labor leader Ira Seward described in 1873 as "the great middle class," people who subsisted on their earnings most of the time but lived always "within a very few days of want, if through sickness, or other misfortune, employment suddenly stops."[11] In an era with no sick pay, no disability benefits, and no health insurance, a day without work was a day without pay. Moreover, many poor New Yorkers lived in crowded, unsanitary tenements. Some had no family members who were free to care for them; others were alone in the city. For such people hospitals offered one indispensable service: the provision of food, warmth, and shelter when they were sick or injured.

The care provided by New York hospitals before the twentieth century served a valuable social function, but it was barely medical in character. During this period a doctor could do little for a patient in a hospital that could not be done as efficiently and often more comfortably elsewhere. Even anesthesia was so rudimentary that it could be provided in a brownstone parlor as well as in a hospital operating room. Moreover, since antisepsis was not widely practiced until late in the nineteenth century, care in a hospital—particularly surgery—often involved higher risks of infection than well-managed home care. When New York Hospital moved to its new building in 1877, its proudest boast was that in the new facility surgery would be " as safe as in the most luxurious home."[12] In general, sick New Yorkers entered a hospital during this period expecting to find not expert medical treatment but care and sustenance. One can understand why a later critic would dismiss the typical nineteenth-century hospital as a "poorhouse with a medical flavor."[13]

Whatever its limitations, New York's entire network of hospitals was exemplary in comparison to those of other cities. Particularly remarkable was the municipal hospital system, which took its modern shape in 1898, when the outer boroughs' public medical institutions were incorporated into the municipal system. Many American cities had no public hospitals, and even the largest cities usually had only one or two. New York now had sixteen, including seven general hospitals and nine special facilities (see Table 1.1).

As for private care, one partial listing drawn up in the 1920s showed that more than 100 private hospitals had been founded in New York between 1870 and 1910.[14] As shown in Table 1.1, only about 80 of these voluntary facilities

Table 1.1. Hospitals in New York City, 1905

	Municipal	Voluntary[1]	Total
General			
Manhattan and the Bronx[2]	6	23	29
Brooklyn and Queens	1	16	17
Staten Island		2	2
Total	7	41	48
Special			
Manhattan and the Bronx[2]	8	30	38
Brooklyn and Queens	1	10	11
Staten Island	0	0	0
Total	9	40	49
TOTAL	16	81	97

Source: *New York Charities Directory*, 15th ed. (New York: Charity Organization Society, 1905).

[1]Private not-for-profit.

[2]Includes facilities on East River islands.

survived; the recession of the 1890s was particularly difficult for the smallest neighborhood facilities, since their financial supporters often had very modest means. Nevertheless, during the nineteenth century, the total number of public and private hospitals in New York City had expanded dramatically. In 1800, the city had had only two hospitals: New York Hospital and Bellevue. By 1905, nearly fifty public and private institutions were providing general care, and about fifty more offered various kinds of specialized treatments.[15]

New York's wealth had played a part in the expansion of these hospitals; so had its strong tradition of reform; so had the bounty of jobs and contracts that swept so many public projects to approval; so had the city's assertive and politically active working class. No matter how many and varied their motives, New Yorkers had built for themselves a remarkable network of medical care.

Hospital Care and Scientific Medicine

New York's rapidly expanding hospitals found a ready demand for their services; between 1890 and 1905, hospital admissions rose about one-third faster than the city's population.[16] What explains this surge in admissions?

Until recently, most historians attributed this increase in hospitalizations primarily to improvements in medical knowledge and practice.[17] For it was during this era that leading American physicians embraced a new approach to their profession, which they called "scientific medicine." During the 1860s and 1870s, the European scientists Louis Pasteur and Robert Koch succeeded in identifying for the first time the specific microscopic organisms that caused several major infectious diseases. As this body of work became generally known in the United States during the 1890s, it was seized upon by the medical profession. The timing was opportune. American physicians were then struggling to differentiate themselves from other healers, such as homeopaths, osteopaths, midwives, chiropractors, pharmacists and Christian Scientists. But substantiating their claims to higher status was difficult when most physicians began their careers with no training except an apprenticeship. Even those who attended medical school usually obtained their degrees in small proprietary (for-profit) institutions that consisted of no more than a series of lectures by one or two physicians. Wholly dependent on student fees, the proprietary schools had little incentive to screen applicants rigorously or to set high standards for graduation.

With entry to the medical profession so easy, several thousand doctors were produced every year, many of them poorly prepared, and the resulting competition forced the majority to accept fee levels that lowered the profession's status still further. Medical leaders—a number of whom were associated with the more prestigious university medical colleges—became convinced that the essential first step in raising doctors' professional status was to reduce their numbers and establish tighter controls over their quality. The reform of medical education became the arena for this campaign, and the new creed of scientific medicine provided its battle hymn.[18]

The reformers took as their guide the great German universities, which were then pioneering an approach to medicine that stressed its relationship to the physical sciences. Instead of simply attending lectures, medical students at the universities of Leipzig and Heidelberg spent much of their time in laboratory work and in direct bedside observation. For those intent on raising the prestige of American physicians, the opportunity to identify their profession with science represented a welcome change from their traditional links to the apothecary and the barber—especially in an era when the marvels of the physical sciences had begun to dazzle Americans and Europeans alike. The reformers preached the new gospel of scientific medicine widely, and in many states they helped pass licensing laws that would enforce their aspirations. Gradually, the better medical colleges (especially those affiliated with universities) lengthened their courses, introduced more laboratory work, and began requiring two years of college before admission. Meanwhile, the many proprietary schools that could not afford to meet these standards began to close down.

The case for the new "reformed" approach to medical education was most memorably articulated in the famous Flexner Report, published in 1910 on a commission for the Carnegie Fund, prompted from behind the scenes by the American Medical Association. Abraham Flexner's scorching indictment of American medical schools—particularly the proprietaries—provided a brief for the prosecution that energized and legitimated the drive for medical reform. In fact, however, the movement to restrict entrance into the profession was already well under way by the time the Flexner report appeared.[19]

Medical education reform proceeded in New York City as it did in the rest of the country. By the early years of the twentieth century, the new style of training was being offered to most medical students in the city and was at least rhetorically endorsed by most of the physicians who taught them. To what extent did this new approach translate into better medical care?

It is true that by 1900 the expanding use of antisepsis had made surgery somewhat less dangerous. In addition, advances in laboratory science had improved the physician's capacity to identify a patient's condition and to predict its course. But medicine's new capacity had a good deal more to do with diagnosis than cure. Most kinds of surgery remained quite risky, since physicians were rarely able to halt the spread of infection once it began. Perhaps the only product of the new scientific medicine that could be used to intervene in a nonsurgical ailment was diphtheria antitoxin.[20] Many of the era's most ambitious claims would come true by mid-century, but public acceptance of the hospital began well before there had been much change in medicine's ability to heal.

Even the limited capacities of the new medical technology seem not to have been fully exploited in the early twentieth century. Rhetoric is not practice, and acquiring equipment is not the same thing as using it. Born to an earlier tradition and looking back on years of practice without the aid of newfangled equipment like X-ray machines and electrocardiograms, most doctors were slow to make practical use of the new medical technology. For example, Bellevue Hospital obtained its first X-ray machine in 1903 but let several years pass before a full-time operator was hired to run it, hardly a feasible arrangement for a machine in active use. During the same period, less than 5 percent of the patients with suspected fractures treated at New York Hospital were given X-rays, and the median wait for an X-ray after admission was twenty-five days—long enough to suggest that the new machines were being used more out of curiosity than to guide diagnosis or treatment.[21]

Infection-control was also erratic. Officially, New York Hospital adopted asepsis in 1888, but a young intern who worked there and at Bellevue fifteen years later recalls that a number of physicians still refused to wear gloves when they operated; the great New York Hospital surgeon Lewis Stimson, when chided for touching an open incision with his bare hand, would explain that he was using only his sterile finger. Nor were those who followed aseptic techniques always praised; as late as 1908, the Superintendent of New York Hospital voiced exasperation over the clinical staff's "craze for the use of rubber gloves."[22]

Similar gaps between theory and practice could be found in most other areas of medicine. This was still a period when the well-regarded Flower Hospital could send a patient to Bellevue with the diagnosis of "Rheumatism and Insubordination." And as late as 1910, surgeons in Bellevue's outpatient department were being reminded to stop performing tonsillectomies without anesthesia. Bellevue's inpatient case records from this period also tend to confirm that medical changes were slow in coming. A sizable fraction of patients were given nothing but cod liver oil, and many others received little more than brandy, whisky, calomel, or mustard paste. Blood and urine tests were generally performed on admission, but there is little evidence that their results influenced treatment.[23]

Still uncomfortable with the new teachings of Koch and Pasteur, many physicians retreated to the more familiar gospel of Florence Nightingale, in which exposure to a bracing breeze counted for more than laboratory analysis. Tour Bellevue's iron balconies on the coldest winter day and you would see patients tucked up in blankets, dutifully breathing in the frosty air; one physician at the hospital boasted that he kept his pneumonia patients outdoors "when the weather was so cold that the sputum froze in their cups." The president of the New York Hospital medical board neatly summed up the kind of care one was likely to receive at most hospitals in the city when he paid tribute to "those two most important therapeutic agents, sunshine and fresh air."[24]

New Reasons for Seeking the Care of Strangers

Whatever the actual limitations of medical practice at the turn of the century, the aura of scientific medicine probably did encourage some New Yorkers to seek hospital care. But given the patchiness of its adoption and the many other changes occurring during the period, technical advances in medicine were probably not the principal reason for the increase in hospital admissions.

Social changes in New York City played a more important role in the rising use of hospitals, particularly those involving the city's increasing population of immigrants. One observer commented in 1878: "Were it not for the never-ending misfortunes of the Irish, most of the hospitals would have many empty wards."[25] Starting in the 1890s, the Irish were joined by several million Jews, Italians, and other newcomers. By 1910 foreign-born residents represented 40 percent of the city's population. These immigrants and their children provided a growing pool of patients for the city's public and private hospitals. Hovering on the edge of subsistence, many experienced all the health problems that are associated with poverty, inadequate diet, overwork, and crowded unsanitary housing. In their densely packed, ill-ventilated tenement houses, communicable diseases like tuberculosis, diphtheria, and typhus spread rapidly. Respiratory diseases of every kind flared in winter, and the new circumstances of urban life helped aggravate health problems that had been relatively minor in the Old World—problems such as diabetes and venereal disease. Recalling his childhood on the Lower East Side, Michael Gold observed: "Earth's trees, grass, flowers could not grow on my street; but the rose of syphilis bloomed by night and by day."[26]

The immigrants also encountered health hazards in their occupations. Many—especially women and children—labored at home, poring over close work in bad light and bad air for hours on end. One physician reported that during the garment industry's busy season, women typically worked nineteen hours a day, seven days a week. Conditions were scarcely better for those who worked in factories. These buildings, too, had little light and air; moreover, they were often crowded and dirty, with minimal sanitary facilities. Such workplaces posed a whole range of occupational dangers, from respiratory problems to accidents. The Triangle Shirtwaist Company won permanent notoriety in 1911 when a fire there took the lives of 146 female employees, but this workshop was hardly unusual with its locked exits, inadequate fire escapes, and profusion of flammable material.[27]

The many immigrant men who did unskilled labor faced their own health hazards on construction sites all over the city. During those years more than a dozen bridges were built; thousands of new residential and commercial buildings went up; the reservoir at Fifth Avenue and 42nd Street was replaced by The New York Public Library; some 500 houses on the west side, near Seventh Avenue and 34th Street, were pulled down to make room for Pennsylvania Station; tunnels were constructed under both the Hudson River and East River; work began on Grand Central Terminal at Park Avenue and 42nd Street and the subway system; and many of the very hospitals where those workmen would be treated were built or expanded. This surge of construction meant jobs but it also meant brutally hard work, often under dangerous conditions. As an example, in just three years of constructing the East Side IRT subway, more than a dozen workers died and hundreds were injured.[28]

As the twentieth century began, more New Yorkers than ever before found themselves seeking hospital admission. Some needed care because of sudden accidents; others were weakened by years of living and working in unhealthy conditions. The growing needs of all these people, as much as medical advances, helped to fill the beds in New York's hospitals.

During this period, reformers in New York were also campaigning for better housing and safer working conditions, but the changes came slowly and the scale of the programs adopted never equaled the scale of the problems. Moreover, in health as in many other social areas, prevention was given the lowest priority. The majority of municipal and private expenditures for health went to hospitals and outpatient services, to the diagnosis and care of physical disorders rather than to preventing them. Although this approach left relatively unchanged the unhealthy conditions under which many poor New Yorkers lived and worked, it ensured that when they were sick or injured, they would have better access to medical care than the residents of any other city in the United States.

Building for the future

Responding to the growing demand for hospital services, the leaders of Bellevue and New York Hospital embarked on plans more visionary than anything their predecessors had ever contemplated. Drawing on their experience in the century just ended and inspired by the heady promise of the one they were entering, both groups set out to transform their hospitals into great modern institutions.

Reconstructing Bellevue

During the early twentieth century, the city's leading private hospitals won growing recognition as exemplars of the modern approach to medical care. But not the public hospitals: staffing and funding in these facilities were generally inadequate and though they served many ordinary workers with ordinary ailments, they carried the stigma of also serving the patients the private hospitals excluded, a group one newspaper characterized as "the dregs of society, the semi-criminal, starving, unwelcome class."[29] In addition, since (unlike the private facilities) municipal hospitals were required to accept every patient who applied to them, the rising demand for care strained their tight budgets and aging facilities. By 1900, New York's public hospitals were in poor condition and were poorly regarded.

About that time the public system was rocked by a series of scandals, of which the most dramatic was the accusation that several Bellevue nurses had murdered a patient. Although these charges were ultimately dismissed, the highly publicized investigation revealed the hospital to be a grim and badly run institution. When a New York Times headline proclaimed: "Grand Jury Denounces Bellevue Management," it seemed to crystallize a growing sense that the municipal hospital system had become an embarrassment to the city. Something would have to be done.[30]

In response, a group of reformers led by Dr. John Brannan proposed to the City Charter Commission (which was then meeting) that the municipal hospitals be removed from city's Department of Public Charities and placed under a separate board of trustees. Brannan had a model in mind: Boston City Hospital, where he had worked during his early years. Many regarded this facility, which had been governed by an independent board since 1880, as the only public hospital in the country that was equal to or better than private institutions. Like other urban boards and commissions of the period, the Boston City Hospital board was intended to insulate the institution from patronage and graft. Brannan was convinced that New York needed something similar, "a kind of buffer between the executive and the appointing power."[31]

The members of the City Charter Commission were inclined to be responsive. Like Brannan, they were part of the city's middle- and upper-class leadership, and most of them shared his conviction that men of the proper background and outlook could manage the city better than grasping politicians. Certainly, the recent past had provided rich examples of incompetence and self-seeking among the hospitals' existing managers. At first, Brannan and his colleagues proposed that the new board should administer the whole public system. When the commission shrank from so sweeping a change, the idea of removing just Bellevue was explored, but it soon became clear that the plan would have to include the three small hospitals that served as Bellevue's feeders: Fordham in the Bronx, Harlem in Upper Manhattan, and Gouverneur on the Lower East Side. That would leave three general hospitals in New York's Department of Public Charities: City and Metropolitan on Blackwell's Island; and Kings County in Brooklyn. This arrangement was accepted, and in 1902 the four municipal hospitals in Manhattan and the Bronx were established in a separate city department, called Bellevue & Allied Hospitals (B&AH).[32] Seven public-minded men were appointed to be the first trustees; among them was Brannan, who was immediately elected chair.

In line with Brannan's original idea, the new B&AH board was structured to protect the trustees against what then Mayor Seth Low described as "the baleful influence of politics."[33] The seven members received no pay for their work. The mayor chose them from a list of nominations submitted by three charitable organizations, he could not dismiss them once they had been appointed, and their terms were longer than his (seven years, compared to the then two-year mayoral term). Brannan exemplified the new model trustee: he had retired from a successful medical career, was active in several other charities, and was married to the daughter of an influential newspaper editor. He pursued his work at B&AH with passion and dedication for more than twenty years, but he did not depend on it for either his livelihood or his community standing.

The B&AH board members were not, however, quite so apolitical as their admirers claimed. Since they were wholly dependent on city approval for their funding, they would have been foolish to ignore municipal officials. In fact, Brannan devoted tireless efforts over the years to keeping a succession of mayors, comptrollers, and city Board of Estimate members informed about B&AH activities, providing them with a flood of explanatory material that must have made them sometimes wish the new regime was as indifferent to the political process as everyone said it was.

Nevertheless, the B&AH board enjoyed considerable administrative freedom, and it successfully rebuffed all requests for political favors or appointments. The Bronx borough president received a polite but noncommittal response when he interceded for a job-seeking friend; so did the city clerk. Even when the Board of Alderman's Finance Committee chairman sought a waitress position for an acquaintance (just when B&AH was seeking the committee's approval for a construction proposal), he was told the applicant would have to apply through the normal channels. When another staff member invoked political support to prevent dismissal, it appears instead to have speeded her departure. "On the whole," wrote Brannan after hearing from both her congressman and the state attorney general, "we think she had better go." As far as can be determined, these refusals produced no negative political fallout. Indeed, Bellevue obtained far more generous city support under the new board than it ever had before. Explaining their success in winning city support for the B&AH hospitals after years of neglect, Brannan had a simple explanation: "No one else asked for it as we did."[34]

Within months of taking office, the trustees decided that Bellevue must be rebuilt. Much of the hospital was still housed in the original 1816 Almshouse, a gloomy structure of brownstone and brick, seven stories high. Newer structures were clustered around and a beautiful greensward sloped down to the East River, but the forbidding central building and the high wall around the hospital complex daunted many a visitor. Physician Emily Dunning Barringer later recalled that passing through the stone archway into Bellevue's central courtyard felt like entering a medieval stronghold. The patients got clean beds and good care, she knew, "but in a place so old and dilapidated that you wondered it could still be used."[35]

The trustees made the scale of their aspirations for the new Bellevue clear when they selected their architect: Charles McKim. His firm, McKim, Mead & White, had made its name with such illustrious commissions as the Boston Public Library, Pennsylvania Station, and a recent renovation of the White House; now Bellevue was to be constructed on an equally grand scale. By 1904, the plans were complete, and Brannan presented them with pride. During the year that followed, the dome that crowned McKim's original design was sacrificed to economy, and the capacity of the projected hospital was cut from 3,000 to 2,000. Nevertheless, the plan as finally adopted remained extraordinarily ambitious, committing the city to spend $1 million per year for eight years. One by one, the old hospital buildings were to be replaced with a majestic new complex, designed from top to bottom to achieve the very latest in medical standards.[36]

Although Bellevue had a distinguished history, studded with examples of heroic service and pioneering medical achievement, it had begun as the Almshouse infirmary and in some ways it had never freed itself from that grudging tradition. Now a new public role seemed possible, quite different from that of the Almshouse, based on shared citizenship rather than demeaning charity. In breaking ground for the new Bellevue, the city leaders were doing more than initiating a construction project; they were asserting their conviction that a municipal hospital could take its place with the noblest public institutions of the day, exemplifying just as they did the inclusiveness and expansive optimism of urban life at its best.

A New Home for New York Hospital

Like Brannan and his fellow board members, the trustees of New York Hospital dreamed of a grander future for their own institution. The main hospital building on 15th Street was a handsome structure of stone and brick, but it was now entering its fourth decade and held only ten wards. Administrative offices and a variety of other services had to be housed in a separate building behind the hospital, while employees' living quarters were squeezed into rowhouses up and down 16th Street. A physician who trained at New York Hospital during these years recalled the main structure as "a nice old building" that was practical "in a clumsy way," but neither its arrangements nor its capacity accorded with the Governor's aspirations.[37]

The trustees of New York Hospital had a second reason for wanting to move: the lack of "sufficient light, air, and sunshine" at the present location.[38] This consideration was absolutely central to hospital design of the period; in an era when infection was a constant threat, medical leaders had an almost mystical faith in the power of breezes and sunshine. Most nineteenth-century hospitals had achieved the desired openness by adopting the "pavilion plan"—a sprawling complex of separate or minimally attached one-story buildings. New York Hospital's 1877 building had been designed according to similar principles, though its "stacked" design allowed for a structure several stories high. Architecture alone could not guarantee a wholesome environment, however; the quality of the surroundings was another crucial factor. By the early years of the twentieth century, the brownstone rowhouses west of New York Hospital were beginning to give way to factories, which generated the kind of noise and dirt that the hospital had moved uptown to avoid in 1877. The nearby garment district, just to the south of the hospital, was expanding, and neighborhood merchants had already begun to move north up Fifth Avenue to outdistance it. As every expert knew, an industrializing district was no place for a hospital; it was time for New York Hospital to seek another location.

New York Hospital's changing neighborhood provided economic as well as environmental reasons for moving. As the city grew northward up Manhattan Island, the land in its path rose in value, making expansion all the more costly and the sale of hospital property all the more profitable. These considerations had encouraged Mount Sinai Hospital, for example, to move from West 24th Street to East 60th Street and then to East 100th Street; six other Manhattan hospitals also relocated farther uptown between 1892 and 1910.

The pressure for such moves came not only from supporters of the hospitals but also sometimes from business interests eager to use the land. Indeed, one of the factors influencing New York Hospital to abandon its first site near the present-day City Hall, according to an early historian, was the fact that some patrons withheld their gifts "through a determination to force the Governors to lease or sell the valuable grounds around the Hospital."[39] Now the need for more space, combined with environmental and economic considerations, was impelling New York Hospital to move again.

In 1909, a board committee recommended that New York Hospital move to White Plains in Westchester County, as their psychiatric facility (Bloomingdale) had done a decade earlier. The committee acknowledged that the Society of The New York Hospital had taken pride in serving the city for more than a century, but relocating in Manhattan would be so costly that the organization would have to pursue one of two unthinkable alternatives: selling off part of its endowment or borrowing money. Far better, the committee argued, to save money for the next ten years or so and then build on inexpensive land in White Plains.

This recommendation was very much in line with the board's previous thinking, and under other circumstances it might well have been adopted. But a Supplemental Report from three men on the committee turned the tables. Defining the moment as "a crisis in the history of the hospital" and reframing the question in terms of the institution's mission instead of its balance sheet, the dissenters insisted that to live up to its historic charter, New York Hospital must construct a "complete modern metropolitan hospital" in Manhattan. Furthermore, the move should be made within the next two or three years. "No large charitable, educational or religious enterprise, like the building of a hospital, a university, or a cathedral, ever has been carried through by waiting until all the necessary funds have been secured. A visible beginning must be made, the imagination and pride of the community must be touched." Nearly a year of doubts and discussion followed, but the trumpet-call sounded by the Supplemental Report prevailed. In the winter of 1910, New York Hospital's board of governors voted to seek a new site in Manhattan.[40]

As with the case of Bellevue, a decision that seemed to deal only with construction had, in fact, much broader implications. Proudly self-sufficient, New York Hospital had run for years on the healthy income from the society's various land-holdings in the city and the handsome gifts and legacies of a small circle of members. Unlike most voluntary hospitals, it had never applied for the subsidies that the city government made available to charitable institutions, because it feared that public support might lead to public interference. Now that new funds would be needed, public money might have to be accepted. A staff member was assigned to consult with other hospitals already in the city program. His report was reassuring; the city's annual inspections produced "no annoyance," and the Finance Department's audits were unlikely to be troublesome since "there are few examiners and many institutions."[41] Thus—and not for the last time—New York Hospital learned that it would be possible to benefit from public money without being subject to close public scrutiny or control.

Bolstered by these reassurances, the board voted to proceed. Unlike Bellevue, New York Hospital had the option of leaving the city altogether, and that choice could still be made if difficulties developed. Yet, like the trustees of Bellevue, the governors of New York Hospital believed that they could build a great urban institution, and they counted on the generosity of the New York community to support them in that effort.

Hospital Life in 1910

The trustees of Bellevue and New York Hospital had grand visions in mind, but to those most directly involved, daily experience spoke louder than future possibilities. It is time to look more closely at the institutions that the trustees were so intent on expanding: how did these hospitals care for their patients? and what kinds of workplaces were they for their staffs?

In both these respects New York City's public and private hospitals had many characteristics in common. Over the course of the twentieth century, the two groups of facilities would move into separate spheres, bound by different obligations, serving different patient groups, and perceived in very different ways. This divergence developed gradually, however, as a result of changes in the city, in medicine, and in public policy. At the beginning of the century, public and private hospitals still belonged to a single network of medical institutions built to serve the city's poor. This shared mission helped define their place in urban life, giving similar meanings to their relationships with both their patients and their employees.

Being a Patient

Imagine that you are walking west on 23rd Street in New York City on a late winter afternoon in 1910. The wind is blowing, snow clogs the streets, and the streetlights shine feebly through the growing darkness. When you reach the corner, the intersection is snarled with horse-drawn carriages and wagons. You start to cross the street, picking your way among the stalled vehicles. Suddenly there is a clatter of hooves, a driver's shout, and you are knocked to the ground. Foggily you hear someone call a policeman and soon an ambulance comes careening around the corner; it is a shiny black horse-drawn carriage with a young doctor perched precariously on the back. You are loaded onto a stretcher and then onto the floor of the ambulance. At a shout from the driver the horse leaps forward and you are rushed away through the darkening city streets to the hospital.

But which hospital? During the first decades of the twentieth century, responsibility for ambulance service in this part of Manhattan was divided between Bellevue and New York Hospital, with Fifth Avenue as the boundary between them. If your westward progress had taken you past Fifth Avenue, the ambulance that picked you up would come from New York Hospital; if you were still east of Fifth, you would ultimately find yourself at Bellevue.

Even before reaching your destination, you would have benefited from one of Bellevue's great innovations: the ambulance itself. In 1869, a physician at the hospital named Robert Dalton, a veteran of the Civil War, became convinced that he could save lives if he could duplicate the swift transport that he had organized for wounded soldiers on the battlefield. Rigging up a horse-drawn carriage with removable floor-slats to serve as a stretcher, he created Bellevue's—and the world's—first hospital ambulance. The idea spread rapidly across the United States and to the major cities of Europe. By 1900, every major hospital in New York had at least one of the new vehicles; a guidebook written around the turn of the century includes a thrilling description of the "startling and imperative" gong of the ambulance, "dead black as to color, swift and furious as to progress."[42]

Suppose the ambulance headed toward Bellevue. Rattling along 27th Street, many a frightened patient must have felt that the carriage was headed straight for the East River. But halfway down the last block it would swerve to the left and rush through the arched gateway into a cobbled courtyard. There stood Bellevue's central building, the old stone Almshouse, now nearly a century old, with its balconied wings reaching out on both sides to enclose the courtyard. Up the stone steps the patient would be carried. Inside the front door was the small admitting office, flanked by long corridors stretching out in both directions, their wooden floors worn down by generations of footsteps. The whole place exuded what generations of visitors had come to recognize as the "Bellevue smell," a mixture of carbolic, soapsuds, dust, and musty wood.[43]

Bellevue did not yet have an emergency room, so new patients were taken directly upstairs. Up, up in the creaking elevator, down the high-ceilinged corridor, and then through a tall door into the heart of life at Bellevue: the ward. There it stood, a long open room with big windows all around. Along each of the two side walls ran a line of iron bedsteads, fifteen or twenty to a side. In the center of the ward was an open area which in summer would be set up like a living room, with chairs and tables for visitors; some wards even kept potted plants there or a rug on the floor. During the winter these embellishments usually had to give way to extra beds, and if the crowding grew bad enough, mattresses might be squeezed in on the floor as well. Even on good days the attractions of the big sunny room had to compete with the sounds and smells of thirty or forty sick people spending their days and nights in close proximity.

Suppose the ambulance had headed for New York Hospital instead of Bellevue. The initial arrival would certainly have been less daunting. Bellevue, with more than 1,000 beds, was the biggest general hospital in New York. New York Hospital was much smaller, serving an average of just over 200 inpatients per day; and it had a newer and better-kept building than Bellevue's (see Table 1.2). Nevertheless, once one arrived on a ward the physical layout was similar, as were the furnishings. More important, life on the ward followed a similar pattern.

Table 1.2. Comparison of Bellevue and New York Hospital, 1910

	Bellevue	New York Hospital
Average daily census	1,113	206
% ward patients	100	96
% private patients	0	4
% free patients	95	74
Outpatient visits per year	110,000	66,000
Ambulance calls per year	9,592	5,237
Cost per patient day	$1.77	$2.68

Source: Annual Reports, Bellevue & Allied Hospitals and The Society of the New York Hospital; NYC Board of Estimate, *Report of the Committee on Inquiry into the Departments of Health, Charities and Bellevue & Allied Hospitals* (New York, 1913), p. 729.

At both Bellevue and New York Hospital, stays in 1910 often lasted many weeks. Since few patients could afford to convalesce at home without a paycheck, they usually remained until they were well enough to work again. As a result, each ward contained a wide range of patients, from people near death to others who were almost well. The sickest were placed at the near end of the ward, next to the nurse's station. At the far end slept those who could take care of themselves most of the time; these healthier patients often spent all day out of bed. As for medication, little was provided that a patient might not have received from a doting aunt. Nature could be helped along with doses of brandy and calomel, laxatives and enemas, outings on the balcony and sponge baths, but the much-heralded new techniques and equipment of scientific medicine played little part in the process.

Compared to hospitals of later years, there was little daily traffic on the ward in 1910. There were no specialized departments to which a patient needed to travel, and few specialized staff to come to them. Support workers appeared periodically to deliver meals or do heavy cleaning, but most of the ward's housekeeping was performed by the nurse, one or two orderlies, and the convalescing patients. Medical students, so ubiquitous in future years, were hardly to be seen. Hospitals around the city had begun getting pressure from local medical schools to let their students have regular access to the wards, now that clinical observation was considered an integral part of medical training. But most hospital boards resisted, because of their concern that the students' presence would trouble the patients or interfere with the institutions' primary mission of healing. No students were allowed on Bellevue's wards until 1907, and New York Hospital held out three years longer.[44]

Both Bellevue and New York Hospital did each have a corps of interns— young doctors just out of medical school—who spent considerable time on their assigned wards. A senior member of the medical staff also appeared every afternoon, making his daily rounds after a morning of house calls to his private patients. Except for these visitors, the nurse and the inmates of the ward spent much of the day alone together. Even so, ward life was by no means tranquil, as thirty or forty people lived their lives more or less in public. Every groan, sob, argument, and private function was audible and often visible to all. Patients were examined on the ward, underwent painful or embarrassing treatments there, and if they died, they died in each other's presence.

Bellevue handled an unusually varied group of patients, because it was the hub of the public system in Manhattan and the Bronx. Smaller municipal institutions referred their most difficult medical and surgical cases there, while mentally ill patients were brought in directly from all over the city. Bellevue in turn sent tuberculosis patients to various sanitoria, chronic patients to the city's long-term institutions on Blackwell's Island, and insane patients who needed more than a few weeks' care to Manhattan State Hospital on Ward's Island. Besides these special categories, the hospital treated more acute patients each year than any other institution in the city.

Bellevue was unusual for its clinical variety, but the socioeconomic status of its patients resembled that of most other large hospitals in the city, including New York Hospital. The range of occupations for one group of Bellevue patients in 1907 included the following: housewife, cook, actor, soldier, salesman, coachman, metal polisher, waiter, domestic, janitor, longshoreman, brakeman, manicurist, bricklayer, painter, and blacksmith. As *Charities* magazine observed, most Bellevue patients were not paupers, but "working men and working women who by reason of illness or injury are temporarily prevented from earning a living." Like New York Hospital, like most public and private hospitals in the city, Bellevue spent the majority of its time caring for the group described by one hospital superintendent as "the great army of unskilled workers, whose wages are too small for a really comfortable living, even when health and times are good."[45]

Middle-class New Yorkers would become intensive users of hospital care only in future decades. During this period, few of them could afford the expense of a private room, and their pride usually rebelled at being lumped with the indigent recipients of charity care on the wards. For this reason, middle-income New Yorkers used hospitals much less than the poor. As for the wealthy, many private hospitals maintained truly elegant rooms designed to attract them, but they accounted for only a small share of the average caseload.[46] It was the city's lower-class citizens, not those from the middle or upper classes, who constituted the great majority of patients in both public and private hospitals.

What set Bellevue apart from private facilities like New York Hospital most sharply was the fact that it was required to accept everyone who sought its services, while private institutions like New York Hospital could choose whom to admit. Private hospitals had often used this privilege in the nineteenth century to exclude those they judged morally unworthy. By 1910, the growing interest in treating medically interesting disorders was starting to work against that distinction; even a dissolute citizen with an unusual ailment might be judged worthy of a private hospital's treatment and study. Nevertheless, the private hospitals' continuing exclusion of patients with alcoholism, mental illness, venereal disease, and chronic illness reflected the continuing distaste for certain kinds of unworthiness, since prosperous citizens tended to associate such disorders with disreputable lives and the more degraded forms of poverty. Therefore, even in 1910, patients in these stigmatized categories were relegated almost entirely to the public system.

Dying patients, too, were often passed along to municipal institutions—sometimes on very short notice, if their conditions showed signs of deteriorating. "No hospital likes to increase its death-rate," observed a contemporary journalist, "and there is always a little feeling on this point." In this respect, patients' income did play a part in the process. While a bootblack with an interesting medical problem might be as welcome in a private hospital as a banker, a bootblack who seemed close to death was far more likely to be transferred to a public hospital. "Open your books," cried one reformer, "and show me one man of wealth who has ever been transferred!" Indeed, private hospitals tried not to admit poor patients at all if they seemed close to death. The supervising nurse at the municipal Harlem Hospital succinctly described one such case, a dying child who had been admitted there after being refused at a nearby private hospital. "The people were poor,—the child very sick. It died at 8 pm."[47]

Besides being free to choose which patients they would treat, private hospitals had another privilege not available to public institutions: when all their beds were occupied, they could close their doors to new admissions. In the municipal hospitals, the doors stood permanently open. In the winter, when respiratory diseases raged through the city, public hospital occupancy rates could exceed 100 percent for weeks at a time. In this sense, public hospitals served as a barometer for the city, reflecting in their busy corridors and crowded wards the same ebb and flow of sickness, injury, danger, and death, that was being experienced in tenements and workplaces throughout New York City.

Given the pressure on public hospitals to accept all applicants, and the fact that they served a disproportionate share of the alcoholic, insane, and chronically ill, they could not function precisely the way private ones did. Yet there were still many more similarities between the two types of hospitals than there would be in future years. Even though voluntary hospitals had begun to court the city's middle and upper classes more aggressively, even though they chose among the charity patients who applied to them, their core role at this time remained the same as Bellevue's: to care for the city's poor. As for the patients themselves, the daily routine on the ward, the staff they encountered, and the services they received were very similar, whether they were treated at Bellevue or at the most elite private hospital.

Working at the Hospital

The hospital's place in the life of the city was defined not only by the kinds of people it served but also by those who served them. Here again there was considerable similarity between Bellevue and New York Hospital in 1910. As workplaces, the sharpest contrasts were to be found not between the public and the private institution, but within the walls of each facility, ranging from the privileged level of the trustees and the volunteer physicians to the lowly status of the cleaners and kitchen help.

Men at the Top.   At both Bellevue and New York Hospital, a governing board sat at the top of the hospital hierarchy. This was standard practice for a private facility, but unusual for a public one, since most municipal departments were run by commissioners, salaried officials who served at the mayor's pleasure. But when Bellevue & Allied Hospitals was established as a city department in 1902, it was given a semiautonomous board of trustees. In general, the members of this board seem to have seen themselves, and to have been perceived by others, in the classic terms of Progressive Era reform—dedicated citizens rather than career politicians, knowledgeable but disinterested defenders of the public good. In this respect, their status was not very different from the men who served on the New York Hospital Board of Governors.

The two boards had social similarities as well. As at New York Hospital, the Bellevue trustees were all male, all white, and all reasonably well-off. Bellevue was unusual in having Jewish trustees from the start—decades before they were appointed to the boards of most non-Jewish hospitals—but even these men came from prosperous German backgrounds and had offices on Wall Street; they were not Eastern Europeans, nor did they live in the neighborhoods served by the hospital. If none of the Bellevue trustees would be called "financier" or "capitalist" in his obituary, as certain New York Hospital trustees were, they shared with these men a comfortable social position in the city and a perception of their hospital work as a kind of civic philanthropy. Neither Bellevue's trustees nor New York Hospital's were *of* the community they served, but each group was convinced of its capacity to work *for* that community in the best tradition of enlightened public service.

At least on paper, the next most significant figure in the hospital after the board of trustees was the hospital superintendent. In practice, however, the active involvement of trustees in the hospital's daily affairs left little room for independent action, and at both Bellevue and New York Hospital the superintendent operated more like an administrative assistant than like a high-ranking administrator. A physician at New York Hospital later recalled the superintendent as a relatively minor figure in the hierarchy, functioning "at a level looked down upon by everybody." Overshadowed by the trustees and often ignored by the medical staff, many hospital administrators experienced, as one put it, "almost heartbreaking strain."[48]

The members of the medical staff had far more authority in both hospitals than did the superintendents. These physicians devoted most of their time to private practice, but three or four time a year each of them spent a month doing daily rounds on the wards. They received no pay for this service, yet membership on the hospital attending staff was seen as a privilege because it offered a combination of facilities and professional connections that were increasingly difficult to find elsewhere. For a busy physician in an expanding city, there were obvious advantages to having one's patients gathered under one roof rather than scattered among a dozen neighborhoods. At the same location, moreover, one might keep in touch with one's colleagues, consult the library, lecture to a group of medical students, discharge one's charitable obligations, and—if one were so inclined—gather data or analyze specimens for a project of medical research. For the physician of 1910, far more than for his predecessor a generation earlier, the hospital had become a vital center for medical practice.[49]

At both Bellevue and New York Hospital, the least senior physicians covered the outpatient department. Only with time and the right connections could they rise to more prestigious appointments on the inpatient service. When one young physician sought to speed up his promotion to the inpatient service, the chair of the B&AH board noted that he himself had spent ten years in various hospitals' clinics before he got a ward service; this was "a common experience," he observed, and would do the young doctor good.[50] Nor was paying one's dues in the outpatient department always enough to ensure an appointment. Staff membership in each hospital came through nomination by the hospital Medical Board and often required letters of recommendation as well; thus, a highly placed friend or enemy could play a crucial part in shaping a doctor's career. This system, which was as solidly entrenched in public as in private institutions, helped ensure that, though both Bellevue and New York Hospital served Roman Catholics, Jews, and blacks, their attending staffs remained male, white, socially elevated, and predominantly Protestant until well into the twentieth century.

Despite their importance in the hospital, the physicians on the attending staff were not the principal providers of medical care. That distinction was held by the interns. By 1904, more than half the country's medical graduates were following their academic education with a hospital internship, paying for this advanced medical training with one or two years of killing hours, spartan housing, and no wages. Unpredictable in their manners, inexperienced in their work, rambunctious in their private lives, the interns provoked a steady stream of incidents and reprimands. Some of the problems they precipitated were administrative, like the floods caused each morning at New York Hospital by fourteen interns splashing boisterously in the single bathroom allotted to them. Others were personal, like the rage of the unmarried supervising nurse at Bellevue when she learned that an intern on the maternity ward had named a new illegitimate baby after her. Despite their misdemeanors, the interns were central to the provision of medical care in the early twentieth century, and no large hospital could manage without them. They had become, as *Medical News* observed, "the real staff of every hospital in the city."[51]

Nurses in the Middle.   Interns were not the only trainees on whom hospitals were learning to depend. In 1873, a group of reform-minded society women founded at Bellevue the first American nursing school to operate under the principles espoused by Florence Nightingale. Learning nursing by doing it, the young women enrolled in the new school worked on the wards twelve hours a day, six days a week, with lectures and homework squeezed into their off-duty hours. The tasks they performed were nearly the same as those performed by their untrained and much-despised predecessors—a class of women whom Nightingale had scornfully described as "too old, too weak, too drunken, too dirty, too stolid, or too bad to do anything else."[52] But the new-style training infused their work with new meaning. Cleanliness, order, and discipline took on an almost sacred significance; in the popular mind the angel of mercy rapidly replaced the drunken harridan as the archetypal nurse. Every major hospital in New York City followed Bellevue's lead; by 1910, there were more than a thousand nursing schools across the country.[53] For the price of board, lodging, and a few dollars' stipend each month, American hospitals had acquired a remarkable new work force of dedicated and enthusiastic young women.

Most nursing school graduates went into private duty, but some of the best were chosen to stay on at the hospital, and by 1910 "trained nurses" represented about one-fifth of the total nursing staff at both Bellevue and New York Hospital. Women had good reasons for choosing to be nurses. In an era of limited opportunities for working women, nursing offered a living wage, occupational status, and considerable independence. The wage was low, the status contested, and the independence restricted by the need to defer to physicians, hospital managers, and private patients. But as Barbara Melosh has observed, "few other institutions in the early twentieth century could provide young women with a comparable experience of female autonomy."[54]

One cannot explore the growth of nursing without confronting at every turn the issue of gender. Nursing leaders explicitly identified their profession with feminine virtues like orderliness, nurturance, and self-sacrifice. The healing touch, the spotless ward, the Bellevue tradition of nurses so deft they could bathe a patient without rolling up their starched cuffs—all these images helped associate nursing with traditional ideas of what women did best. When in 1906 the New York Hospital superintendent warned that his hospital's training school showed signs of evolving from "a feeble institution" into a "virile, dominant power," the gendered implications of his remarks were unmistakable.[55]

The hostility of physicians toward independent-minded female nurses was paralleled by the difficulties encountered by males when they entered this now feminized occupation. The pattern was clearly visible in Bellevue's continual problems with its school for male nurses, which opened in 1888. Perhaps the Bellevue superintendent was correct when he observed that "a much larger proportion of male nurses are rough, unkind, dishonest, addicted to the use of alcohol, or neglectful."[56] Yet Bellevue leaders continually revealed their deep-seated antipathy to the whole idea of male nurses. When the hospital decided to close the male nursing school in 1910, little was said in public; but Bellevue's internal documents make clear that the action followed a chaotic summer during which accusations of homosexuality swept the school and almost one-quarter of the students resigned or were dismissed. In retrospect, it is impossible to tell whether the accusations were true, but it is clear that the hospital's leaders were more than ready to believe them. Bellevue's head psychiatrist expressed their perspective clearly: "The average man does not select the profession of nurse unless there is something wrong with him."[57] Nursing as a profession had carved out an important place in the life of the hospital, but only within the boundaries of traditional gender roles.

Support Workers on the Bottom.   If nurses' standing in the hospital was defined by their gender, the status of support workers was defined by their class. Male or female, native-born or foreign, support workers functioned on the lowest rung of the hospital's occupational ladder. As a group they were poorly regarded, ill-paid, and ill-housed (either in staff dormitories or in whatever quarters of their own they could afford to rent). Yet these employees—orderlies, engineers, painters, clerks, cooks, maids, plumbers, electricians, laundryworkers, clerks, butchers, porters, and laborers—played a critical role in keeping New York's hospitals functioning.

Many support workers were never seen by the patient, and most have remained out of sight of historians as well, partly because they left so few written records of their experience. Only occasionally can one catch a glimpse of them at work. Dr. Emily Barringer recalls her visits to Bellevue early in the century, and through her eyes we see the long corridors, peopled by "a faithful army of scrubwomen, forever on their knees." Another visitor remembers the scrubwomen, too, "on their knees all day long with brush and pail, just scrubbing the floor over and over again." A few years later, Bellevue ambulance drivers complain to the mayor that they are required to be on call twenty-four hours a day, six days a week.[58] From New York Hospital come similar voices. In 1903, a petition from the hospital's maintenance men pleads for the resumption of free laundry service, explaining that the $3 they are being charged each month represents one-fifth of their salary. "We respect our superiors," says the petition. "We work hard, our hours are long, our position is by no means easy." Two years later a New York Hospital clerk deferentially asks the Board of governors for a raise, citing "the long hours, the Sunday work." The request is filed, neatly marked "Declined."[59]

The Bellevue trustees frequently argued that if the city would set higher wages for the hospital's support workers and improve their working conditions, a better class of employee could be recruited. But raises came rarely, and employees continued to work long hours at difficult jobs in the gloomiest corners of the hospitals' old buildings. Their only recourse was to quit, which they did in large numbers, joining many others who were fired every month. During most of the years between 1902 and 1910, Bellevue's annual staff turnover rates ran close to 150 percent. Bellevue's superintendent illuminated the facility's continuing dilemma when he described one troublesome Hospital Helper. The man had been hired, dismissed, rehired, and recently dismissed again, but he had been asked to stay on a few more days until a replacement could be found.[60]

New York Hospital was, according to one of its trustees, "by far the most extravagant hospital in New York," which "almost invariably" paid its staff more than other facilities. In fact, its wage-levels were about the same as Bellevue in most job categories.[61] In 1907, one private patient wrote to the New York Hospital Board of Governors to express his distress at having learned how little the institution's orderlies earned. He noted the hospital's "extremely prosperous condition," as described in its annual report, and its record for "noble charities." Surely, he suggested, the hospital would not wish "to dispense charity with one hand and to withhold justice with the other."[62] But not until the union movement of the 1960s would there be a systematic effort at either Bellevue or New York Hospital to win for non-medical workers the respect and financial rewards that their importance to hospital operations warranted.

Looked at level by level, considerable similarities existed between the work forces of Bellevue and New York Hospital in 1910. Bellevue employed some raffish souls who would probably not have been hired at New York Hospital, but in general the two hospitals seem to have drawn their employees from similar groups. There must have been considerable similarity between the two facilities from the workers' point of view as well. Although Bellevue's buildings were larger, older, and more crowded, the pay levels were roughly equivalent, as were the tasks performed and the hierarchical nature of hospital society; and both sets of workers shared the experience of providing relatively untechnical care to a population of predominantly poor patients, most of whom were treated without charge.

The characteristics that would distinguish Bellevue so sharply from New York Hospital in the future were plain to see by 1910. They were the core characteristics of a public institution. Bellevue was expected to show greater inclusiveness by admitting patients with every kind of disease and social behavior. It was expected to maintain continuity of care, even if it meant putting beds in the corridors and mattresses on the floor. It was expected to be responsive to the city's priorities and deferential to its public officials. And its every act had unique visibility because of Bellevue's status as a symbol of the city's legal obligation to the poor. None of these characteristics applied to New York Hospital. Nevertheless, in an era when the philanthropic tradition of private hospitals was still very strong, and when middle- and upper-class citizens had not yet begun to make much use of hospital care, Bellevue and New York Hospital were more similar to each other than they ever would be again. In this they were united: their common mission to serve the poor.

Assessing their position during the early years of the twentieth century, the leaders of Bellevue and New York Hospital had reason to feel both pride and optimism. Bellevue's leaders believed that their hospital's new facility would finally put its Almshouse past to rest; New York Hospital's were convinced that their expansion plans would establish their institution as one of the city's premier medical facilities. In their different ways both were flourishing institutions, embodying the community's highest aspirations toward science and public service.

Yet even in these expansive times, certain questions simmered below the surface: Could Bellevue attain the distinction to which it aspired while continuing to serve as provider of last resort? Could New York Hospital increase its services to private patients without eroding its historic responsibility for serving the poor? How did the missions of public and private hospitals differ, and who was empowered to define them? The need for answers to such questions would help set the agenda for the decades that followed.

2

Maintaining the Mission
1910–1930

Imagine yourself at Bellevue Hospital again, this time in the 1920s. Strolling the grounds, you can see how much has been achieved since the plans for the new Bellevue were launched in 1904. All the old structures around the perimeter of the complex are gone, and in their place stand half a dozen new McKim, Mead & White buildings, handsome four-square brick structures with white trim and big windows—visible steps toward the ambitious goal that John Brannan laid out twenty years ago. But look more closely, and you will see that Bellevue's past is also still very much in evidence. The heart of the hospital complex remains untouched: there is the same central courtyard; the same giant old elm tree; and, looming above them as it has for generations, the grim main building, now more than a century old, still housing several hundred patients.

What is true for Bellevue's architecture is true for the whole institution: however hard Bellevue's leaders may work to modernize their institution, they cannot leave behind its history, its longstanding obligation to care for everyone in need, no matter how destitute. This inclusive role represents a vital contribution to the community, but it also signifies Bellevue's growing isolation from the path taken by the city's major private hospitals. During these years—in New York and around the country—a new understanding is emerging of what it means to be a modern hospital. Instead of acting primarily as a hospice for the poor, the modern hospital will become a center for medical science—a center so technically advanced that even the most

43

respectable members of the community will come to depend on it. Energized by this vision, New York Hospital will virtually transform itself in the decades ahead. But for Bellevue, the same vision represents a daunting challenge: to match the rising standards of private facilities like New York Hospital, while remaining faithful to its own historic mission—ensuring that every New Yorker who needs care has a place to turn for help.

Besides the drive for modernization, another change is underway that has important implications for Bellevue: private hospitals are providing less and less free care. The two changes are closely related. Modern health care is expensive, and to meet these costs the voluntary hospitals have begun charging fees, not only to their private patients but also to most ward patients. In one sense voluntaries are becoming broader-based institutions, since they are attracting more middle- and upper-class patients than ever before. But of course they have always been eager to serve such patients when they could get them; the more significant change in social terms is the private hospitals' weakening commitment to serving the poor. Charity care is still available, but by the 1920s it is declining. Only in public hospitals like Bellevue can one count on receiving free care as a right. Elsewhere it is becoming more like a commodity—usually sold, sometimes given away, but recognized as having a cash value.

Under other circumstances, Bellevue's continuing commitment to including the poor in the community's circle of care might earn it special regard, but in New York City as in other cities, it is the leading private facilities like New York Hospital that define the terms of medical excellence. The modern hospital is to be a temple of science, attracting the city's most solid citizens while concentrating its free care on patients whose treatment will be most useful for research and educational purposes. This view of the hospital leaves little room for an institution that is obligated to accept everyone in need. Together, the drive for modernization and the private hospitals' retreat from charity care are establishing a new set of standards for medical excellence—standards that open new vistas for New York Hospital but which Bellevue will find increasingly difficult to harmonize with its own inclusive mission.

Making Hospitals Modern

Although scientific medicine represented at least a rhetorical ideal for New York's hospitals from the 1890s on, most of the concrete actions that actually reorganized hospital practice around that ideal occurred between 1910 and 1930. In those years, many of the characteristics that now are associated with the modern hospital first became visible in New York City: highly specialized staff, highly specialized space, and expensive technical equipment. These changes were effected to varying degrees and at varying paces depending on the facility, but by 1930 nearly all the hospitals in the city had become larger, more complicated institutions.

Ironically, from 1910 to 1930, hospitals changed the least in the arena that would seem most important: their ability to cure their patients. During those years, the use of modern techniques and equipment steadily improved physicians' diagnostic capacities, but few of the innovations offered much help in treatment. As a result, the wards remained full of patients suffering from the same diseases that had haunted their parents' generation—illnesses like pneumonia, typhoid, meningitis, and tuberculosis (still a major killer, though the rates were declining). Surgical successes progressed more rapidly, thanks to asepsis, yet surgery too was still an uncertain art and postoperative infection remained a grave reality. Not until antibiotics became widely available after World War II would there occur the dramatic advances in healing that the heralds of scientific medicine had been promising since the turn of the century.[1]

Nevertheless, if the 1910s and 1920s brought only modest improvements in treatment, they still represented a revolution in medical care because of the new way in which hospitals defined their mission and organized themselves to carry it out. Even changes that occurred only in private hospitals, like the reduction of charity care, inevitably altered conditions in the public sector. In many other areas, such as staff organization and hospital architecture, the public institutions made every effort to keep pace with leading private institutions. By the end of the 1920s, New York City and, indeed, most communities in the United States, were well on the way to what Morris Vogel called "the invention of the modern hospital."

The Changing Nature of Hospital Care

Between 1910 and 1930, New York City hospitals expanded their physical plants, their staffs, and their scientific facilities. At the same time, their buildings, their work forces, and their services were divided and subdivided into new specialized functions. This trend was part of a process of increasing differentiation that was occurring throughout American professional life during the late nineteenth and early twentieth centuries. In many fields, from academic endeavor to business management, tasks that had formerly been undertaken as part of a single broad activity were being isolated and elaborated into separate occupations.

Nowhere was the trend toward specialization more visible than in the medical profession. Once the new scientific medicine made it possible to isolate the defective bone or organ or germ, there appeared to be little need for a broad understanding of the patient's life or familiarity with the many branches of medicine that had seemed so essential to earlier physicians. "The general practitioner as such is nearly extinct," reported one visiting Britisher in 1929. American physicians started specializing as early as their internship years, he observed, a process that "excludes any dangerous broadening of their interests." Celebrating that trend, the New York Hospital medical board president called specialization "the spirit of modern medicine."[2]

During these years, medical students found themselves in the midst of a remarkable transition. At Cornell Medical College, Dr. Connie Guion studied first with a general surgeon of the old school, who would not even let her use a stethoscope but insisted she listen to the heartbeat directly, her head on the patient's chest. A few months later, she rotated through Cornell's teaching service at Bellevue, where she helped a young faculty member do pioneering research in the physiology of metabolism.[3] The conflicting messages Guion received were part of a wider debate about the whole direction of modern medicine; about the relative value of bedside diagnosis versus scientific measurement; about professional lives devoted to general practice versus careers in which specialized research and teaching played a major part.

The general practitioners who dominated most hospital medical boards managed to keep their specialist rivals out, at least at first, by denying them inpatient appointments. The specialists, however, rapidly established footholds in the less valued territory of outpatient departments, opening dozens of clinics devoted to particular disorders. Demand for their services grew, as did the perception that medical specialization was the wave of the future. Each time one hospital added a specialist to its staff, others felt pressed to do the same. By the late 1920s, specialists were well established in most hospital outpatient clinics and many had obtained inpatient appointments as well.

These changes were reflected in the staff rosters of each hospital. At Bellevue, for example, the great majority of senior attending staff in 1910 were general physicians or surgeons. By 1925, the senior staff had expanded to include specialists in pediatrics, children's surgery, tuberculosis, laryngology, urology, dermatology, obstetrics, syphilology, ophthalmology, radiography, pathology, and dental surgery. The same trend occurred, even more dramatically, at New York Hospital. House staff was expanded at both hospitals, too, with new postinternship residencies offered in various medical specialties. Those familiar with either facility a generation earlier would have been astonished by the size and variety of the two medical staffs by 1930.

The trend toward expansion and specialization reached well beyond the physicians. Hospital administration also came into its own during these years. As more money changed hands, as equipment proliferated, new buildings rose, admissions increased, and the staff expanded, the hospital's superintendent no longer functioned merely as a deferential assistant to the trustees. Gradually the idea emerged that administration, like ophthalmology or urology, was a professional specialty. The superintendent's powers were expanded, and instead of working alone he now directed a team of subordinates. At the same time—and not incidentally—hospital administration increasingly was seen as an occupation for men. Nurses still supervised many of the smaller hospitals, but men ran the large institutions and they dominated their emerging profession. Within the Bellevue & Allied Hospitals (B&AH) organization this attitude was reflected in the decision to replace the nurse who ran Harlem Hospital; the place had become so busy, the *Annual Report* explained, "that a trained man at the head is quite necessary."[4]

Another line of new specialties was created when nonmedical technicians began to be added to departments like radiology, electrocardiography, pathology, and physical therapy. The chair of the Bellevue Medical Executive

Committee noted that physicians were happy to "carry on" while the program was being established, but he explained that once the procedures became routinized, physicians would "look to the hospital to supply trained technicians to do the work." A scandal at Bellevue during the mid-1920s revealed how the system worked in practice. A city investigator exposed the fact that the head of the radiology department generally came to the hospital only two or three hours a day, although he was paid a full-time salary. The department head was dismissed, despite the strong support of senior physicians at the hospital (many of whom, cynics noted, had similar arrangements of their own). Nevertheless, the system of which the radiologist was an example continued. Throughout Bellevue and most hospitals at that time, physicians directed the special departments and provided general supervision, while their nonmedical subordinates provided most of the daily services.[5] Here, as in so many areas of the hospital community, distinctions of occupational status both reflected and reinforced distinctions of gender. Since the overwhelming majority of medical specialists were men and the overwhelming majority of the subordinate technicians were women, their relative positions must have seemed natural to many of those involved. The new sorority of technicians might have sought to challenge the physicians' command in some corner of their shared domain, but instead they adapted themselves to existing power relations and accepted their own niche within the expanding hospital hierarchy.

Technological advances made much less difference to the lower-level support workers. Sometimes they even took jobs away, as happened at New York Hospital, when the purchase of new washing machines permitted the laundry to double its output while dismissing three employees. The advent of automobiles, too, meant chauffeurs' jobs for drivers who qualified and demotion for the rest. A poignant note in the *New York Times* in 1924 recorded the departure of the last two ambulance horses from Bellevue. Their driver, John O'Neill, stood by with bowed head as the old horses were led out of the yard. Yet the horses faced a more comfortable future than he did. O'Neill no longer qualified to serve as superintendent of ambulances, since he could not drive a car. Instead of retiring to an upstate farm like the horses, however, he was being transferred to another position with the city, probably one involving—as most support jobs did—hard physical labor.[6] For O'Neill and thousands like him, the elaboration of the hospital hierarchy brought few benefits, and it devalued even more the unskilled jobs at the bottom of the ladder.

The Changing Character of Hospital Space

Like the work force, the physical space within hospitals was expanded and subdivided between 1910 and 1930. Across the United States during these years, hospitals grew larger, their institutional ambitions supported by the growing population and its increased willingness to seek hospital care. Even long-neglected municipal hospitals began to receive attention; those in Cincinnati, Philadelphia, Washington, D.C., Baltimore, Chicago, and Boston all initiated major rebuilding projects between 1910 and 1930. By the end of the 1920s, American hospitals represented a capital investment of nearly $3 billion, a level then exceeded by only a few industries, such as iron and steel.[7] Nearly every large hospital in New York City had more beds in 1930 than it did in 1910.

As hospitals increased in size, they echoed in spatial terms the specialization that was occurring in hospital jobs. Each of Bellevue's new buildings was designated for a specific category of patients—surgery, medicine, or tuberculosis—and pathology also got a building of its own. Hospitals established separate spaces off the wards for admissions, for treatments, and for emergencies, while laboratories and operating rooms multiplied. At the turn of the century, the ward had been the center of hospital life. Birth, death, and every event in between had occurred on that open stage. By the end of the 1920s, only about 20 percent of the space in most new American hospitals was allocated to patient rooms.[8]

Nonmedical hospital spaces were also rebuilt and expanded during these years. Significantly, of the first four structures erected in the new Bellevue project, two were support buildings: the laundry and the powerhouse. As more employees provided more elaborate treatment to more patients, more elaborate support facilities were needed as well. At the same time, the ordinary standards of urban living were rising. The hospitals' demand for modern conveniences like elevators, telephones, and motor vehicles soared, generating a parallel need for new spaces to install and maintain them. From its garage to its operating room, the hospital of the late 1920s had undergone an extraordinary physical transformation from the generic and uncomplicated spaces it encompassed in the nineteenth century.

Stepchildren: Outpatient Clinics and Social Service Departments

New developments in outpatient clinics paralleled and even led the changes in inpatient care, causing hospital leaders to congratulate themselves on the distance they had traveled from what one called the "medical soup-kitchen," the old-style dispensary that had treated so many working-class patients during the nineteenth century. The number of outpatient visits soared between 1910 and 1930, and the number of specialty clinics increased dramatically. During these years, hospitals added their first evening clinic sessions, introduced special outpatient services for children, and adopted the newest diagnostic equipment long before it reached the offices of most private practitioners. Yet as late as 1922, an American Hospital Association committee agreed that in the world of hospital care, outpatient services remained "the dark horse, the Cinderella, the step-child, the poor relation."[9] Why was this so?

For one thing, young physicians no longer depended on outpatient work to introduce them to patient care, since they now entered practice with years of clinical training behind them—in both medical school and as hospital interns. And with fewer physicians available (because of the tightening of medical school criteria) and larger hospital medical staffs, a larger proportion could obtain the coveted inpatient appointments. In addition, the outpatient ambiance was hardly appealing. Working in Bellevue's outpatient department as an intern in 1920, Dr. Connie Guion saw as many as ninety patients in an hour. "I didn't spend more than a minute on 75 percent of my patients," she recalled. Clarence de la Chapelle, who came to the department a few years later, described it as "a madhouse . . . horribly crowded and odoriferous, too." Bellevue served an unusually large number of outpatients and its physical plant was particularly poor, but contemporary comments suggest that its problems were not unique. The low quality of outpatient care in the city was noted frequently, and one critic observed: "Common courtesy is as rare in many New York City clinics as in the subway."[10]

The new specialty clinic sessions offered some opportunity for focused research and training, but most outpatients still needed the traditional medical and surgical services, and few physicians found that work rewarding. As the president of the New York Hospital medical board explained: "No competent man wishes to bury himself in a clinic where there is no opportunity for special thought and study." Indeed, in the evolving pattern of American medical care, it is hardly surprising that the clinics' array of coughs, backaches, and colicky babies should have struck physicians as medically uninteresting. De la Chapelle, who was primarily interested in research, described his outpatient work as boring and frustrating, "almost assembly-line stuff."[11] And so in 1930—as in 1910—clinics remained overcrowded by patients and undervalued by staff.

Outpatient service could not even serve as a significant adjunct to inpatient care, since the emerging approach to hospital treatment was highly episodic. In the nineteenth century, patients often returned to the ward on which they had been treated to have dressings checked or prescriptions refilled. Now, once they left the ward, the staff there might never hear of them again, even if the patients spent years receiving other services from the same hospital. Inpatient care itself had become a specialty—more sophisticated and elaborate but increasingly isolated from the rest of the patient's life.

Observers had been troubled for years by the gaps that existed among hospital departments, as well as by the even greater gap between the hospital and the patient's life in the community. "Our patients shoot by us like comets," said Dr. Richard Cabot in Boston, "crossing for a moment our field of vision, then passing out into oblivion."[12] Seeking to help patients after discharge and prevent readmissions, Cabot opened the nation's first hospital social service department at Massachusetts General in Boston in 1905. This example inspired Bellevue in 1906 to establish the first such department in New York, and within a few years most large hospitals in the city had followed suit. The new departments were staffed by nurses and supported by large, enthusiastic women's auxiliaries. They helped discharged patients find work, housing, and financial support; arranged for placements in sanitoria; assisted families while their breadwinners were in the hospital; supplemented sparse diets with extra milk and eggs; and taught discharged patients the principles of hygiene and nutrition. The Bellevue Auxiliary also bought an old Staten

Island ferryboat and tied it up at the 27th Street pier; it served as a fresh-air camp for tubercular children during the day and a residence for tubercular adults at night.

Hospital leaders praised the social services departments, and the social workers' own reports provided heartwarming anecdotes of families served and problems solved. On the whole, however, the evidence suggests that they made little fundamental difference to the way their hospitals functioned. At New York Hospital, for example, the 1927 record of a Brooklyn heroin addict reads: "Brought in on the ambulance as an interesting study of a large heart with mitral stenosis and auricular fibrillation." The file contains no indication that the patient's heroin addiction received attention during his stay or was considered in connection with his release, although the ambulance had originally been called because the patient was suffering from drug withdrawal, not heart problems. About this time, a physician at Bellevue sculpted a statuette of an all too typical departing patient, a man dressed in shabby clothing, jacket collar turned up against the cold, carrying only a paper bag; the title read: "Discharged Cured."[13] Despite the efforts of Dr. Cabot and his followers, patients were still shooting by the hospital like comets.

"I make a plea," wrote one hospital social worker, "for keeping always before us the living palpitating human being."[14] This appeal both affirmed the social workers' high aspirations and suggested why their aspirations went unrealized. Stressing the importance of the whole person and the whole society rather than specific disease organisms and processes, addressing daily problems of living rather than acute illness, directed by nurses and female volunteers instead of male doctors, social service departments were out of step with the dominant trends of American medicine. In the end, instead of providing the overarching continuity between home and hospital that Cabot and others had intended, they settled into being one more specialty, one more narrow segment of the complex world of hospital care.

By 1930, Bellevue and New York Hospital had changed both clinically and structurally. Larger than their founders could have imagined, divided into new departments and administrative layers, focusing increasingly intensive services on increasingly narrow episodes of care, both had become far more elaborate and fragmented institutions.

Meeting the Cost of Modern Care

As hospitals in the United States grew larger and more complex, they also grew more expensive. The cost of living was rising and most hospitals were increasing in size, but another factor was at work as well: the growing importance of money in the hospital economy. This trend would make it increasingly difficult for Bellevue and other public hospitals to keep pace with the private hospitals they hoped to equal.

At the turn of the century, many hospital transactions still depended on the exchange of in-kind services rather than money. Some scientific equipment was starting to become available, but it was not yet an integral part of patient treatment. Physicians worked for free, the great bulk of nursing was performed by students who received only tiny stipends, and the low salaries paid to the rest of the staff were further reduced by the custom of exchanging free housing for part of workers' wages. Few patients then paid for their care. By 1930, expectations of what constituted adequate care had changed, and meeting the new expectations required capital as well as labor. During their hospital stays, patients now saw a variety of physicians, were subjected to more tests, and underwent more ambitious surgery than ever before. Laboratory tests multiplied, radiotherapy began, blood transfusions became more common, and electrocardiography changed from a scientist's hobby to an accepted diagnostic tool. Other machines were also being added to the hospital scene, from washing machines to typewriters, from elevators to switchboards.

Most hospital leaders were convinced that the more technical the services and the more money spent, the better the care. The United Hospital Fund of New York noted approvingly in 1927 that outpatient costs in its member hospitals had risen 50 percent while the number served had grown less than 25 percent. "No single item," said the report, "is more indicative of general advance." Higher costs were appropriate, explained a 1929 report from New York Hospital, because the patient "gets more than the greatest optimist of half a century ago would have ventured to predict." And were the new services of genuine value? There, the reasoning became circular. "The importance of cystoscopy is indicated by the number of examinations made annually."[15]

Money not only bought equipment; it also bought staff. In 1910, nearly every physician at both Bellevue and New York Hospital lived by private practice, contributing their extra hours to the hospital as a charitable donation. By the late 1920s, dozens of physicians had joined the two hospitals as full-time salaried employees. Graduate nurses were also hired in growing numbers to supervise student nurses, to run various departments, and to take on additional treatment responsibility as care became more technical.

Each purchase of equipment and each addition of salaried staff involved cash, and this further committed hospitals to the exchange of money rather than services. Hospital expenses increased rapidly; between 1910 and 1930, the cost per patient day at both Bellevue and New York Hospital more than doubled.[16] This rising cost presented a challenge to every hospital, and in meeting it the paths of public and private institutions diverged. The different ways that Bellevue and New York Hospital managed to pay for the new style of care brought into sharp focus their differing resources, constituencies, and obligations.

Bellevue Struggles to Keep Up

Bellevue's trustees were determined to make their institution a first-class modern hospital. They did not expect to attract an elite clientele, but they were convinced that they could create an institution for working-class New Yorkers that would do the city proud. The first step in achieving this goal was to carry out the grand plan for the new Bellevue designed by the firm of McKim, Mead & White. Once again money was the key, and for a time the city provided it consistently. Close to schedule, the first of the projected buildings opened in 1908; it was Bellevue's first major new patient building in half a century. Construction proceeded steadily for the next several years, supported by capital expenditures that totaled, as planned, about $1 million per year. By 1912, Bellevue had a new nurses residence, a laundry, a power-house, and a pathology building; a second patient building was nearly fin-ished and excavations had begun for a third. Once this newest structure be-came available, the board planned the most decisive break yet with the past: the demolition of the gloomy and dilapidated main building, which had served as the center of Bellevue Hospital since 1816. Then, and only then, would the new Bellevue really overtake the old.

Meanwhile, however, there were two changes going on in the city that would soon halt the municipal spending that was bringing the new Bellevue to life. The first had to do with urban geography; the city was spreading out-ward. At the turn of the century, Bellevue's status as the city's leading public hospital had been reinforced by its proximity to the crowded immigrant neighborhoods of lower Manhattan, most notably on the Lower East Side. By the 1920s many downtown residents had begun following the subways and elevated railways to new homes in the outer boroughs. Bellevue continued to be busy and full, but the growing dispersal of the municipal hospital clien-tele around the city led many to conclude that Manhattan was getting too large a share of the city's hospital dollars; perhaps the money allocated to the new Bellevue should go instead to the other boroughs.[17]

The work on the new Bellevue would probably have continued despite these concerns, given the deterioration of the hospital's old buildings, but soon a second obstacle entered the picture: the city's debt crisis. In an era of majestic expectations for public institutions, borrowing money had proved increasingly seductive to municipal leaders. In theory, city borrowing was to be limited to projects like toll bridges, which would produce revenue to pay off their own construction bonds. But one round of debt followed the next and by 1910 the city had even begun borrowing for ordinary operating ex-penses like supplies and salaries. The end came in 1914, when an economic downturn caused a drop in the city's tax base (its collateral for most loans). That fall, with Wall Street's gun to its head, the Board of Estimate passed a law stipulating that capital projects must hereafter be paid for with funds on hand.[18] Bellevue managed to complete the two buildings that were already under way, but thirteen years would pass before another one opened. If Belle-vue was going to become an outstanding hospital in the near future, it would have to do so in its old buildings.

Upgrading services inside the hospital did not cost as much as construct-ing new buildings, but it too was expensive, as every hospital was discover-ing. Here, as so often in Bellevue's history, it becomes necessary to acknowledge both the generosity of the city's investment in its public hospitals and the inadequacy of that investment in relation to what was needed. Bellevue's expenditures rose dramatically during these years, from about $710,000 in 1910 to $2.8 million in 1930. But unlike what happened at private hospitals, most of the increase in Bellevue's expenses was accounted for by inflation and an increased patient load. As a result, much of the new salaries, services, and equipment that Bellevue added had to be paid for by reducing other costs below the rate of inflation.[19] (See Table 2.1.)

Staffing patterns reveal one way in which Bellevue managed to keep pace with the rising cost of medical care during these years. On the whole, city employees' political clout and periodic rabble-rousing served to keep municipal salaries at least equal to the dismal levels set by the voluntary hospitals. But the ratio of staff to patients at Bellevue was significantly lower than that of private hospitals; in 1922, for instance, when Bellevue had less than one employee per patient, the citywide average for hospitals over 300 beds was 1.6 to 1, while the ratio at New York Hospital was 1.76 to 1.[20] Bellevue's administrators complained more frequently about the quality of their workers than about their inadequate numbers, but the hospital's tight staffing must have made it even more difficult to attract and retain the best employees.

Besides the halt in its capital spending and the growing pressure on its operating budget, Bellevue was less free than before to control the resources it did receive. Reform Mayor John Purroy Mitchel (1914–1917) began the process of eroding the power of the B&AH trustees when, in a drive to rationalize municipal government, the city began centralizing and systematizing many procedures that until now had rested, either officially or by default, within the control of individual departments. Among other things, Mitchel established a Central Purchasing Committee for the city, moved payroll preparation from the

Table 2.1. Comparison of Bellevue and New York Hospital, 1910 and 1930

	Bellevue Hospital		New York Hospital	
	1910	*1930*	*1910*	*1930*
Average daily census	1,113	1,960	206	255
Cost per patient day:				
Current dollars	$1.77	$3.93	$2.68	$7.67
Constant 1930 dollars	$3.16	$3.93	$4.79	$7.67
Change in % cost per patient day,				
1910–1930, in 1930 dollars		+24		+60
Bellevue's cost per patient day,				
as % of New York Hospital's cost	66	51		

Source: Annual Reports, Bellevue & Allied Hospitals, NYC Dept. of Hospitals, and New York Hospital; constant dollars calculated from "Consumer Price Indexes (BLS)," *Statistical History of the United States* (New York: Basic Books, 1976), p. 211.

departments to the Municipal Building, gave the Department of Plant and Structures authority over major repair and maintenance allocations, and intensified the city's auditing procedures.[21] Each of these changes made the B&AH board's sphere of control a little smaller.

Mitchel's successor John F. Hylan (1918–1925) exerted another kind of pressure, subjecting the B&AH management to a barrage of criticism and restrictions. Bellevue drew the mayor's particular attention in 1919, when staff at the hospital helped lead a campaign for higher salaries and even engaged in a brief flurry of union activity. But even without these provocations the mayor would probably have come to dislike Bellevue and its trustees. He particularly distrusted the kind of gentleman reformers who dominated the hospital board, and his antipathy was undoubtedly confirmed when his attempt to have a friend appointed to the Bellevue medical staff was frostily rebuffed by Brannan. Hylan's solution was to replace the entire B&AH board, one by one, with members more to his liking. In February 1923, Brannan was the last of the old group to come up for reappointment. When he, too, was dismissed, the rout was complete. "The present Board of Trustees," observed a Brooklyn newspaper in 1924, "is admitted to be a Hylan board in its entirety."[22]

Hylan's new board had some strengths that the old one had lacked: it brought new blood to a department that had been run for years by the same close-knit group; it reached farther down the social scale; it added representation from Queens and Staten Island; and it introduced the first woman trustee (thirty years before New York Hospital did so). But it had one crippling weakness: it lacked community stature, and thus could no longer serve as a countervailing power center to mediate and influence city policies toward Bellevue and its allied hospitals.

The diminished stature of the B&AH board probably eased the way for its final dissolution. Mayor James J. Walker (1926–1932), who succeeded Hylan, showed unusual personal interest in Bellevue and even helped to revive its construction program. But he also made a decision that marked a dramatic change in Bellevue's fortunes; he implemented a plan developed under Mayor Hylan to create a citywide Department of Hospitals, bringing together all the medical institutions that until then had been administered separately by the Department of Public Welfare, the Department of Health, and the B&AH.

Walker's principal advice on how to create the new department came from a committee composed of leading New York physicians. In forming this committee, Walker chose a course that would be followed repeatedly by his successors: to design public medical care based on the advice of physicians whose own past experience and future prospects lay primarily in private hospitals and medical colleges. The policy of relying on elite medical advisers with close ties to the private system was understandable, since these men stood at the top of the New York medical profession, but it was based on two assumptions that might at least have been questioned: first, that ascertaining the needs of public hospitals was a purely medical, rather than a sociomedical, question; and second, that because these physicians were free of ties to party politics, they had no other agendas that might diverge from the public interest. Walker's medical advisors seem to have approached their work seriously and in a spirit of public service, but their view of the public hospitals' mission was necessarily shaped by their own experiences, and like most people associated with private hospitals, they tended to see public institutions as existing primarily, in the words of S. S. Goldwater, "for the purpose of filling gaps in the voluntary system."[23] The more expansive vision that had animated the B&AH trustees would find little place in the new department.

The formation of the new Department of Hospitals marked the end of an era for Bellevue. It remained the largest hospital in the city, but after 1929, instead of being the heart of the small B&AH network, it became just one institution in a large city department that included eighteen hospitals spread across five boroughs. Bellevue's resources had always been limited, considering the scope of its responsibilities; now new limits had also been placed on the hospital's freedom to manage those resources.

By the end of the 1920s, Bellevue had developed many of the services and facilities that were considered essential to a modern medical institution, but the old Almshouse still standing at the center of the hospital offered a sharp reminder of the goals that remained to be reached. And the growing importance of money in the provision of health care left Bellevue at a disadvantage that would only increase during the years ahead.

New York Hospital Finds a Way to Pay the Bills

Like Bellevue, New York Hospital also faced the challenge of paying for the modern style of medical care. Unlike Bellevue, the strategy it adopted to solve this problem was to revise its historic mission of serving primarily the poor.

By the 1920s, many of New York City's private hospitals were having trouble covering their expenses.[24] As noted, costs were rising rapidly. In addition, the growing emphasis on medical science was beginning to influence the philanthropic contributions that had always played such an important part in keeping the hospitals running. Many of the wealthiest patrons were now earmarking their gifts for research, education, or highly specialized equipment. This trend both reflected and reinforced the idea that the hospital's highest social value lay in its contributions to the future—training physicians, advancing scientists' understanding of disease—rather than in curing the ills and meeting the needs of today's patients. The two sets of goals were not unrelated, but medical science rather than medical care became the principal focus of private philanthropy.

Most hospital leaders were as bewitched as their donors with the idea of advancing the frontiers of medicine. Nevertheless, they still had to meet the rising cost of their day-to-day operations. They therefore turned to their best alternative revenue source: the patients. They focused first on that perennial object of desire, the private patient. New Yorkers of all classes were using hospitals more often, and private hospitals made every effort to ensure that their services, their furnishings, and their rates would attract what a Mount

Sinai report called "the better conditioned of people."[25] This was not an easy task, since private patients expected attractively furnished individual rooms, prompt service, good meals, special orders from the kitchen on demand, and comfortable accommodations for their visitors. New York Hospital, like its fellow voluntaries, worked hard to provide these amenities and to encourage patient referrals from community physicians.

Through these efforts, the hospital managed to raise its proportion of private patients from 4 percent in 1910 to about 20 percent by the early 1920s. But the special services provided to these patients cost money, and many private rooms stood empty each summer when wealthier New Yorkers generally left the city. As a result, the patronage of the upper class did very little for hospital balance sheets. At New York Hospital, the Private Patients Department generated a surplus in only three of the sixteen years between 1910 and 1925.[26] Trustees and physicians continued to stress the importance of serving private patients as a symbol of hospital status, as a convenience for medical staff members, and as a potential revenue source for the future. Nevertheless, at New York Hospital as at most private facilities, the immediate financial problems remained unsolved.

Ward patients were soon called upon to fill the financial gap. Between 1910 and 1930, the proportion of patients at New York Hospital whose care was entirely subsidized by the hospital dropped from 74 percent to 13 percent. The rest either were partially subsidized by the city or had to pay for their own care as best they could. Smaller private hospitals had taken this course even earlier; now leading facilities like New York Hospital followed their example. Commenting in 1920 on the widespread reduction in charity care, the United Hospital Fund attributed the change to "better financial circumstances" and the fact that "working people are not inclined to impose on the hospitals." However, the report also noted that "tactful pains" were being taken "to guard against imposition."[27]

Hospital trustees sometimes presented the transition to pay wards as an effortless process, suggesting that it involved little more than asking patients for a contribution that they were glad to make. Yet it seems most probable that the change must have involved turning away at least some people in need, especially when one finds the New York Hospital Superintendent observing for the first time in 1921 that it was now "not uncommon" for the hospital to have vacancies on its wards. We catch a glimpse of the running duel between patient and hospital in the complaint by a hospital worker that Jewish patients were difficult to screen financially, since they often did not seem to know how much money their families made. In fact, these patients probably understood their families' finances very well, but they also understood the advantages of evasiveness.[28] Such gambits could not turn the tide by themselves, however; each year fewer ward patients were treated for free.

The new policy was codified in 1919 at New York Hospital, when it was decreed that the executive committee of the board of governors "shall carefully examine and pass on the admission of all free cases" by the superintendent.[29] Selected poor patients would always be accepted for their teaching potential, and they would be treated well; but they were no longer the hospital's primary patient population. Nor was meeting the health needs of their communities the hospital's primary purpose.

City subsidies helped cover the expense of treating some patients who could not pay their way under the new policies. The private hospitals rarely referred to the government funding they received; for instance, in a typical report the United Hospital Fund (UHF) announced that its members had met their deficits that year through money from gifts, UHF allocations, investment income, and "other unusual sources." During this period UHF hospitals were actually receiving nearly $900,000 a year in city subsidies, but the statement made no reference to this fact.[30] The patients to whose care the city contributed—increasingly referred to as "city patients"—seemingly belonged so entirely to the government that there was no need to refer to them in reports. Little by little, private hospitals were starting to abdicate to the public sector their own former responsibility for providing free care to the poor.

In some ways, the private hospitals' circle of patients was widening during these years. Their growing focus on ward patients as "clinical material" for teaching and research eradicated virtually all vestiges of a moral criterion for hospital admission. When, in the words of Joel Howell, "patients started to become organs," their character failings became irrelevant. But even when serving the poor, the private hospitals continued to concentrate on patients with acute and medically interesting illnesses; they passed the more routine or chronic cases on to the public system. Nearly every private facility routinely rejected patients "under the rules" for such conditions as scarlet fever, measles, erysipelas, mental illness, venereal disease, epilepsy, and alcoholism. Even when physicians at New York Hospital initiated a research study on cancer, the superintendent of Saint Luke's Hospital advised them to exclude "all cancers of an incurable and offensive nature."[31]

The private hospitals also continued to shift dying patients to the public system during their final days or hours. In 1914, a Board of Estimate committee reported that within the previous three months, private hospitals had sent Bellevue eighteen transfers who died on the day of arrival. At New York Hospital, a senior physician censured a house physician for requiring a patient terminally ill with influenza to walk from her ward to the ambulance that would take her to Bellevue. But the rebuke focused on the fact that the woman had been forced to walk, not on the question of whether she should have been moved at all. The painful effect of such transfers on patients is suggested by the case of one delirious man, close to death, who was moved from Polyclinic Hospital to Bellevue when his condition took a turn for the worse. Because his name was misspelled in the medical record, hospital officials could not find his family. As he tossed and moaned through his final hours, the nurse by his bed could make out only one word: "wife." He died three hours after being transferred.[32]

Patients without money had always been disproportionately affected by transfers like these and by the private hospitals' exclusion of certain medical conditions. Now the private hospitals' services to the poor were curtailed more sharply by their search for revenue. So at a time when moral and social criteria for admission were relaxing, thus opening the door to a few new impoverished patients, economic criteria arose in their place, closing the door to many more.

During the same years that private hospitals were cutting back on their charitable services to the poor, their growing number of private patients also contributed to changing the institutional climate. Private patients had always been given special treatment, but as their numbers increased, the type of care they received took on new meaning. By 1930, instead of representing one small corner of privilege in an institution designed primarily for the poor, the private service had become a visible and familiar standard of hospital care, making ward care seem all the more undesirable by contrast. This trend, along with the growing pressure for even ward patients to pay their way, helped to transform the private hospitals' charity medicine from a tolerable norm to a degrading exception.

These changes raised difficult questions for the private hospitals, which had long based their public image and private sense of worth on their charitable mission. Was serving patients who could pay for their care betraying the hospital's mission or enhancing it? To what extent should pay-ward patients be treated differently from free patients? The private hospitals struggled with these issues throughout the 1910s and 1920s; but all their uncertainties arose from a single social fact: in private hospitals most care was no longer a gift—it had become an item for sale, like any other commodity. Making this change helped private facilities like New York Hospital move toward the more elevated social role they now envisioned for the modern hospital. But it also represented a step away from the broadly inclusive tradition that until now they had shared with public institutions like Bellevue.

The Medical School Connection

How does a public hospital like Bellevue make its mark in modern medicine when most of its buildings are antiquated, its budget is strained, and it is feeling strong pressure from City Hall? Bellevue's answer, at least in part, was to strengthen its relationship with the three medical schools that used its wards for teaching. New York Hospital, too, established its first medical school affiliation during these years, going from an initial agreement with Cornell Medical College in 1912 to plans for a huge shared facility by the end of the 1920s.

In establishing these relationships, Bellevue and New York Hospital were following a course that was central to the principles of medical education reform. The president of Columbia University, Nicholas Murray Butler, expressed the philosophy clearly if brutally when he explained that a first-class medical school must have "complete and permanent control of the hospital staff and of the facilities for clinical teaching which the hospital affords."[33] Few hospital leaders would have offered the total abdication that Butler seemed to expect of them, but most did agree that closer cooperation was needed. They recognized the appeal of identifying their institutions with the revered accomplishments of medical science, they were eager to attract top-rated physicians, and they were acutely conscious that rival institutions were moving in the same direction. So Bellevue's decision to strengthen its medical school affiliation, though given special urgency by its needs in other areas, was not unlike the choices being made by other hospitals.

Bellevue Builds New Alliances

Bellevue's wards had long been divided into four divisions, and for many years three of these divisions had had informal ties to local medical schools: one to Columbia, one to Cornell, and one to New York University. (The fourth division, designated as "open," was reserved for community doctors who had no academic affiliations.) Each division initiated its own staff nominations, and the appointments went to doctors connected with that division's medical school. The staff members selected took turns during the year in making daily rounds on the wards in their divisions; many also taught at the hospital, giving lectures and performing surgery in the big amphitheater or supervising students who were serving as clinical clerks on the wards. One medical student of the era recalled that Bellevue was "our classroom, our home. We lived at Bellevue."[34]

In theory, this arrangement was exactly what Butler was prescribing. In practice, however, the organization at Bellevue was considerably looser. All members of the attending staff had equal status on the hospital medical board, regardless of their rank in the affiliated medical school, and they depended on one another, not on their universities, for their appointments. No medical school controlled Bellevue's laboratories, nor did technical staff from the various schools have access to the hospital's patients. These constraints on the medical schools gave Bellevue greater power in the relationship. Of course, few medical reformers of the day would have seen that as an advantage; most felt that the more control a medical school exerted over a hospital, the better. The case seemed even more compelling where city government was involved. In the public hospitals of Baltimore, Philadelphia, and Cincinnati, aggressive improvement campaigns were being launched during these years by academically connected physicians. Perhaps, given greater power, Columbia, Cornell, and New York University would do the same for Bellevue.

Bellevue took its first step in 1913, when eight chiefs of service were chosen from among the senior faculty members of the affiliated medical schools. This ended the democratic arrangement under which responsibility had rotated among the whole medical staff. At the same time, clinical policymaking shifted from the hospital medical board to a new medical executive committee, composed only of the eight new chiefs (plus the general medical superintendent and the hospital's pathologist). Next, Bellevue undertook what Brannan described as a "radical reorganization" of its wards, for the first time grouping together patients with similar diagnoses, to facilitate specialty training. All four divisions were still to provide some general care, but each specialty area—urology, ophthalmology, neurology, pediatrics, orthopedics, and the others—now came under the sole control of one medical school. In addition, the hospital began to solicit staff nominations directly from the universities, rather than obtaining them from the hospital medical board, and it dropped its longstanding rule reserving the "open" fourth division for physicians without medical school affiliations.[35]

By the time the restructuring was complete in 1917, Bellevue had become as much a "teaching hospital" in the reformers' sense of the term as any institution in New York City. In its reach for scientific excellence and political allies, Bellevue had opened the facility to three powerful outside institutions, each with its own resources and priorities. The challenge would be to ensure that Bellevue remained a full partner in the relationship, rather than becoming a colony shared by three empires. The following story of a gift made to the hospital at about this time suggests the delicate trade-offs involved.

Most of the people treated at Bellevue were poor, but now and then the ambulance brought in a relatively prosperous patient. Such a man entered Bellevue in the early 1920s, the victim of a street accident. Patients of this kind were usually swept away by their families to private institutions as soon as possible, but in this case the family was delayed and by the time they arrived, the patient refused to leave. Enthralled by the raffish variety of life on a Bellevue ward, impressed by the quality of patient care and bedside teaching, he remained till he recovered, drinking in the unfamiliar scene. For him it was, as the intern who treated him observed, "a liberal education." When the man died some years later, he left $40,000 to Bellevue. At once, the hospital's status as a public institution came into play, as municipal accountants argued that the money should go to the city's general fund. Struggling to defend its prize, the hospital claimed the money for itself. In the end, lawyers on both sides agreed to interpret the gift as having been made not to Bellevue but to the New York University College of Medicine, since the ward on which the patient had stayed was in a division affiliated with NYU.[36]

This outcome, apparently perceived on both sides as an acceptable compromise, illuminated the complicated world within which the city's municipal hospitals operated. As a branch of city government, Bellevue paid for the tax support it received by having less control over its own resources. Partly in reaction, it began to cede other kinds of control to its affiliated medical schools. The compromise over the legacy reflected a policy that was established, though not quite articulated, between 1910 and 1930. Scientifically, the medical school affiliation had the same meaning for Bellevue that it had for any teaching hospital, promising access to the best clinical resources. Institutionally, it offered Bellevue something more: an apparent refuge from the bureaucratic and political pressures of city government. The validity of this assumption would be tested and retested in the decades ahead.

An Alliance for New York Hospital

Bellevue built its medical school relationships gradually over many years, but New York Hospital was precipitated into an affiliation with Cornell Medical College by a single gift of $250,000. The offer came to the board in 1912 through Dr. Lewis Stimson, a retired New York Hospital surgeon who counted among his friends and patients many of the city's most prosperous men. One of these was the gift's donor, George F. Baker, the seventy-year-old president of First National Bank and a member of the hospital board of governors since 1899. Described by the *New York Times* as a "colossus of the financial world," Baker moved in three overlapping New York worlds: Wall Street, the upper levels of white Protestant society, and the circle of wealthy contributors who sustained New York's voluntary institutions. His offer to New York Hospital reflected all three worlds; while the gift drew upon the financial proceeds of his business career, the conditions he set for its use were the direct result of his social ties with Dr. Stimson. At the same time, by making so large a donation, Baker affirmed his standing as a generous contributor to the city's institutional life.

Baker's gift came with conditions: to receive it, New York Hospital must establish a formal relationship with Cornell Medical College. The possibility of such an affiliation had been discussed occasionally at hospital board meetings, and the members were keenly aware that medical affiliations were the wave of the future. As the trustees of Presbyterian Hospital had recently asserted, a close association with a medical school was "important and indeed essential" to building a modern hospital.[37]

Presbyterian Hospital's alliance with the Columbia University College of Physicians & Surgeons, signed in 1911, probably nudged New York Hospital to move in that direction, especially since Presbyterian was considered to be its principal rival. As it happened, several New York Hospital board members were involved in the 1911 negotiations, because they were also trustees of either Presbyterian or Columbia. In any case, when Stimson presented the proposal for an affiliation with Cornell, the New York Hospital board accepted it promptly.[38] Besides immediately obtaining the right to name half of New York Hospital's medical staff, Cornell also gained access for its faculty and students to "clinical material," that is, patients on the New York Hospital wards. In return, the hospital benefited from the medical school's technical facilities and from the stimulation of its focus on education and research.

Gradually, New York Hospital and Cornell began discussing a closer alliance, including the possibility of a shared facility. During one brief period in 1917–1918, it appeared that Presbyterian Hospital and Columbia University might join them in the project. These discussions foundered, however, and in 1927, New York Hospital and Cornell signed a formal agreement to build a new medical center that would house their two institutions. Board chairman Edward Sheldon described New York Hospital's participation in the planned center as "the most important and progressive event of its career."[39]

Agreeing upon the new center was one task; paying for it was another. A

$7.5 million grant from John D. Rockefeller's General Education Board helped finance Cornell's part of the project, but for New York Hospital one donor mattered above all others: Payne Whitney, the hospital's resident angel. As a young man, Whitney had inherited millions from his father and millions more from his uncle, Colonel Oliver Hazard Payne, who had been Cornell Medical College's founding patron; in 1924, Whitney was the third largest taxpayer in the United States. He spent more time on horse-breeding than on good works, but his uncle got him interested in New York Hospital, which soon became his primary philanthropy. Whitney donated most of the land for the new medical center: two entire blocks along the East River, from 68th Street to 70th, as well as parts of a third block to the north. Then in 1927, in the middle of a tennis game, Whitney fell dead of a heart attack at the age of 51. His personal leadership was missed thereafter, but his bequest of $20 million to the hospital was an enormous help, and plans for the new center rushed forward.[40]

In theory, New York Hospital and Cornell were collaborating on the building plans, but in fact, as one center physician explained: "From the beginning the Board of Trustees of the New York Hospital had the feeling that they were the predominant factor in the combination."[41] The trustees had reason to feel this way, since the hospital alone owned all the land in the new center, had a far larger endowment than the medical school, and was contributing most of the money for the project. The biggest contribution to Cornell's part of the medical center—the Rockefeller grant—came through the active intervention of New York Hospital leaders, and most of it was simply passed over to the hospital as soon as it arrived, to pay for the medical school's use of the new buildings. Cornell's place in the planning process is suggested by the head of the medical school faculty, who later described poring over a news story about Payne Whitney's will, hoping to pick up information about the center's finances that he had been unable to obtain from the hospital board chairman.[42] The futures of the two institutions were now linked, but New York Hospital dominated the partnership.

The hospital's primacy was emphasized one hot, cloudy day in June 1929 when, with a crowd of supporters looking on, its board chairman shoveled the first spadeful of dirt for the new project. The medical center would include fifteen buildings, house nearly 1,000 patients (four times the old hospital's capacity, though only half of Bellevue's), and cost $60 million.[43] Columbia–Presbyterian was making hospital history about that time with its new twenty-two-story tower, but architect Henry Shepley gave the New York Hospital–Cornell Medical Center a tower three stories taller, with a facade inspired by a fourteenth-century architectural gem, the Palace of the Popes at Avignon (France). Clothing the buildings in bricks of a gray so pale they gleamed in the sun, and using Avignon's tall, pointed windows arranged in vertical strips, Shepley's design created an extraordinary effect, an improbable marriage of Chartres Cathedral and Rockefeller Center.

A generation earlier, the New York Hospital board had debated for months before allowing even a few medical students on the wards; at that time the trustees had still made a sharp distinction between the mission of a hospital and that of a medical school. By 1930, the two missions had become intertwined. Responding to national trends, nudged by George F. Baker's gift, stung by the progress of rival institutions, and supported by Whitney's millions, the trustees had come to share a very different vision of the ideal hospital. As the main tower rose above the surrounding buildings, so the new center would rise above the limitations and obligations of the old hospital on 15th Street. From that point on, it would concentrate not on charitable care for the poor but on benefiting society through scientific treatment, high-level research, and the training of physicans.

Bellevue's Door Stays Open

From 1910 to 1930, New York's private hospitals helped finance their transformation into modern medical institutions by restricting the amount of charity care that they dispensed. Yet it is important to note that they were not alone in choosing this course; similar policies were being adopted by private institutions across the country.[44] In that sense, the decisions made in New York were significant not because they were unique but because they were part of a pattern that was being established in most American communities.

The unusual factor in New York was that as poor citizens found it more difficult to obtain free private care, they could turn to a large and generous public system. Public hospitals existed in cities other than New York, but few cities had more than one, and many offered little besides long-term custodial care under the most dismal circumstances. New York, by contrast, had twelve public general hospitals located in neighborhoods all over the city, as well as six long-term institutions. This public system had its problems, but it was among the best in the country, with the most generous eligibility criteria. New York's voluntary hospital trustees were giving less free care to the poor, but unlike trustees in many other cities, they knew that the patients they did not serve had an alternative source of care. Would they have preserved more free care if the city had had no public hospitals? It seems unlikely, given the evidence from other communities. Nevertheless, the trustees of New York's private hospitals could pursue their own priorities with a clear conscience, because hospitals like Bellevue were there to assume the responsibilities they left behind.

Whatever Bellevue's academic aspirations, it remained a public hospital, tightly connected to the community and its demands. "It is not to be commended to those who look upon life from a pedestal," observed the *New York Times* in 1926. "It lives on the pavement and vibrates with the doings and undoings of a gigantic city."[45] Bellevue's inclusiveness gave the public hospital a unique urban role, impelling it to provide medical care to patients who were welcome nowhere else. Even Bellevue's hiring practices reflected this greater openness, widening access to hospital employment just as its admission policies widened access to hospital care.

An Open Door to Patients

In terms of actual treatment, a patient in 1930 would probably have received similar therapies whether he entered Bellevue or almost any other large New York City hospital. But a patient's experience at Bellevue was not like that in private hospitals. As the voluntary institutions began to serve more private patients and reduce their proportion of charity cases, public hospital admissions increased.[46] Although their budgets also rose, the funding never quite kept pace with the rising number of cases. As a result, patients at a hospital like Bellevue were much more likely to encounter crowded wards, poor food, and inadequate staffing. Nevertheless, Bellevue's patients also continued to enjoy one distinctive privilege they could not have received in a private hospital: the assurance of receiving free care as a right rather than a charity. Entering Bellevue, you did not have to prove your worthiness, persuade an admissions clerk that you were destitute, or obligate yourself to fees you could not afford. Nor did you have to wonder how many of your fellow patients were paying for their care, and how many of them knew that you were not.

Patients at public hospitals like Bellevue had another distinctive experience: they were all treated alike. In the voluntary hospitals, a world of space and privilege separated the private patients from those on the ward, and even private patients received varying levels of service depending on how much they were paying. At Bellevue, the trustees waged unceasing war against distinctions of any kind. Every patient went through the same admission process, slept in the same kind of bed, wore the same hospital-issue gown, ate the same food, and followed the same schedule. In 1915, the board reprimanded an attending physician for having arranged a special room and privileges for a wealthy out-of-towner. This practice, the doctor was told, was "at variance with what the Trustees expect in the administration of this hospital."[47]

This principle was laudably egalitarian and should in no way have detracted from the hospital's renowned capacity to give good care to the city's poorest citizens. But as private hospitals offered increasingly luxurious arrangements to increasingly prosperous patients, Bellevue's even-handed austerity tended to reinforce its image as the place you went when you could go nowhere else. Two events around the time of World War I highlighted the ambiguous nature of Bellevue's standing among the city's hospitals.

As testimony to its eminence, Bellevue was one of only three New York City hospitals that was invited by the American Red Cross to organize a medical unit for service overseas during the war. Outpacing the other two institutions selected—New York Hospital and Presbyterian—Bellevue put its unit together so quickly that it earned the proud title of Base Hospital Unit #1. The company set sail for France in January 1918, established a military hospital near the front, and served with distinction until the end of the war.[48] In being chosen for this mission and in carrying it out so successfully, Bellevue affirmed its place beside New York Hospital and Presbyterian in the top rank of New York City hospitals.

Bellevue's wartime service would always be remembered with pride, but by the time it was over the hospital was already involved in another kind of war on the home front: the virulent influenza epidemic of 1918–1919, which killed millions around the world, including 33,000 New Yorkers in six months. Bellevue's experience in this epidemic provided a brutal reminder that in many respects its position was far removed from the city's private hospitals. Bellevue treated what may have been New York's first victims of the epidemic—three sailors from the Brooklyn Navy Yard. Within a week of their admission, all three were dead; within another week, the hospital was overflowing with cases of "flu," as it was called. As the epidemic spread across New York, no hospital escaped unscathed, but Bellevue carried the heaviest load in the city. Cots filled every aisle and when the cots ran out, screens and bathroom doors were pressed into service as well. Children crowded the pediatrics division, three to a bed. Deaths, which usually ran about ten per day, peaked at sixty-two on one terrible day in October. An intern recalled: "It got to the place where I would only see patients twice—once when they came in and again when I signed the death certificate. It was horrible."[49]

At the height of the siege, the B&AH board debated closing the hospital to new admissions until the overcrowding subsided, but concluded that it must continue—as it always had—to accept every person who applied. Since private hospitals were limiting their admissions, Bellevue's decision only reinforced its role as an escape-valve for the rest of the system. At one point, ambulances from ten hospitals waited on the Bellevue grounds to discharge their passengers.[50] The experience left a tangled legacy. On the one hand, tales of heroism and self-sacrifice among Bellevue's staff became part of the hospital legend. On the other hand, the epidemic emphasized the fact that whenever a choice arose between maintaining quality of care and admitting all who applied, Bellevue would be required to choose the second.

The persistence of this understanding was illustrated in the bitterly cold winter of 1923, when once again a combination of flu, pneumonia, and other diseases filled the city's hospitals. The *New York Times* reported that Bellevue's beds were filled and cots lined every corridor. Nevertheless, since the private hospitals were also full, they were continuing to send Bellevue all their ambulance cases. A spokesman for New York Hospital explained that they might start putting up cots once Bellevue ran out of vacancies.[51] Of course in New York Hospital's sense of the term, Bellevue had run out of vacancies long ago, but the transfers were continuing unabated. This accessibility did little for Bellevue's professional status; superb care for the few was what won recognition, not harried care for the many. But thousands of impoverished New Yorkers owed their lives to that harried care, to that door that remained open when many others had begun to close.

An Open Door to Staff

Staff as well as patients found an open door at Bellevue. Between 1910 and 1930 Bellevue pioneered in providing occupational opportunity to several groups of health professionals who generally faced exclusion and discrimination. In part, Bellevue's inclusiveness reflected its continuing struggle to keep the hospital staffed; perhaps if it had been a more pleasant workplace, it might not have been so welcoming, but its hiring policies also reflected its openness to community pressure. Far more than any private institution, Bellevue was obliged to listen and respond when citizens pressed their claims. The arrival of the hospital's first female doctors is a case in point.

Women who wanted to become doctors had to pass through three narrow gates, each one guarded by men. First, they had to be admitted to medical school. In this respect, opportunities in New York were slowly improving; by the mid-1920s, about 125 women were enrolled in New York City medical schools. Second, the female graduate had to win a hospital internship, a form of training that had become so integral to a medical career that those excluded from it were left at a professional disadvantage. In 1910, the New York Infirmary (an affiliate of the city's sole women's medical college) was the only hospital in the city that offered internships for women, but this institution offered little help as an entrée to the masculine community of New York medicine. This was an important consideration, since the support of an established male physician was usually needed to pass the third gate: establishing oneself professionally—obtaining patient referrals, consultancies, hospital appointments, and teaching positions. Dr. Connie Guion, one of those who made it through all three gates, later recalled that there were so few practicing female physicians in the city in 1920 that they were able to hold their monthly meetings in each other's living rooms.[52]

The Bellevue & Allied Hospitals board pioneered in opening hospital internships to women in New York. As soon as the department was established in 1902, it began admitting women to the interns' examination for Gouverneur, its small hospital on the Lower East Side. When Emily Dunning won an appointment in 1903, the house staff in all four B&AH hospitals circulated a petition warning that the appointment would be "decidedly distasteful to us." But Dunning took her appointed place and a few months later a reporter offered a spirited account of her first ride as ambulance surgeon. Dozens of male hands were proffered to help her onto her perch on the back of the carriage, said the reporter, but she brushed them aside. "'Never mind,' said Dr. Dunning, 'that is easy,' and with a light spring she mounted the step and vaulted over the tailboard."[53]

Dunning's appointment to Gouverneur Hospital set an important precedent, but the road to professional success in New York lay through training in the major hospitals. Here again, B&AH broke new ground by opening Bellevue's internships to women in 1913. The board's decision was barely voluntary. Four young women, star graduates of Cornell Medical College, laid political siege to the institution, calling personally on every Bellevue chief of service and arranging to meet hospital board members, city leaders, and physicians at teas and dinners held by their supporters. When the four women then scored high on the interns' examination, the B&AH board took what it called "a step of far reaching importance" and gave them the appointments they had earned.[54] By 1920, twelve of Bellevue's ninety-nine house staff were women. Meanwhile, except for a brief period during World War I when male applicants were unavailable, no other major New York hospital accepted female interns until late in the 1920s.

Accepting female physicians was not, however, the same thing as welcoming them. When Edith Lincoln arrived at Bellevue as an intern in 1918, she was assigned to eat her meals with the nurses, and the supervising nurse reported her for insubordination when she refused to lengthen her skirts. A few years later, Connie Guion and her fellow female interns found themselves shut out of the modern house-staff quarters, and assigned instead to "a regular rat-trap of a room" in the attic of the hospital's oldest building, because the superintendent wanted to house them as far as possible from the male interns. In the dining room, if one of the women stopped to talk with a male colleague, all the house staff seated nearby would beat on the water pitchers with their spoons. Nevertheless, the women persevered with good humor and received the training and the credentials they sought at a time when they were obtainable at no other institution of Bellevue's caliber. In 1929, Bellevue pioneered again by appointing a woman to the last bastion of privilege: the inpatient attending staff. No other major hospital in the city took this step until World War II, when men's absence overseas reopened the doors of opportunity.[55]

Bellevue also pioneered, again somewhat reluctantly, when it opened its medical staff to black physicians. In 1915, Roscoe Conkling Giles, a black graduate of Cornell Medical College, enraged B&AH trustees when he maintained that he had been rejected for a Bellevue internship because of racial prejudice. The trustees grew even angrier when Giles took his case to the mayor and the National League on Urban Conditions Among Negroes. "In plain English, he was outclassed, and that is all there is to it," wrote a member of Bellevue's medical executive committee. He had warned Giles before the exam, the physician said, that if Giles failed, he must take it "in a sportsmanlike manner, and not go about claiming that he had a race grievance."[56]

Perhaps the matter was as simple as Bellevue's leaders maintained, but the debate over Dr. Giles helped prepare the way for his successors. In 1918, in the face of continuing pressure from the National League, as well as wartime manpower shortages, Bellevue bypassed the examination process and took its first black intern as a transfer from Fordham, one of its allied hospitals. A few years later, when house-staff members protested the acceptance of a second black intern, the medical executive committee blandly responded that "the same was considered," and proceeded with the appointment. Black physicians would still have to fight well into the 1930s for positions on the attending staff, but a beginning had been made and Bellevue had played an important part.[57] As with its acceptance of female physicians, the B&AH board had opened its doors to black interns reluctantly, yet it had done so well ahead of the city's other leading hospitals.

Bellevue's record was less admirable when it came to nursing students. In this field, black applicants were systematically excluded until the 1940s by every public and private New York City hospital except Harlem and Lincoln.

The arrangement drew periodic criticism from the black community; in 1927, one Harlem newspaper described Harlem Hospital as a "jim-crow nurse system and training school, used as a vicious and un-American excuse for barring them elsewhere."[58] Nevertheless, Bellevue hired no black nurses until forced to do so by the staffing shortages of World War II.

Bellevue performed better in respect to another health-care field dominated by women: midwifery. In 1911, the hospital opened the nation's first school for midwives. At the time, midwives were locked in a battle they would ultimately lose. Obstetricians, fighting to establish their new medical specialty, blamed America's high maternal mortality rates on midwives' ignorance and ineptitude. Since most midwives were uneducated, foreign, and female, they were vulnerable targets; at the same time, they had delivered 40 percent of all babies born in New York City in 1909, which made them targets worth taking on. In some cities, physicians and their allies concentrated on driving the midwives out of business, but in New York, the independent-minded director of the Health Department's Bureau of Child Hygiene, Dr. Josephine Baker, initiated a plan of public registration and regulation. She then persuaded the B&AH Board to establish a school for midwives at Bellevue. Any midwife who had not received satisfactory training abroad would have to attend the free six-month course at Bellevue before she could be registered.[59]

The School for Midwives did well for more than two decades, enrolling many New York women who could not have met the educational criteria for nursing school or afforded the three-year training period that nursing required. Immigrant women, in particular, took advantage of the course; a typical graduating class consisted of twenty-five women from nine countries. Serving an active patient load in the course of its teaching program, the school provided prenatal care and home deliveries to thousands of women; it also gave medical students the opportunity to observe normal childbirth at a time when only problem pregnancies were seen at most hospitals. Baker, for one, asserted that Bellevue's midwives knew more about delivering babies "than three-quarters of the recently graduated interns now entering medical practice."[60] By enabling hundreds of relatively uneducated women to earn the legitimacy and security of recognized training and licensure, the school served to broaden the social range of Bellevue's (and the city's) circle of health-care providers.

We cannot know how the city's private hospitals would have responded to the kinds of social and political pressures that nudged Bellevue toward more open hiring practices during these years. For better and for worse, Bellevue's policies and services were always subject to appeal through the political process. The hospital superintendent was reminded of this fact one day in 1918, when he asked a cook's helper why he had complained directly to the mayor about conditions in the kitchen. "He said he knew the Mayor but he did not know me."[61] This kind of responsiveness to external pressure was almost entirely foreign to private hospitals. As private institutions, they received praise and support for their quasi-public role, but no one demanded of them the kind of inclusiveness—in hiring or in patient care—that Bellevue was expected to provide.

By 1930, New York City's leading private hospitals had traveled a long way from the original mission defined by their founders. The choices they made between 1910 and 1930 demonstrated their range of concerns—the determination to provide good care to the patients they accepted, the desire for high institutional status, the need to cover their costs, and the aspiration to serve humankind by furthering medical education and research. Still, the responsibility for ensuring that all New Yorkers received the hospital care they required, no matter what their diagnosis, class, or income, had been delegated, more than ever before, to the public sector. In the community of hospitals, as in the individual institutions, there were now two tracks; private hospitals would concentrate the great majority of their services on patients who could contribute to the cost of their care, while public institutions dealt with the others.

As the private hospitals redefined their mission, the public hospitals' mission was redefined as well. This process was a social act. It required the participation of trustees, staff, donors, public officials, and the general public. Although the private hospitals did not necessarily publicize each individual policy change as they made it, their drift away from charity care was clear and could have been contested. By the end of the 1920s, the private institutions were not as invulnerable to public opinion as they had been in earlier decades. Most received money from the city and all needed to be acknowledged as charitable institutions in order to attract private gifts, protect their tax-free status, justify the low wages they paid, and sustain their own sense of institutional identity.

If community leaders had systematically pressed the private hospitals to take a larger share in caring for the city's poor, they could not easily have been ignored. Such pressure was not exerted, however, because many community leaders shared the private hospitals' perspective. In general, influential New Yorkers seem to have believed that private institutions merited public support because of their community service, but that they should be left free to define for themselves the nature and the limits of that service.

The private hospitals' decision to reduce their own investment in charity care between 1910 and 1930 was made more palatable by the emerging redefinition of the hospital's role in society. The new conceptualization placed much more emphasis on serving society generally through medical science than on ensuring that every member of society had access to care. Now more than ever, the residual burden was left to the public hospitals; they alone would be expected to act as truly inclusive institutions, fulfilling the mission that no longer quite fit the definition of the modern hospital.

3

Help in Time of Trouble

1930–1950

I n 1938, an accident victim was admitted to New York Hospital, and then transferred an hour later to City Hospital, the nearest municipal institution. Since the move did not seem to have been motivated by the patient's medical needs, reporters asked Dr. S. S. Goldwater, the commissioner of hospitals, to comment on the case. He defended New York Hospital, explaining that there were "scores of transfers every week under comparable conditions." Perhaps the decision was unfortunate, he said, "but if New York Hospital was wrong, so are they all." Only by making such transfers, Goldwater explained, could the voluntary hospitals remain "in the relatively advantageous position of being able to avoid overcrowding and the heavy stresses and strains to which the city's own hospitals are constantly subjected."[1]

Thus the municipal hospitals' leading spokesman articulated with perfect clarity the unequal balance of responsibility that existed between the public and private hospital systems—an inequality rooted in the past but reinforced by the austerities of the Depression. Private facilities like New York Hospital would define for themselves the limits of their capacity. Public facilities like City Hospital and Bellevue would pick up where they left off, accepting whatever "overcrowding," whatever "stresses and strains" were necessary to ensure that care was continuously available to everyone in New York who needed it.

This incident took place during one of the most difficult periods in New York's history. Between 1930 and 1950, the city was jolted first by the Great

Depression, then by World War II, and finally by the challenges of postwar adjustment. Drawn into the crises around them, both Bellevue and New York Hospital faced problems of a severity they had rarely experienced before, but their experiences were not identical. Instead, the social and institutional distinctions that had emerged in previous decades were reinforced, ensuring that the burden of providing continuity of care in troubled times would be distributed unequally between the public and private hospitals.

Hard Times, Unequal Burdens: The Depression

"Once They Were Citizens"

In many American communities, the Depression began with the stock market crash of October 1929. New York, with its light industry and highly diversified economy, took longer to feel the effects; but by 1931, the Depression had engulfed the city. "Go just a few blocks from Fifth Avenue," wrote one visitor, and you see "hardship, misery and degradation, accentuated by the shoddy grimness of the shabby houses and broken pavements." New York State officials estimated that more than 1.5 million people in the state were out of work; New York City, with half the state's factory workers, was hit hardest of all. The streets filled with sidewalk vendors selling apples, flowers, ties, or rubber balls. One observer counted nineteen people shining shoes on one block, ranging in age from twenty to seventy. In the tenements south of Bellevue, investigators found that a quarter of the families had no income at all. A few hoboes built a cluster of shacks on the riverbank some dozen blocks south of Bellevue; within a few months, the colony had mushroomed to sixty shacks and acquired a name: "Hardluck-on-the-River." More than twenty such settlements grew around the city, including the huge "Forgotten Man Gulch" in the empty reservoir in Central Park.[2]

In 1933, President Franklin D. Roosevelt's relief administrator, Harry Hopkins, sent a group of "reporters" out to survey conditions around the country. One of them, Lorena Hickok, captured the growing sense of despair and dislocation felt by so many unemployed Americans when she wrote: "Once, and not so long ago, they were citizens." Visiting New York, Hickok found more than 1 million people wholly dependent for food, clothing, shelter, and medical care on a faltering, overburdened system. "There they are," she wrote, "all thrown together into a vast pit of human misery, from which a city, dazed, still only half awake to the situation, is trying to extricate them."[3]

Several events helped stabilize the situation. First was the election of Fiorello H. LaGuardia as mayor, on an anti-Tammany, Fusion ticket in November 1933. His zestful energy helped to shake New Yorkers out of their despair and make recovery seem possible. By cutting the city budget and promising future fiscal restraint, LaGuardia won permission to resume selling municipal bonds and to levy a new set of emergency taxes dedicated to unemployment relief. Federal dollars, too, began reaching the city as President Roosevelt's

New Deal programs took hold. Soon federal construction projects were rising all around New York, funded by the New Deal's Public Works Agency (PWA) and later by the Works Progress Administration (WPA). The talent for attracting federal money displayed by LaGuardia—and by members of his administration like Robert Moses—is suggested by the fact that New York became the only municipality in the country to have its own independent WPA unit.[4]

Robert Moses was only one of many able administrators brought in by LaGuardia. Another was S. S. Goldwater, the commissioner of hospitals. The mayor's friend, George Baehr, recalled that at LaGuardia's request he spent long hours persuading Goldwater to become commissioner of health. Soon after Goldwater agreed, the mayor told Baehr he had made a mistake: "The most difficult problem is the Hospitals Department. Can't we get him to take this terrible job?"[5] In the four years since its creation by Mayor James J. Walker, the Hospitals Department had drifted under a series of lackluster appointments; LaGuardia was determined to do better. Baehr reopened the conversation with Goldwater, and the mayor got the commissioner he wanted—the first man who had both the will and the capacity to run the department with a firm hand. Besides Goldwater's long experience in running Mount Sinai Hospital, one of the best private facilities in the city, he was a former commissioner of health, had served on innumerable national committees, and had consulted for hospitals around the globe. Goldwater was not without his flaws; his style was autocratic and his temperament testy. He also believed that one of the principal functions of the public system was to care for the patients the private hospitals chose not to serve; this reasoning had led him to defend New York Hospital in the transfer case cited above. Whatever Goldwater's limitations, however, he was a talented administrator, and he managed the department with skill and integrity during one of the most difficult periods in its history.

Even with officials like Moses and Goldwater, as well as LaGuardia's personal drive and the new federal largesse, the Depression did not go away. New York City's relief rolls continued to rise, doubling in 1934 and not peaking until late in 1935, when one-third of the people who had been employed in 1930 were out of work. "I am not a coward," wrote one New Yorker to President Roosevelt, "but good Lord it is awful to stand helpless when you need things." The decision of the federal government to shift responsibility for unemployable persons back to local government in 1935 brought new burdens to the city, and the sudden cutback of WPA funds in 1937 triggered another surge in the relief rolls. As late as March 1941, some 3,000 applicants showed up, many sleeping in line overnight, to apply for about 1,000 jobs in the municipal hospitals. As one applicant explained: "If I am going to eat, I have to have a job."[6] Not until the United States entered World War II did the New York City economy regain the resilience it had had during the 1920s.

For many New Yorkers, the economic catastrophe of the 1930s became a health catastrophe as well. Bad times meant both more sickness and less care. When an official at Metropolitan Life stated: "There is no evidence at all that anybody in these United States is starving," a researcher for the Welfare Council checked with New York's four biggest hospitals. She found that these institutions had admitted ninety-eight starving patients in recent months, and that twenty of these patients had died. Nor were all cases of hunger identified as such. Dr. Milton Slocum, who interned in New York during these years, recalls giving a starving girl a diagnosis of pneumonia, which he knew she did not have, so that the hospital would provide her with food and shelter for a few days.[7]

Other health problems multiplied as well. Mount Sinai Hospital's Orthopedic Department reported a sharp increase in foot troubles among the many patients who could afford neither carfare nor shoe repairs. Many adults on work relief were doing hard physical labor for the first time in their lives; for them, injuries and muscle-strain were added to the general debility engendered by the Depression. In one immigrant neighborhood near Bellevue, investigators found that almost 40 percent of the families interviewed had someone sick in the household.[8] These physical troubles provided a grim commentary on city life during the Depression, an existence of sparse meals, ragged and outgrown clothing, broken shoes, and unheated apartments.

Private Hospitals Retreat from Charity Care

While New Yorkers' health needs were increasing, the services available to treat them were melting away. With few patients able to pay their bills, many physicians found they could no longer afford to practice. The head of the Medical Association in Brooklyn reported that 30 percent of the doctors there had closed their doors; he estimated that the figure was even higher in Manhattan. The voluntary hospitals were in trouble, too. Their philanthropic contributions were declining, their endowments were losing value, and their private rooms were standing empty. Meanwhile, a parade of impoverished patients knocked at the door. After an extensive survey in 1937, the United Hospital Fund (UHF) warned that many private hospitals would soon have to close, merge, or be taken over by the government.[9]

Few of the voluntary hospitals did any of those things. Instead, they moved to limit their costs and increase their revenues. The UHF president acknowledged in 1935 that most of its member hospitals had resorted to "the deplorable but necessary length" of closing ward beds. As for the beds that remained open, he said, hardly any of those hospitals had been able "to maintain the honored creed of admitting, without regard to the ability of the patient to pay, all who need their aid." A popular summary of the citywide Hospital Survey described the situation with painful clarity in 1938: "Taken all in all, what are your chances of getting into a hospital if you cannot afford to pay? Not very good."[10]

New York City was not unusual in this respect, since private hospitals throughout the United States were feeling similar pressures and responding in similar ways. E. H. L. Corwin, author of *The American Hospital*, estimated that during the 1930s most private hospitals devoted no more than 10 percent of their beds to free care. (The average in New York was a bit higher, about 16 percent, but it still represented a retreat during the time of the city's most acute difficulties; see Table 3.1) It is hard to document precisely the methods used to reduce charity care; as an official of the Cleveland Welfare Federation observed: "The thing which cannot be measured statistically is the extent to which persons needing hospital care are having it refused."[11] Nevertheless, the outcome seems clear: as the need for free care was rising, private hospitals were funding less of it.

New York Hospital faced all the fiscal problems of the Depression and another problem as well: the burden of a huge and expensive building. Having broken ground for its new medical center just a few months before the stock market took its plunge, the hospital found both its investment portfolio and its real estate holdings decimated in value, just when they were needed to finance the project. The center's director later observed that the hospital lost millions of dollars by having to sell so much stock at the bottom of the market during the early 1930s, just to keep going. Foreseeing at least some of the problems ahead, the board of governors decided not to occupy the whole new building at once. So when the New York Hospital–Cornell Medical Center officially opened its doors on September 1, 1932, nearly half the rooms in the hospital stood empty and unequipped. The new edifice received a rapturous welcome; medical scholar and reformer Henry Sigerist of Johns Hopkins joined a chorus of admirers when he called the center "the last link in the chain of hospital evolution," a building "of really overwhelming beauty."[12]

Table 3.1. General care services in New York City hospitals, 1930–1934.

	Municipal Hospitals			Voluntary Hospitals[1]		
Patients served per year	*1930*	*1934*	*% Change*	*1930*	*1934*	*% Change*
Free patients	150,278	191,714	+28	53,508	47,416	-11
"Public charge" patients[2]	none	none	—	30,288	69,363	+129
Pay or part-pay patients	6,947	10,822	+56	188,594	176,495	-6
Total	157,225	202,536	+29	272,390	293,274	+8
Distribution of patients						
% Free	96	95		20	16	
% "Public charge" patients	none	none		11	24	
% Pay or part-pay	4	5		69	60	
% Average occupancy	92.8	97.7		72.1	67.1	
Average cost per patient day		$3.90			$6.40	

Source: Haven Emerson, *The Hospital Survey for New York* (New York: United Hospital Fund, 1937)

[1] Private not-for-profit hospitals

[2] City-subsidized patients in voluntary hospitals

Yet though it looked complete, the project remained unfinished for many years. Not until well into the 1940s would New York Hospital open the 1,000 beds so proudly proclaimed in its initial announcements.

Even with some beds closed, the costs of the new facility outran New York Hospital's resources. During the next few years, the hospital adopted many cost-cutting measures, including reducing wages, laying off employees, lengthening staff hours, and raising patient rates. In addition, it reduced the amount of free care provided. The hospital continued throughout the 1930s to stress its charitable tradition, but in fact that tradition—already well eroded by 1930—was nearly abandoned. In the course of the 1930s, the hospital's proportion of free patients was reduced from 13 percent to 5 percent (down from 74 percent in 1910). As the *Annual Report* explained in 1937, patients who could "share in the expense" of their care were increasingly "given an opportunity to do so." Meanwhile, those who could not so share came to form a smaller and smaller proportion of the patient population.[13]

An institution can hardly be faulted for seeking to limit its losses; but all through the 1930s, as New York Hospital reduced its level of free care, it also directed a number of sizable legacies and grants to various research programs. The donors may well have preferred projects of this kind and perhaps their minds could not have been changed; but the hospital's leaders do not seem to have tried very hard. In fact, the hospital's fund-raising appeals, which set the context for the donors' gifts, placed their strongest emphasis on contributions for research and medical education. New York Hospital's circle of supporters included many of the wealthiest people in the city. As a reminder, just when relief rolls hit their highest point in 1935, a frivolous book entitled *Society Circus* let New Yorkers know how the other 1 percent lived. The author's description of the staffing requirements in nine of the city's grandest households (twenty-six to forty employees per household) included four families with New York Hospital connections: the Bakers, the Morgans, the Astors, and the Whitneys. Along with many other wealthy New Yorkers, these families made generous contributions to the medical center during the 1930s; perhaps they and other donors like them might have expanded or redirected their contributions if the hospital's leaders had shown the same concern for the city's current crisis that they did for the future of medical science.[14]

In 1938, a New York Hospital report identified the three goals of modern medicine: "Care of the sick, here and now—Teaching of doctors and nurses, to serve the community tomorrow—Research which aims to help everyone, everywhere and for all time."[15] During the 1930s, the first of these goals—the care of the sick—often seemed to be given less primacy at New York Hospital than it might have merited, considering the problems of the Depression. As for the care of the sick poor, that seemed to rank lowest of all.

Turning to the Public Hospitals

When sick New Yorkers failed to find a place in private institutions like New York Hospital, they turned to public hospitals like Bellevue. At the depths of the Depression, about half the people in the city were eligible for free care in the municipal hospitals because they qualified as "medically indigent"—that is, they could not afford private health care.[16] Not all availed themselves of the privilege, but hundreds of thousands did.

Serving this great number of patients put a tremendous strain on the capacities and the environment of the public hospitals. A journalist in 1933 contrasted the city's half-empty private hospitals to the chaotic scene at Bellevue, where the wards were packed with row upon row of beds—"not high hospital beds, but miscellaneous cots, some unpainted, some sagging so low that reaching down to care for their occupants taxed the back muscles of the scurrying nurses." Out on the balconies, the journalist discovered still more patients, lying in beds barely sheltered from the falling rain. Four years later another reporter visited Bellevue and found matters even worse. "Were ever the sick and suffering packed in more wretchedly anywhere," he asked, "except in military hospitals after a great battle?"[17]

The spartan conditions took a toll on everyone treated at Bellevue during the 1930s. Yet many of the patients must also have recognized the value of the service the hospital was providing. This juxtaposition of positive and negative can be seen in one woman's description of a night on the wards. Her account (written originally in Yiddish) portrays Bellevue as both awesome and protective, an institution that is huge and overcrowded but also somehow nurturing:

> It is night. . . . From time to time I fall asleep and wake again. . . . Nurses and orderlies [are] still keeping watch over the sick. Meanwhile, I observe the titanic task of Bellevue Hospital. Row upon row of occupied beds. . . . It is indeed a gigantic factory where healing is brought to mortal flesh. . . . I see the patients, statuelike in our beds . . . and all around us the doctors and nurses constantly laboring to relieve our fevers and diminish our pains.[18]

Who were these patients, "statuelike" in their beds? There are no statistics that profile precisely the people who sought help at Bellevue during the 1930s, but anecdotal accounts suggest that many individuals who had previously used private hospitals turned to the public system because of the Depression. One visitor to a clinic at New York Hospital noticed how well-to-do the patients appeared and asked an employee where the poor ones were. The employee explained that now that the hospital was in financial trouble, "we don't get as many of them as we used to." About the same time, a New York City radio commentator reported that Bellevue Hospital was serving more middle-class patients than ever before. Three years earlier, he said, the hospital had treated "few so-called Americans who could speak English and very few of that class known as the white-collar man." Now New Yorkers of all kinds were appearing at Bellevue's door. A WPA artist who painted murals at Bellevue during those years puts the matter even more simply: "I saw everybody at Bellevue," he says. "Everybody was poor."[19]

Like all social institutions during the Depression, the municipal hospitals were straining to make ends meet. For the first time, the city assigned a team of full-time staff to ascertain whether patients could help pay for their care. Collections rose, but even in the banner year of 1939, patient fees covered only 1 percent of the department's total costs. And although municipal hospitals did make some attempt to screen out those who could afford to go elsewhere, they virtually never rejected patients for lack of space. As early as 1930, the commissioner of hospitals turned down a proposal by some Bellevue doctors to limit daily outpatient admissions, and his explanation set the tone for the municipal hospitals' performance throughout the 1930s. "Treatment cannot be refused cases in public city hospitals," he wrote, "because of limitations of time or space."[20] This principle was followed faithfully, under circumstances of extraordinary difficulty, ensuring that everyone in New York had a place to go for medical care throughout the Depression, though the care often took place under less than optimal conditions.

The public hospitals managed to serve their multitudes of patients, in part, by spending nearly 40 percent less per patient day than the private hospitals (see Table 3.1). A portion of the savings came from what they paid their senior staff. The $13,000 a year that Commissioner S. S. Goldwater earned for presiding over twenty-four hospitals was less than the chief administrator at New York Hospital was paid for managing one institution. Goldwater was not shy about publicizing the inadequacy of his pay. When a citizen wrote to complain about municipal services and signed his letter "Contributor to your salary," Goldwater replied that he could tell the complainant was a reluctant contributor, so he was returning his contribution herewith. "The 1¢ stamp which is enclosed represents probably a little more than your fair share of my salary for the current year, but you may keep the change, and welcome."[21] Other top municipal staff also earned much less than their private hospital counterparts.

Even at the lower staff levels, where wages were generally competitive with the private sector, the work in public hospitals was more difficult because there were more than twice as many patients per employee. Like many municipal institutions, Bellevue filled in as best it could with WPA workers, but many were underqualified or, as the director of nursing said, "of the floater type," putting in as brief a spell as possible until something better turned up. A reporter visiting Bellevue's maintenance department observed: "Patients and maintenance workers have one thing in common: both groups wants to leave the hospital just as soon as they possibly can!" And leave they did. Staff turnover rates exceeded 80 percent, even during the worst years of the Depression.[22] Not until 1938, when public hospital workers finally won an eight-hour work day and received their first raises since 1932, did Bellevue's staffing begin to stabilize.

The private hospitals were well aware of the strain on the municipal institutions, but they insisted that they could not afford to accept more charity patients unless the city subsidies for treating the poor were increased. Indeed, they maintained that the current insufficient level of subsidy would soon force them to close, throwing the whole burden of charity care on the public system. City officials often demonstrated the effectiveness of this argument by repeating it back to the public. The Brooklyn borough president, for example, rose to the private facilities' defense at a hearing on subsidy rates. "These hospital men are not professional agitators," he proclaimed, "and I will do what I can to keep these hospitals from closing up."[23]

The city's $3 per day subsidy was indeed little more than half the reported per-diem cost of ward care in the private hospitals, but given their high fixed expenditures—whether they ran full or empty—it probably cost them less than their official rate to care for additional patients. The private hospitals showed their awareness of this by more than doubling their number of city-subsidized patients between 1930 and 1934, despite their continuing insistence that the reimbursement scale was driving them to ruin (see Table 3.1). By the late 1930s, the number had nearly doubled again, and the city was subsidizing nearly 40 percent of the ward patients served in the voluntary hospitals.[24]

Overall, between these subsidies to private institutions and the hundreds of thousands of patients served each year in the municipal system, public funds played a decisive role in maintaining the continuity of hospital care in New York City during the Depression.

Shoulder to Shoulder? The 1940s

When the United States entered World War II, the financial crisis that had caused voluntary hospitals to decrease their charity care during the Depression eased. Yet the 1940s brought new challenges, and both public and private hospitals experienced new difficulties in carrying out their missions. In some respects they shared similar problems, but in other respects their differing circumstances produced very different results.

"There Is No War Here"

The United States entered World War II in December 1941, after Japan bombed the U.S. Navy base at Pearl Harbor in Hawaii. The city did not feel the effects of war immediately, but within a year of Pearl Harbor, military installations like the Brooklyn Navy Yard began filling with workers, while small factories and machine-shops all over town started humming with war production. New York also become a major transfer point for people and materials; goods flowed in and out of the harbor, while service personnel, war workers, and executives arrived on every train and plane.

With consumer goods rationed, highlife became one of the few ways to spend wartime earnings. So vigorously did New York embrace the business of entertainment that the city struck many observers as callous. Carlos Romulo, a member of the Philippine goverment-in-exile, looked around a New York restaurant and exclaimed to a friend: "But there is no war here!" In this town, he observed, "One read of rationing and shortages, but one also seemed able to buy pretty much anything one desired if the price were in his pocket."

Harry Woodburn Chase, the chancellor of New York University, wrote to the dean of the medical school, who was serving in the armed forces overseas: "The most amazing sight in New York these days is Times Square on a Saturday night. . . . If you can imagine New Year's Eve with most of the people in uniform, you won't be far off."[25]

Not all New Yorkers could buy whatever they wanted, nor did they all spend their Saturday nights in Times Square. For most of them, the war brought jobs, but it also brought long hours, rising prices, shortages, and anxiety about friends and family overseas. Social divisions persisted in the city as well, making a noticeable contrast to the wartime rhetoric of democratic unity. Women defense workers, for instance, frequently encountered hostility and exploitation from male coworkers and supervisors, while many black New Yorkers continued to face persistent discrimination. For the most part, racial tensions remained below the boiling-point, but when a black soldier was wounded by a white policeman in Harlem in August 1943, the incident drew hundreds of people into the streets. Protest turned to riot, and in the end it took appeals from black community leaders, a carefully controlled police response, and the on-site presence of Mayor LaGuardia to restore order.

New York City's wartime experience reflected many of the best and worst characteristics of the American home front during World War II. On the positive side, many New Yorkers rose to the occasion valiantly, displaying courage and innovation, along with the heroic ability to make do with insufficient resources. Romulo, for one, came to admire New York's "gay and absurd, seemingly heartless bravery." The city, he said, had "a fighting spirit of its own." New Yorkers enlisted by the thousands on the first morning after Pearl Harbor, donated huge quantities of blood, contributed millions of dollars to war bond drives, and kept vital services running with a patched-together combination of retirees and volunteers. On the negative side, the city also provided numerous examples of discrimination, profiteering, and casual self-seeking. If New York was a city of courage and voluntarism, it was also a city where a military order was necessary to enforce civil defense rules for dimming public lights, where the black market flourished, and where influential people seemed to know a way around every rule.[26]

Making Do

New York's hospitals began their own wartime activities in the winter of 1942, with preparations for mass casualties if the city should be attacked by German bombers. The New York Times carried a picture of Bellevue with windows newly bricked up and a bombproof entrance rigged outside the emergency room. Air raid fears gradually diminished, but by then, the hospitals had become immersed in the struggle that would preoccupy them for the rest of the war: how to keep going with most of their staff on military leave. In line with draft restrictions, medical students squeezed four years' education into three, and interns rushed through their training in nine months; one of their teachers called this generation "the rat-race boys." By the summer of 1942, 6,000 New York physicians had departed for the service, one-third of them from the municipal hospitals. Among them were the members of Bellevue's and New York Hospital's World War I field units, both reorganized and dispatched overseas in the summer of 1942. When a New Jersey hospital administrator wrote Mayor LaGuardia asking whether New York hospitals could lend him any medical staff, the mayor responded: "We cannot help you, but, in return, would ask your help."[27]

Nurses joined the services even faster than physicians. The *New York Times* reported in 1943 that they were leaving the city at the rate of 3,000 per month. The U.S. Cadet Nursing Corps helped keep many hospitals going, including Bellevue and New York Hospital, by training its recruits in existing nursing schools and attracting the largest classes in history. But eager young students could not make up for the departure of hundreds of experienced nurses. By 1944, Bellevue had about half as many trained nurses as it had had in 1940. New York Hospital did somewhat better, but only by constantly hiring replacements; in 1944, the hospital experienced a 96 percent turnover rate among its staff nurses.[28]

Not all staff departures were service related. During those years many of the lower paid employees left hospital work for higher paying civilian jobs. A United Hospital Fund spokesman chided these people for being lured away by "the false prosperity of the times."[29] Yet the reviving economy of the war years must have seemed to workers a long-awaited deliverance after the spartan years of the Depression. When the new opportunities opened up, many jumped at the first chance in a decade to better their positions.

Meanwhile, as wartime spending revived the city economy, the need for free care declined and with it the demand for Bellevue's services. The hospital's one source of extra patients during this period was its new 200-bed unit for venereal disease—a fact that illuminates both the particular health problems of wartime and the kind of disease still consigned, for the most part, to public care. Even so, Bellevue's total patient census decreased for the first time in years; between 1941 and 1945, its occupancy rate fell from 101 percent to 71 percent. Unfortunately, the hospital's staffing fell even faster.

Wartime staffing shortages opened new opportunities for several groups of health providers who had long faced job discrimination. For instance, once the men began going into the service, women doctors found themselves in demand at hospitals all over the city. The total number appointed was still not very large—Bellevue, with thirty-eight female house staff out of 242, had the most in the United States—but the trend was notable and widespread. The *New York Times,* praising the change at Bellevue (while using wording that helped explain why it had taken so long), assured its readers that "the girl doctors work on an equal footing with their men colleagues."[30]

Blacks as well as women found new opportunities at Bellevue. During the Depression, Bellevue had added a number of black attendants; by the late 1930s, they represented about 20 percent of the hospital's nonprofessional nursing staff. Black nurses waited even longer for their opportunity, but when Bellevue lost a third of its trained nurses during the first year of the war, it began hiring black nurses to replace them. Other municipal hospitals followed suit, and by 1943, more than a quarter of the nurses and half the attendants in the public system were black.[31]

The city institutions' acute need for staff drove this change in hiring policy, but it was spurred on as well by continual lobbying from community groups and from City Councilmen Stanley Isaacs and Adam Clayton Powell, Jr. Later in the war, after black nurses were well established in the public system, the same groups turned their attention to the private hospitals, but there they made little headway.[32] The exigencies of the war were not enough to give all Americans equal opportunity, not even for such a mixed blessing as hospital employment. Under wartime conditions, women physicians might be acceptable in the private hospitals, but not black nurses.

Bellevue's greater openness to black and female staff members did not solve its desperate staffing shortage, so in 1943, the hospital turned to a source of workers that no private hospital would have considered: the prison on Riker's Island. Starting in 1943, many of the Riker's inmates convicted of petty crimes served out their sentences at Bellevue, where they helped in the kitchen and laundry, did painting and carpentry, ran elevators, and even worked on the wards as orderlies. By the end of the war in 1945, nearly 200 prisoners were working at Bellevue, their presence bearing eloquent testimony to the distance between Bellevue's aspirations as a leading medical institution and the reality of its position as an impoverished city hospital.[33]

Bellevue's prison workers were housed in the hospital's empty wards—an indication of how much the patient load had dropped from the overcrowded days of the 1930s. By contrast, New York Hospital found itself serving more patients than ever before. As wartime profits and military salaries began to enrich the city's economy, private patients reappeared, and for the first time since the medical center began operation, New York Hospital was able to open all of its beds. For the rest of the war, it struggled hard to maintain the facility it had finally managed to fill. Like Bellevue, it found itself skimping on services, giving trainees unprecedented levels of responsibility, and using thousands of hours of volunteer assistance. At the same time, again like Bellevue, it had to navigate a morass of wartime shortages and rationing requirements. Keeping food on the table and fuel in the boilers often proved to be as much a struggle as keeping nurses on the wards.

If Bellevue and New York Hospital faced a number of the same problems during the war years, this did not mean that their situations were identical. The hiring in public institutions was much more tightly regulated than in the private sector, since Mayor LaGuardia's reforms had put many more positions under civil service hiring restrictions. In addition, most municipal jobs were still limited to persons who were city residents and American citizens. Those limitations excluded many potential employees that private hospitals were free to hire. As for purchasing, municipal hospitals were tied into an elaborate month-by-month bidding process within a narrow circle of approved vendors, whereas private hospitals could establish long-term relationships with their best suppliers, venture as far afield as necessary to obtain what they needed, and stock up on extra provisions as they became available.

New York Hospital actually prospered financially during the war, since the heaviest costs of the new medical center had been paid, the demand for its services rose, and wartime restrictions kept its operating expenses in check. In fact, the hospital resorted to subterfuge in order, as Board President Langdon Marvin put it, "to avoid the evidence of too much prosperity." Because its progression from red ink to black might discourage potential contributors, the hospital made a practice at least through 1946, according to Marvin, of transferring up to $500,000 a year in capital expenses to the operating budget so as to show an operating deficit. This procedure, Marvin noted, "certainly puts us in the red."[34]

Leaders of private hospitals often suggested that their institutions were able to serve the community better than the public hospitals because they were free from political pressure. But just as New York City's wartime performance displayed both bravery and self-interest, so its private hospitals during those years combined a commitment to serving the public with nearly total freedom from public scrutiny. Early in the war, a United Hospital Fund spokesman defined New York's private hospitals as "a working example of democracy and free enterprise, intrinsic to the way of life the United States is arming to defend."[35] However, the private hospitals reflected more about the American way of life than this speaker acknowledged. In their division of responsibility with the city's municipal hospitals, in what they were asked to do and what they were excused from doing, those hospitals also reflected the American tendency to give private institutions more latitude than public ones, to ask few questions about their operations, and to exempt them from the more disagreeable demands of public service. Praised for their contributions to society during the war, yet rarely criticized when their institutional self-interest limited such contributions, private hospitals demonstrated—in war as in peace—that the burdens of community service were not equally distributed.

When "After the War" Arrived

When World War II ended with Japan's surrender in August 1945, the event was hailed by a two-day bacchanal in Times Square and welcomed in quieter ways all over the city. Within months, the troops began to come home and rationing was ended. For the first time in fifteen years, Bellevue and New York Hospital went about their business without either economic or military crises hanging over their heads.

Within a year of Japan's surrender, however, the municipal hospitals found themselves struggling to accommodate a new surge in demand. Once again, New Yorkers were having trouble paying for private care. Responding to the inflation that followed the end of wage-and-price controls in 1946, private hospitals raised their rates precipitously. At the same time, as discussed below, they began converting their cheapest areas—the wards—to semi-private rooms. Unable to afford these accommodations, many New Yorkers turned back to the system that had seen them through the Depression: the public hospitals. "Our wards are bulging today," wrote Commissioner Edward Bernecker, "overflowing their burden of human misery into every corner of each hospital."[36]

Another strain on the public system came from the tradition that the municipal hospitals should take sole responsibility for certain categories of patients. A not untypical report by the New York Academy of Medicine in 1947 revealed that New York urgently needed more services for alcoholics. The report confirmed that private hospitals were systematically excluding these patients, then concluded by recommending that the municipal hospitals should take in more of them. The chronically ill, too, were routinely referred to the public institutions on Welfare (formerly Blackwell's) Island. As one physician from Columbia-Presbyterian Hospital explained: "Chronic disabilities at present cannot be handled by private hospitals. . . . Chronic patients are happier on the Island."[37] By the postwar years, chronic and degenerative illnesses were becoming more prevalent, as more New Yorkers were living long enough to develop such disorders. This changing pattern might have inspired dialogue about a new distribution of clinical responsibility. Instead, the city Department of Hospitals continued to accept primary responsibility for these patients, dedicating a significant part of its postwar budget to developing new facilities for their care.

Many other city departments had undertaken equally ambitious commitments, causing municipal expenses to outpace municipal revenues despite the city's healthier economy. Taking office in 1946, Mayor William O'Dwyer found himself trying to balance soaring inflation, a civic expectation of free-handed public spending, and an abrupt end to the federal dollars that had poured into New York during the Depression and the war. Even maintaining the many public structures erected with New Deal funding became a challenge. During the 1930s, someone had asked the grandest builder of them all, Robert Moses, how the city's growing array of facilities was to be maintained. He answered: "That's the next generation's problem."[38] The expansion of municipal services—schools, hospitals, parks, highways, bridges, and sewers—had been one of the glories of the LaGuardia administration, but by the late 1940s, his successors were struggling to live with the results.

The public hospitals were a case in point. New York was spending millions of dollars every year on these institutions, but the investment was modest compared to the scale of the system the money was meant to maintain. For example, in 1950, when the Department of Hospitals spent about $3,800 per patient bed, New York Hospital averaged more than $8,000.[39] Capital funds were also short; Mayor O'Dwyer obtained state permission to borrow $150 million in hospital construction bonds, but this was not nearly enough to do all the renovation and rebuilding needed, let alone to maintain the structures once they were completed. Besides the one-time bond issue, the city needed more spending money every year to keep its hospitals going.

Locations Over Time
Bellevue Hospital & New York Hospital

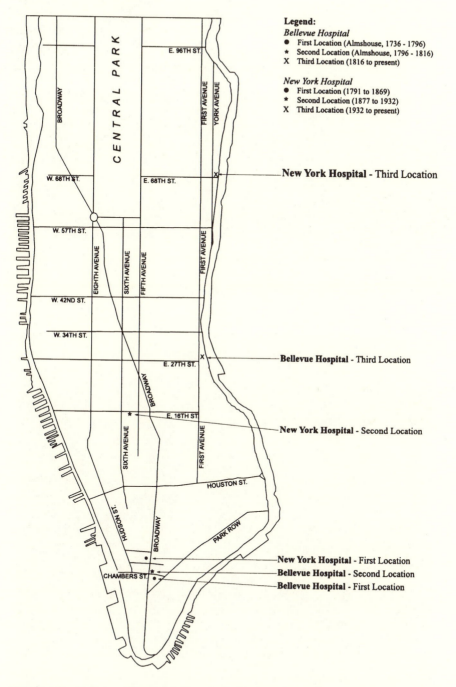

Legend:

Bellevue Hospital
- First Location (Almshouse, 1736 - 1796)
- ★ Second Location (Almshouse, 1796 - 1816)
- X Third Location (1816 to present)

New York Hospital
- First Location (1791 to 1869)
- ★ Second Location (1877 to 1932)
- X Third Location (1932 to present)

New York Hospital - Third Location

Bellevue Hospital - Third Location

New York Hospital - Second Location

New York Hospital - First Location
Bellevue Hospital - Second Location
Bellevue Hospital - First Location

Map locating Bellevue Hospital & New York Hospital throughout their histories. Map designed by Elizabeth O Mlulu Geary.

New York Hospital's first building, in lower Manhattan, operated from 1791 until 1869. At the time the hospital opened, it was so far north of town that its grounds were sometimes used for clandestine duels. *Courtesy of the Archives, New York Hospital–Cornell Medical Center.*

Private patients represented only a fraction of New York Hospital's patients until well into the 1920s. After the new hospital opened on West 15th Street in 1877, however, it exerted every effort to attract more such patients, offering them attractive rooms like this one. *Courtesy of the Archives, New York Hospital–Cornell Medical Center.*

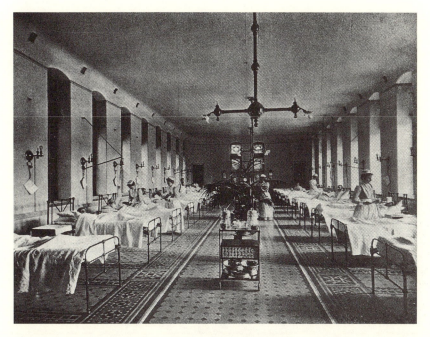

Most New York Hospital patients stayed on wards like the one shown in this 1894 photograph, with bare floors and little furniture other than the rows of iron beds under the big windows. Bellevue's wards looked much the same and served a similar patient roster, mostly working-class New Yorkers in need of charity care. *Courtesy of the Archives, New York Hospital–Cornell Medical Center.*

Bellevue Hospital, seen from the East River in 1848. The architecture was similar to that of New York Hospital, shown on the preceding page. The Bellevue building, which opened in 1816 and originally also included the Almshouse, took its name from the Bellevue Farm that had previously occupied the site. Portions of this building continued to be used by the hospital until it was finally demolished in 1938. *Courtesy of New York University Medical Center Archives.*

Medical students watch an operation in the Bellevue Hospital amphitheater in 1895. Senior students observe from the lower rows, while lowerclassmen crane their necks for a view from above. Medical students of this era learned by observation, not practice; as one student recalled, "We didn't come within a mile of touching a patient." *Courtesy of Board of Managers Collection, Bellevue Hospital Archives.*

This student nurse, photographed in 1891, wears the Bellevue Training School's official student uniform: dress of blue-and-white striped gingham, crisp white apron, and the distinctive cap of pleated organdy. Her small patient, too, is immaculately dressed. *Courtesy of Board of Managers Collection, Bellevue Hospital Archives.*

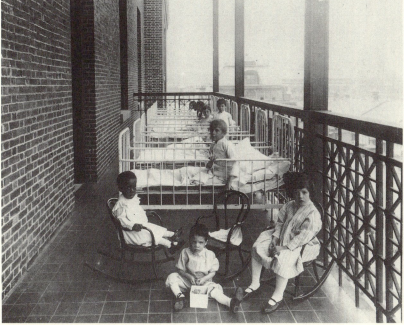

Children take the air in 1913 on one of Bellevue Hospital's many balconies. During this period, sunshine and fresh air were seen as vital elements in the treatment of disease. Then as now, however, some "boarder babies" remained at Bellevue long after they recovered, because of the difficulty of finding homes for them. *Courtesy of Bellevue Hospital Archives.*

Bellevue's historic invention—the hospital ambulance—responds to a street accident in 1915. By that year, most hospitals in the city were using only motorized vehicles, but Bellevue did not retire its last horse-drawn ambulance until 1924. *Courtesy of Arthur Zitrin, M.D., Bellevue Hospital Archives.*

The Ringling Brothers and Barnum & Bailey Circus entertained at Bellevue every year from 1908 until 1967, when demolition for the new hospital tower eliminated the courtyard and balconies that had created an arena for the circus. Here, in 1919, young patients mingle happily with clowns, cowboys, and two elephants. *Courtesy of Allan E. Dumont, M.D., Bellevue Hospital Archives.*

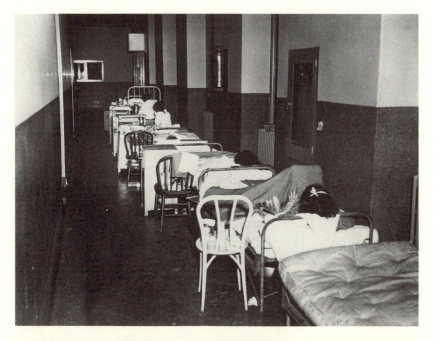

During the years after World War II, as private hospitals expanded semiprivate care and cut back on ward beds, the public hospitals experienced a surge of admissions. In this 1948 picture, patients who cannot fit into Bellevue's wards are accommodated in the corridor, some in beds and some on spartan cots. *Courtesy of the Collections of the Municipal Archives, Department of Records and Information Services, City of New York.*

In 1976, during New York City's fiscal crisis, Bellevue's hospital workers staged a four-day wildcat strike to protest a scheduled layoff of several thousand staff. Those particular layoffs were averted, but only after the strikers agreed to forego cost-of-living raises for two years—a giveback worth about $10 million. *Courtesy of Bellevue Hospital Archives.*

A Bellevue volunteer transports her young patient in the most serviceable conveyance available: a grocery cart. In this corridor may be seen both the handsome detailing of the original building and the deterioration that had occurred by the early 1970s. *Courtesy of Bellevue Hospital Archives.*

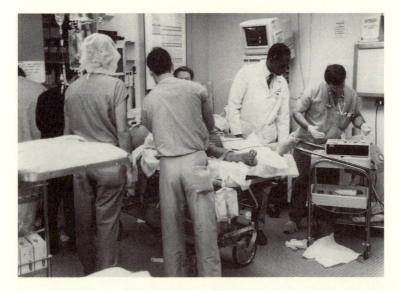

The Bellevue emergency room is the crossroads of the city, where policemen and prisoners, wealthy accident victims, and homeless drug addicts are brought for trauma care. The crowded conditions shown in this 1993 picture were much improved after a major renovation in the mid-1990s. *Courtesy of Bellevue Hospital Archives.*

One obvious way to improve city finances was to reduce the transit system's huge annual deficit by raising the subway fare. But the five-cent fare, which had remained unchanged since the turn of the century, had become an icon of civic culture; as a travel guide to the city observed, "The New Yorker is extremely sensitive on this point." Casting about for a politically palatable way to sell a fare rise to the public, Mayor O'Dwyer shrewdly chose to base his appeal on the need for new hospitals. Raising the subway fare became, in effect, a vote for health. "It is time we all quit playing politics with the sick in the hospitals," he told one audience in 1947. Transit deficits were taking $31 million a year "from the health of the people." The following month, he put the matter even more simply: "As long as New York City has a five-cent subway fare, it will have a five-cent hospital system." Events took many more turns, but on July 1, 1948, O'Dwyer raised the subway fare to ten cents; the nickel ride was gone forever. When the city budget was prepared the following spring, the Board of Estimate found itself with $40 million more to spend. Out of this surplus, the Department of Hospitals got only $4 million, far less than O'Dwyer had led the public to expect. To a considerable extent, a campaign stressing the hospitals' needs had been used to win funding for other departments.[40]

This episode says a good deal about the status of municipal hospitals in postwar New York. The fact that O'Dwyer chose to link the fare rise to the well-being of the hospitals testifies to their continuing importance in civic life; the prospect of saving them, he believed, would encourage New Yorkers to swallow the higher fare they had resisted for years. At the same time, the fact that the hospitals received much less than was expected emphasizes the complicated political trade-offs that shaped their world, trade-offs shaped by the city leaders' altruism, by their political calculations, and sometimes—as in O'Dwyer's case—by both at once. Finally, despite a $150 million construction campaign and a $67 million annual budget, the hospitals were still in trouble, and that suggests the magnitude of the challenge that New York had set for itself in building so expansive a system. Compared to other cities, New York's hospital spending was extraordinarily generous. Compared to what it would have cost to maintain the system adequately, its allocations were far too small, and every year the gap widened between what was needed and what the city could afford to spend.

New York's private hospitals, too, were facing spiraling costs in the postwar years, and they insisted that the city had an obligation to help them by raising the rate at which it reimbursed them for serving the poor. Private hospitals had always complained about the inadequacy of the city reimbursement rate, which had hardly changed since 1930; after the war, when their costs rose steeply, the complaints intensified. This time their lobbying was successful. Starting in 1946, Mayor O'Dwyer increased their subsidy rate almost every year. The rate did not yet match the hospitals' full costs, but by making an effort to bring the two into line, O'Dwyer endorsed for the first time, at least in principle, the idea that private providers should not have to bear any part of the cost for serving New York's poorest residents. Originally the private hospitals had taken pride in the fact that philanthropic funds financed most of their services to the poor; by the middle of the twentieth century, they had established the principle (if not yet the practice) that government alone should carry that responsibility.

The city was not the only level of government from which the private hospitals received useful assistance during the postwar years. For example, the Veterans Administration's decision to create its own medical system after the war protected private institutions from having to deal with the many veterans who had long-term disabilities. Also, the federal Hill-Burton Act of 1946 provided generous public funding for private hospital construction. Perhaps even more important were the actions the federal government chose *not* to take. In 1933, private hospital representatives had persuaded Congress to exempt them from the National Recovery Administration's rules on hours, wages, and collective bargaining. Two years later they managed to have their workers excluded from the Social Security Act. Finally, in 1947, the Taft-Hartley Act put private hospitals beyond the reach of the National Labor Relations Act.

When private hospitals appealed for public support, they made a virtue of their nongovernmental status, stressing their independence and voluntarist heritage and associating themselves with all the values of American democracy. One New York Hospital publication explained that the hospital's story was "the story of an American institution . . . developing in the wholesome atmosphere of American freedom." As the Cold War succeeded the World War, this idea was turned into a clarion call. New York Hospital was a free hospital, wrote John Hay Whitney, board president in 1947, not in the sense of treating most patients for free, but "in the sense of being free to avoid bureaucracy or politics, free to investigate in the whole field of medicine, free to experiment in the better organization of medical care, free to innovate, to initiate new plans, to progress, perhaps to lead the way."[41]

By the time Whitney wrote these words, the private hospitals had redefined their social role in a way that would have astonished the trustees of an earlier generation. In 1948, the president of the United Hospital Fund explained that caring for the medically indigent was the responsibility of the public system, although private hospitals were "called upon to help."[42] His words marked the final stage of the voluntaries' disengagement from a formal obligation to the city's poor. Many poor patients would still be admitted, to meet educational needs or to "help" the municipal hospitals, but they would only be visitors in the private system. The city hospitals were their institutional home.

Legacies of Hard Times

As New York City's hospitals prepared to enter the 1950s, they could take pride in having survived twenty traumatic years. Indeed, they had done more than survive. Like their patients, these facilities and their employees had urgently needed help in hard times, and out of their need they had established new patterns of behavior, new institutions, and new relationships that would live long into the future. In particular, two trends emerged during the 1930s and 1940s that would permanently affect the pattern of hospital care in the city. First, private hospitals needing revenue introduced hospital insurance and semiprivate rooms. Second, a combination of economic need and Depression-era politics sparked the city's first sustained union activity among hospital workers.

In different ways, these two trends increased the distance between New York's public and private hospitals. Hospital insurance made private care affordable for many middle-income New Yorkers, thus further marginalizing the patients left in the public system; and the public sector's openness to labor activism gave unions a voice in the municipal hospitals that they would not attain in private medical institutions for several decades. The years of Depression and war presented the city's public and private hospitals with many similar problems, but they also accentuated the differences between them.

Help for the Hospitals: Semiprivate Care and Hospital Insurance

During the 1930s, as private hospitals reduced their role in charity care, a new patient group arose to take the place of the poor: the middle class. This represented a change that hospital leaders had been seeking for years. As early as 1910, the head of Presbyterian Hospital had told a gathering of fellow administrators that they should not be satisfied with serving a few rich patients and many poor ones. Instead, they must find a way to accommodate the one group whose needs remained unmet: "the real citizenship . . . the brain and brawn upon which the very life of the state depends." Yet these solid citizens remained underserved for two more decades, primarily because hospitals of the time offered no accommodation that suited both their pocketbooks and their pride. As the United Hospital Fund explained in 1920, middle-class New Yorkers "feel unable to pay full rates and do not wish charity." This delicacy of feeling was generally applauded. A *New York Times* editorial in 1926 noted that the instinct to pay one's way was "deeply engrained in the American ethic." If people saved their lives by giving up on this point, observed the editors, "then every instinct tells us that their lives are not particularly worth saving."[43]

It was sometimes difficult to tell precisely who belonged to this underserved class, since descriptions tended to focus more on their sensibilities than on their occupations or income. All observers agreed on one point, however, that these individuals were the social bedrock of the city—the hard workers, the taxpayers, the good citizens—struggling to live exemplary lives on little money. Many apparently belonged to the city's growing population of low level white-collar workers. This group expanded during the 1920s, as many second-generation Americans gained a firmer foothold in the city. Leaving behind the tenements and sweatshops that had dominated their immigrant parents' lives, these New Yorkers had little taste for the kind of medical care that their parents had had to accept. They felt no need for the special services and elegant rooms that facilities like New York Hospital provided to their private patients, but neither did they wish to share a ward with twenty or thirty people and be grouped with domestics and laborers.

In 1930, Massachusetts General Hospital in Boston broke new ground when it created a semiprivate service for this "middle" class of patient. Semiprivate patients shared both their rooms and their nurses with three or four other patients, and they paid much less than they would have for private care, but in the hospital's most important social dichotomy—the division between the private service and the wards—they stood on the private side. Mount Sinai Hospital brought semiprivate care to New York in 1931, and soon voluntary hospitals all over the city followed Mount Sinai's example. By the late 1930s, New York Hospital had opened 100 semiprivate beds.

Even semiprivate care might have proved too expensive for middle-income families, especially during the Depression, had not hospital insurance emerged as a way to pay for it. Health insurance of various kinds had existed in the city for generations, offered by neighborhood associations, fraternal lodges, mutual benefit societies, immigrant societies, and many other groups; but these plans tended to offer very limited benefits, and many did not cover inpatient care at all. In any case, by the 1930s, fewer such plans were available, since by then many families had left behind both the old neighborhoods and the old organizations.[44]

Into this void, in 1933, stepped the voluntary hospitals. By that time, the Depression had hit New York with full force, and the hospitals were desperate for revenue. They turned to an experimental insurance plan that had been pioneered by Baylor University Hospital in Houston a few years earlier and had since been adopted by groups of hospitals in several U.S. cities. A committee of the United Hospital Fund was established to plan a similar program for New York, and in May 1935 the Associated Hospital Services (AHS, which evolved into New York City's Blue Cross program) opened its doors.[45]

The AHS launched a vigorous campaign for its "3¢ a Day Plan," focusing (like many earlier schemes) on employed workers. Advertisements made clear that buying hospital insurance was one way a responsible man looked after his family. Some might have argued that the need for this service was not urgent in New York, since a sizable proportion of the city's working families were already eligible for free care in the public hospitals. In addition, private philanthropy and a broad program of city subsidies supported inexpensive ward care in voluntary hospitals throughout the city. The AHS dismissed these alternatives, portraying ward care as demeaning and second rate. A typical ad in 1935 explained: "The average man, with the average income, has pride. He is not looking for charity; he is not looking for ward care. He wants the best of attention for himself and his family."[46] The subtext was clear: the "best of attention" was to be had in the semiprivate rooms of AHS's participating private hospitals, not on their wards, and certainly not in public institutions, where the sole offering was the despised charity care.

The AHS campaign struck a responsive chord; the plan met its first year's enrollment goal in six months and by 1938 had 500,000 subscribers. Indeed, it offered an attractive package. In these years of low salaries and minimal fringe benefits, a sudden illness could simultaneously stop a worker's wages and cost several months' pay in hospital bills. Now, anyone who could afford 90¢ per month could count on twenty-one days of semiprivate care per year in any participating hospital. By the end of 1940, its fifth year of operation, AHS's membership topped 1 million, making it the largest Blue Cross plan in the country. And as AHS grew, so did semiprivate care. In 1940, one quarter of the patients in New York's voluntary hospitals stayed in semiprivate rooms.[47] Because of hospital insurance, semiprivate care was on its way to becoming one more middle-class entitlement—not necessarily accessible to all, but part of the package of services that many average Americans could afford, and to which many more could reasonably aspire.

AHS was as welcome to the providers as it was to the patients. A United Hospital Fund official asserted in 1935 that the program was "in no way a money-making scheme for hospitals. It is rather a public service made available to persons of modest means by hospitals." In fact, AHS was very useful to hospitals—as it should have been, since they designed it. After years of empty rooms and unpaid bills, these facilities could hardly help loving a plan that brought them many new patients while sparing them from either having to negotiate reduced fees or engage in costly bill collection. In addition, AHS paid slightly better than the going rate for semiprivate care.[48]

Under other circumstances, the medical establishment might have shown little enthusiasm for a Blue Cross program like AHS, which introduced a fourth player into the already complicated interaction among physicians, patients, and hospitals. But, during the mid-1930s, the possibility that the federal government might enact compulsory national health insurance put the matter in a new light. Recognizing the appeal of insurance, the physicians threw their support behind the most acceptable form available: the private Blue Cross plan, within which they had considerable influence.[49] The immediate danger of federal action was averted when medical opposition succeeded in keeping health insurance out of the Social Security Act in 1935. But the issue remained alive, guaranteeing AHS and its fellow Blue Cross plans continued support from those who feared a public program. In this political atmosphere, voluntary insurance became more than a method of financing health care; it was seen as an emblem of loyalty to the medical profession, a bulwark against socialized medicine, and a symbol of patriotic values. A revenue source from one perspective, a benefit program from another, Blue Cross gained not a little from being presented also as an affirmation of the American way of life.

During World War II, new factors fostered the growth of health insurance. For the first time in a decade, New York City was experiencing a tight labor market, and once wages were frozen in October 1942, health insurance became an alternative that employers could offer their workers. The U.S. Internal Revenue Service soon ruled that firms could deduct their contributions to their employees' health insurance as a business expense; it also ruled that employees need not count these payments as taxable income or as raises that were subject to the wage freeze. Thus, supported by public policy, enrollment in private insurance plans grew dramatically.

AHS did have its limitations. It addressed only minimally the needs of part-time workers, temporary workers, the unemployed, the elderly, and the chronically ill; even many New Yorkers with fulltime jobs could not afford the AHS monthly premium. Consequently, its very success within the private system reinforced the necessity for the public hospitals to treat those who were excluded. Nevertheless, the AHS health plan was highly valued by many employed workers and their families, and it spread rapidly after World War II. Compulsory national health insurance soom reemerged as a possibility, intensifying the political passions of those who preferred voluntary plans. AHS ads fed the fire, describing the growth of programs like Blue Cross as "the only answer to socialized medicine." Meanwhile, employers continued to use hospital insurance as a job benefit to attract and hold workers. In New York, the municipal government began paying half the cost of Blue Cross coverage for its huge work force, and this encouraged even public employees to turn to private facilities for their health care. Unions, too, took an increasing interest in health benefits, and once the Taft-Hartley Act of 1947 made health insurance a legitimate area for collective bargaining, it became a common element in contract negotiations. In New York City, a contemporary observed: "We are now watching a parade . . . a mass migration" of unions into AHS.[50]

Even the municipal hospitals began to get an occasional insured patient, but that trend was peripheral to the intense and symbiotic bond between the AHS and the voluntary hospitals. Now these institutions could pass their increasing costs on to their patients, not just through highly visible increases in their fees but through quiet negotiations with the friendly staff at AHS. As the *New York Times* remarked during a period of widespread increases in hospital fees in 1946, insured patients would not be directly affected "as the insurer takes up any of the increase in rates."[51] This perspective, which was widely shared, glossed over the fact that higher hospital rates must ultimately be reflected in higher insurance premiums.

The hospitals' negotiation process with AHS became even more painless in 1948, when AHS announced that its reimbursement rate to hospitals would be automatically readjusted four times a year to account for inflation. In later decades, major payers' concern over rising health costs would help produce wrenching changes in American hospital care, but few complaints were recorded in the years just after the war. Instead, AHS joined the hospitals companionably on the escalator, passing the increasing costs on to subscribers who seemed equally satisfied with the arrangement.

By 1950, the social geography of New York City's hospitals had changed significantly. During the Depression, thousands of New Yorkers of every class had needed free hospital care. While private rooms stood empty and the voluntary hospitals cut back on charity care, the municipal hospitals attracted patients from an ever widening social spectrum. A second surge into public hospitals occurred during the late 1940s, when the escalating price of private care sent many patients back to the public system. But the difficult conditions they encountered in the city hospitals during these two periods must have left many New Yorkers determined to avoid them in the future if they could.

Even if conditions in the city hospitals had been better than they were, the public system still had to contend with the widespread conviction that what one gets for free cannot be as good as something that costs money. As the editor of *Modern Hospital* observed in 1946, "However superbly our present medical system may provide for the patient at Bellevue or Cook County [Chicago] . . . he is generally convinced that what he gets is inferior to the care that is provided in Park Avenue consulting rooms and the top floor at Passavant Hospital [Chicago]."[52] This perception, already well entrenched, was reinforced by the wide publicity for hospital insurance, which stressed the idea that responsible citizens—the real Americans—were "too proud" to accept free care on a ward. Responding to all these messages, as well as to their own experiences, many New Yorkers chose to use private hospitals when they got the chance, and the expansion of hospital insurance gave that chance to thousands of employed New Yorkers and their families. By the end of the 1940s, they were using semiprivate care in record numbers.

Meanwhile, the private hospitals were beginning to close beds on their wards. (See Figure 3.1) Some of the former ward patients could now afford

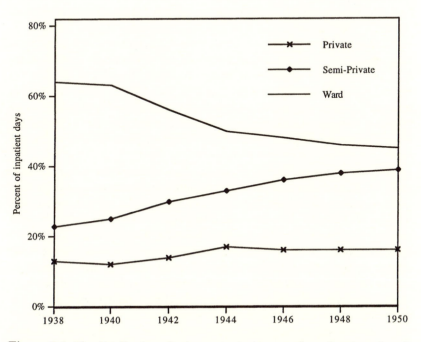

Figure 3.1 The distribution of private, semiprivate, and ward patients in voluntary hospitals, New York City, 1938–1950. Source: United Hospital Fund.

semiprivate rooms, but the soaring admission rates at Bellevue and other municipal hospitals during those years suggest that at least some uninsured patients had been squeezed out of the private system. Nourished by the Depression and the war years, by private initiative and public policy, hospital insurance had defined more sharply than ever the division between public and private care.

Help for the Workers: Labor Unions

Whatever its other functions, hospital insurance began as a well-organized and highly effective response by private hospitals to the problems they encountered during the Depression. While this was happening, another kind of collective response was emerging from quite a different quarter: the hospitals' employees. During the 1930s, for the first time in history, labor unions became a significant factor in the affairs of New York City hospitals.

The wave of union activism that swept across America in 1919 generated a small rivulet of militance among hospital workers in New York City, but it ended quickly, and, for many years, hospital workers remained organizationally mute. In the private hospitals, no union activity of any kind is recorded between 1919 and the mid-1930s. In the public hospitals, employees had a quasi organization, the Civil Service Forum, but that was hardly a union; it opposed check-offs for union dues, collective bargaining, and strikes, and it included many supervisors among its members. Furthermore, the Forum had little to offer the many municipal employees who were not part of civil service.

The hospital workforce was characterized by ethnic diversity, high turnover, many unskilled workers, and a preponderance of women. These were exactly the wrong characteristics to interest the dominant labor organization of the early 1930s, the American Federation of Labor (AF of L), which had built its strength on craft unions of skilled workers, most of them white males. Once President Roosevelt's New Deal opened new opportunities for labor organizing, a dissenting group within the AF of L began to protest the narrowness of their leaders' focus. Dissent led to rebellion, and in 1935, labor leader John L. Lewis and his followers bolted the AF of L to found the Committee for Industrial Organization (in 1938 renamed Congress of Industrial Organizations, CIO), promising to concentrate on industries and workers that the AF of L had ignored. Initially the CIO showed no more interest in hospitals than did the AF of L; instead, it organized mass-production industries like rubber, steel, and automobiles. Nevertheless, the CIO's success helped create a better climate for hospital unions by demonstrating that unskilled workers could be stalwart union members and that effective labor organizations could be built across whole industries, instead of approaching each trade separately.

Within a year of the CIO's birth, things began to simmer in New York City hospitals. One of the new CIO unions—State, County and Municipal Workers (SCMW)—hired a hospital pharmacist, Elliott Godoff, as an organizer. More or less on his own, Godoff began working with hospital maintenance and laundry staff, soon forming them into the Hospital Employees Union, SCMW Local 171. About the same time, an AF of L organizer, Luciel McGorkey, established a union aimed at white-collar hospital workers: pharmacists, secretaries, hygienists, social service workers, and nurses. Organizing mostly in the private hospitals at first, Godoff and McGorkey found grievances aplenty. Few hospitals had restored the wage cuts they had made in the years just after the 1929 stock market crash, and resentment over that issue exacerbated employees' longer standing grievances over oppressive working conditions, punishing hours, and squalid housing.

Private hospital leaders had argued for years that unions had no place in the world of charitable care. They maintained that since there were no profits to be shared, wages and working conditions could only be improved by diverting resources from the patients. Many Americans found this argument compelling, and workers themselves were not immune to it. In particular, workers were hesitant to unleash their only significant weapon: the strike. Nevertheless, a tragic incident in January 1937—the death of a nurse by fire in a dilapidated residence at Israel Zion Hospital in Brooklyn—provided, in the words of one journalist, "the tinder that set off the strike." Soon after the fire, maintenance workers at Israel Zion and at Beth Israel Hospital in Manhattan walked off their jobs, while employees at Brooklyn Jewish Hospital seized the kitchen and laundry. A scattering of workers in other facilities joined the action, but the strike died quickly and, within a short time, only the core membership at Brooklyn Jewish still held out. A magazine picture of the time shows the strikers, both black and white, crowded convivially around a long table in the hospital kitchen.[53]

Mayor LaGuardia insisted that peaceable strikers should not be arrested without warrants, but a Tammany judge quickly provided the warrants, explaining as he did so that in his opinion the maintenance workers were all bound by the Hippocratic Oath. In a brutal confrontation, the police broke the strike, arresting more than fifty people. None of the strikers ultimately served time, although the hospital trustees tried to invoke an obscure section of the penal code that could have sent some of them to prison for twelve years.[54]

The hospital rising of 1937 produced both a precedent and a lesson. The precedent was established when the unions sought to protect themselves from an injunction by invoking two recent state labor laws protecting collective bargaining and the right to strike. Although neither law mentioned hospital workers specifically, the unions hoped that a favorable court decision would confirm their rights under the two statutes. They lost on both counts. The court held that private hospitals, since they received payment from the government for treating city patients, were a kind of governmental agency and thus were exempt from the two laws. In any case, the court argued that the state Legislature could not have meant to cause harm, and since forcing the private hospitals to accept unions and strikes would promote "hardship, suffering and disaster," the Legislature must have meant to exclude them. This decision did not make hospital unions illegal, but it freed hospital leaders from any obligation to bargain with them, and it assured that any strike, however orderly, would face an immediate injunction. In effect, there was to be no New Deal for hospital workers.[55]

If the events of 1937 revealed an unsympathetic legal establishment, they demonstrated one promising fact: the municipal hospitals were not as closed to union pressure as the private hospitals were. Even before the Brooklyn Jewish Hospital strike began, the labor-friendly *Evening Journal* ran a nine-part exposé on conditions in both public and private hospitals, documenting the workers' complaints in bitter words and searing pictures. The private facilities gave no quarter; but three days into the *Evening Journal* series, Mayor LaGuardia suddenly announced that he would seek an eight-hour day for nursing staff in the public hospitals. The city Board of Estimate rapidly expanded his proposal, and soon nearly all municipal hospital employees began working eight-hour shifts instead of the former ten or twelve.[56]

Union leaders were not blind to the implications of the city's sudden concession, and for the next decade they focused the majority of their attention on the municipal institutions. They knew that the mayor had spent twenty-five years as a lawyer and a congressman advocating for labor, and they were also aware, as he was, that the city work force represented 150,000 voters. La-Guardia preferred the submissive good manners of the Civil Service Forum to the unions' noisy activism, but he could hardly treat labor representatives with the hostility they received from private hospital boards. Shop steward Rudy Mitarittona learned this when he was fired from a municipal hospital for objecting too boisterously to the dismissal of two fellow union members. After dozens of workers besieged LaGuardia with telephone calls that afternoon, the hospital superintendent begged Mitaritonna to stop the barrage "because the Commissioner called and he's coming over within an hour." Mitaritonna and both his friends were reinstated.[57] Only in the public system did the workers have recourse to such powerful forces outside the hospital.

As the Depression gave way to World War II, the unions remained active participants in the life of the city hospitals. An example of the role they played is the occasion on which reporters learned from a CIO official that there had been an outbreak of dysentery at Bellevue because of unsanitary conditions in the kitchen (which the union blamed on inadequate staffing). Both the superintendent of Bellevue and the commissioner of hospitals were then obliged to respond to the allegation, further publicizing the problem and the workers' complaints.[58] Epidemics were hardly unknown at the hospital, but since kitchen staff rarely had access to the press, news of the incident would probably not have reached the public without the union's intervention. In this case and many others, advocating for the employees helped publicize issues that were of serious concern to patients as well as staff.

After World War II, Mayor William O'Dwyer assumed the task of following the legendary LaGuardia, while facing a backlog of workers' demands that had accumulated over more than a decade of economic and military constraints. One strike followed another during O'Dwyer's first winter in office. Western Union workers walked out and so did the Teamsters, while a tugboat worker's strike nearly crippled the whole city. Among municipal employees, only the transit workers were strong enough to engage in explicit strike threats, but dozens of other labor organizations began sharpening their rhetoric and making their presence felt through speeches, press releases, radio broadcasts, circulars, petitions, and delegations to City Hall. In 1946, the SCMWA, the next strongest city union after the transit workers, merged with another left-leaning employee organization to form the United Public Workers of America (UPWA, CIO). The UPWA was now one of the largest public unions in the country, with a membership that included several thousand of the city's hospital workers. Its main rival in New York, Associated Federal, State, County, and Municipal Employees (AFSCME, AF of L), enrolled another 1,700 hospital workers, nearly half of them at Bellevue. Together, the UPWA and AFSCME represented less than 10 percent of the city's municipal hospital work force, but they provided a base for advocacy and agitation that the unions exploited exuberantly.[59]

Many Americans believed that public employees (like the employees of private hospitals) should be forbidden to join unions. The New York State Supreme Court, for example, stated that for civil service employees to do so would be "not only incompatible with the spirit of democracy but inconsistent with every principle upon which our Government is founded." For a time, it appeared that New York State might outlaw public unions. That did not occur, but public strikes were declared illegal in the Condon-Wadlin Act of 1947 and, throughout the 1940s, New York's municipal unions derived more power from their political clout than from their legal rights. Yet their clout was considerable. Having played a major role in O'Dwyer's nomination and election, the unions were in a position to make their voices heard once he took office. In 1946, a record-breaking city budget provided for raises to every city employee earning less than $4,000 per year. Eight months later, the Board of Estimate added another $32 million in cost-of-living raises for most city employees. It was pleasant, if perhaps extravagant, the *New York Times* observed, "to ease the burdens of nearly 100,000 workers on a single afternoon."[60]

Despite the increases, city salaries continued to trail the rising cost of living, and the unions continued to press for more money. As they fought for higher wages, however, they were experiencing a fierce battle within their own ranks. The fear of Communist subversion that had flared in the late 1930s reappeared with the Cold War, and it destroyed the UPWA. This was a loss, since the union's principal rival, AFSCME, maintained a rather cozy relationship with city officials despite its sharp public statements. The UPWA had important flaws and prejudices, but its gradual weakening after 1947—culminating in its expulsion from the CIO in a purge of left-wing members in 1950—deprived the city of a vital and militant voice for workers' interests. As the UPWA sank out of sight, so did many of New York City's most articulate labor leaders. Meanwhile, those who survived settled into a pattern of quiet, behind-the-scenes negotiations with the city administration, enlivened only by occasional public fireworks for the benefit of the membership.

Henceforth, union leaders were more likely to be seen at Democratic Party dinners than on the barricades. But if they had little formal power, they were ready to settle for influence—and under O'Dwyer they had a good deal of that.

To appreciate the ground that labor had gained in the municipal hospitals, one has only to compare it with the total defeat that the unions experienced in private medical institutions during the same two decades. Drawing on their formidable community influence, their reputations as hard-pressed charitable institutions, and the legal protections provided them by public policy, New York's private hospitals managed to repel every effort to organize their workers between 1930 and 1950. One decisive chapter in this drama took place at New York Hospital, which in 1945 became the target of the first major strike among New York hospital workers since the Depression.

As soon as World War II ended, organizers for the AF of L's New York Building and Construction Trades Council (BCTC) took up the cause of hospital maintenance workers. New York Hospital followed the campaign with interest, especially in October 1945, when the BCTC organized an eight-minute work stoppage at four other private hospitals. Then a few weeks later, the New York Hospital administrator arrived at work one morning to be greeted by pickets lining the sidewalk and the news that more than 100 hospital maintenance men and elevator operators had stayed home from work. The trustees obtained a temporary injunction that dispersed the picketers and then brought suit to make the injunction permanent. During the month that elapsed before the trial, the workers remained off duty while the hospital administration issued a stream of press releases designed to show that the facility was managing to carry on without its disloyal workers. One newspaper picture portrayed the hospital elevator being run by a B-29 bombardier, newly returned from overseas. He had come to visit a sick friend at the hospital, it was explained, and had stayed on to help a good cause. The story made it very clear which side of the strike was favored by patriotic Americans.[61]

New York Hospital's petition for a permanent injunction came to trial in December. The judge, Ferdinand Pecora, was known to be sympathetic to labor, but the union lost its case. Upholding the precedent established at Brooklyn Jewish Hospital in 1937, Pecora confirmed that charitable institutions were legally free to reject collective bargaining. He gave New York Hospital its permanent injunction, explaining that a strike against a private hospital could not be permitted, since it might result in loss of life. He did express sympathy with the workers, observing that a hospital's "shining lights of benefaction, mercy, and charity should at least be reflected to the basement of their own structure." Nevertheless, there was no question who had won the case. New York Hospital's administrator promptly announced that any workers who were still on strike had been replaced.[62] The next union action at New York Hospital would not occur for fourteen years.

In showing greater responsiveness to its workers' demands, the city government demonstrated again that municipal hospitals were community institutions, open to all the stresses and strains of urban life and politics. Motivated by a combination of private conviction, public consensus, and political calculation, city officials made it clear throughout the 1930s and 1940s that municipal hospitals were obligated to respond to community demands. Just as city residents could not be denied medical care, so city workers could not be denied a hearing. The private hospitals were free to define their obligations, but the municipal hospitals claimed no such luxury.

The years between 1930 and 1950 were as traumatic as any that New York had experienced. Yet through it all the city managed to continue running the most generous system of public medicine in the country. Mayor LaGuardia, in particular, was a staunch supporter of the municipal hospitals. He devoted scarce city resources to them, as well as every federal dollar he could get. He appointed the abrasive but talented S. S. Goldwater to head the Department of Hospitals and supported him loyally. He exempted the department from most of his budgetary reductions, and he gave it a larger proportional increase during the Depression than any other city department.[63] Mayor O'Dwyer, too, though his relationship with the department was more ambiguous, worked hard to maintain the hospitals during the early postwar years; he kept them relatively free of politics, and he launched a major campaign to rebuild them.

Yet if the years from 1930 to 1950 represented a continuing commitment to public medicine, they also cast in stone the idea that the municipal hospitals should function primarily as a safety valve for the private system. During the 1920s, the private hospitals had shown an increasing tendency to pass the primary responsibility for charity care onto the public sector. This tendency was legitimized by their genuine economic crisis during the Depression, and practices that gained acceptance in a time of trouble lived on in the years that followed.

In many ways, the years between 1930 and 1950 were a time of impressive achievements. Yet through these years there ran a dark connecting thread: the persistent presence of social inequality. Because of this inequality, the deprivations of economic crisis and wartime necessity imposed different burdens on Bellevue and New York Hospital. Because of it, the private hospitals' collective response to adversity—hospital insurance and semiprivate care— achieved considerably more than their employees' efforts to improve their own situation through labor unions; and, because of it, the world that emerged in the postwar years reproduced many of the power relationships of the old one.

Never wholly absent from American life, such inequality is particularly striking during an era like the 1940s, when public rhetoric stressed so emphatically the goals and purposes that all American shared. Shoulder to shoulder in vanquishing the Axis powers, Americans were more united during those years, one might think, than ever before or since. But the old inequalities remained as well, doing their own part to determine what happened and what the legacy of those years would be. In New York City, as in the nation, the dominant events of the period were shadowed by the continuing separation of rich from poor, white from black, native from foreigner, manager from worker, and male from female. The same separation could be seen in the world of the hospitals, with private facilities being left free to serve the community more or less as they saw fit, while public hospitals carried the unique burden of ensuring that—in good times or bad—care would be available to everyone in New York who needed it. The world that Bellevue prepared to enter in 1950 was, in some senses, a world of brand new possibilities; in other ways, it was already shaped by the habits and values established in earlier years.

4

Many Voices, Many Claims
1950–1965

Throughout Bellevue Hospital's history, its status as a public institution had required it to respond, not only to the needs of its patients, but also to the needs and demands of the surrounding city. Fulfilling this broader obligation had inspired a variety of policies in different eras, ranging from the training of midwives in 1910 to negotiating with labor unions in the 1930s. But perhaps no time period illustrated more vividly than the 1950s and 1960s the diversity of the demands on Bellevue and the practical implications of the hospital's responsiveness to those demands. One incident sets the tone for the era.

One day in December 1956, Dr. Dickinson Richards set out on his regular ward rounds at Bellevue. This routine event usually drew only about a dozen people—primarily the house staff that Richards supervised as chief of Columbia University's medical service at Bellevue. But three times the usual number appeared on this particular morning, and their sparkling white coats and freshly brushed hair made it clear that this was no ordinary day. Richards had just returned from accepting the Nobel Prize in Sweden, and they were here to celebrate his homecoming.

Richards had come to Bellevue in 1945, after spending most of his career at Presbyterian Hospital and its affiliated medical school, the College of Physicians and Surgeons (P&S) at Columbia University. When another man was chosen to head the P&S Department of Medicine, Richards left the uptown campus for what amounted to a colonial outpost—Columbia's teaching service at Bellevue. He was joined in his exile by Andre Cournand, who had been working with him for a decade, studying the heart. Neither the plant nor the equipment at Bellevue compared to their facilities uptown, but Richards and Cournand made the best of their new circumstances and within a year had set up the world's first cardio-pulmonary laboratory. For the next decade, with the enthusiastic assistance of their house staff and the indispensable participation of Bellevue's patients, the two men broke new ground in understanding the workings of the heart and heart disease. Their pioneering work on cardiac catheterization won them the Nobel Prize for medicine in 1956.[1]

No medical staff could be indifferent to having their colleagues gain such recognition, but the house staff at Bellevue was intoxicated by the triumph of Richards and Cournand. To them, it was as if someone working with home-made equipment in Calcutta had outperformed the best minds at the Royal Academy of Science in London. They knew that Richards's move to Bellevue from the medical school campus had represented a professional step backward, and they knew that, for all Bellevue's fame, it lacked the status of the city's top private teaching hospitals. This Nobel Prize had elevated them all. That is why so many of them had come that December morning, dressed in their Sunday best, to join Richards's rounds on his first day back from Stockholm.

With his entourage at his heels Richards entered the first ward, where he greeted the nurse on duty and looked around at his patients. He and his followers approached the first bed, in which an elderly woman lay flat beneath the sheets. Just as the great man was about to address her, the woman silently beckoned him to bend nearer. Then, in a heavily accented stage whisper that echoed around the room, she said, "Doctor, darling, could you bring me a bedpan?"[2]

The incident became part of the Bellevue legend, handed down from one generation of house staff to the next. The tension exemplified in the story— between the institution's head in the academic stratosphere and its feet in the city streets, between Bellevue as a teaching facility and Bellevue as New York's hospital of last resort—had existed for years, but it sharpened during the 1950s and 1960s. Who represented the true voice of Bellevue? The Nobel Prize winner? The patient needing a bedpan? Or was it one of the many other people involved with the hospital: the taxpayer, the mayor, the hospital worker? In truth, each played a part, along with dozens of others. In many respects, the key to understanding Bellevue during those years is to understand the growing chorus of voices—sometimes harmonious, often dissonant—that shaped hospital life.

And what of New York Hospital? We can understand Bellevue's relation to its many constituents still better when we look at the way that New York Hospital responded to similar forces during the same years. Between 1950 and 1965, New York Hospital also faced a number of new challenges. Academic medicine came into its own; real estate development transformed the surrounding neighborhood; and labor unions mounted their first sustained effort to organize New York Hospital's employees. Yet by making the most of its many resources (including its private status) the hospital was able to survive the postwar decades with its identity and its autonomy almost unaltered. The events of the 1950s and 1960s display in high relief how differently Bellevue and New York Hospital functioned in relation to the city around them.

New York City: Capital of the World

Despite their differences, Bellevue and New York Hospital had one important characteristic in common: their shared time and place in history—that distinctive combination of generosity and selfishness, egalitarianism and inequity, cosmopolitanism and provincialism, that was New York City in the two decades after World War II. Those years were, in most respects, a time of buoyant self-assurance for New York. Having overcome the terrors of the Depression and the war, the city entered a new era. Essayist E. B. White captured the scope and promise of the postwar city in his elegant *Here Is New York*. "The city is like poetry," he wrote: "it compresses all life, all races and breeds, into a small island and adds music and the accompaniment of internal combustion engines. . . . New York is not Spokane multiplied by sixty or Detroit multiplied by four. It is by all odds the loftiest of cities."[3] Because of its place in the United States, and the United States' place among nations, New York had become the capital of the world; it seemed quite appropriate that the United Nations' new headquarters should find its home on the bank of the East River. And if further proof of New York's eminence were needed, what other city had baseball teams like the New York Yankees and the Brooklyn Dodgers—teams so successful that in six of the years between 1947 and 1956, they faced each other in the World Series, giving New Yorkers the chance to travel to every game of these "Subway Series" for the price of a token.

On the political scene, many heaved a sigh of relief in 1950, when Mayor William O'Dwyer resigned his office one step ahead of the investigators, accepting a hastily arranged ambassadorship to Mexico. The former City Council President, Vincent Impellitteri finished O'Dwyer's term. Then, in 1954, Robert F. Wagner was elected mayor and held the position for the next twelve years. Wagner was a career Democrat with a liberal bent, and although he preferred behind-the-scenes negotiation to fiery crusading, he built a solid record of public programs and reforms, reinforcing—to the nation and to New Yorkers—the idea that this city was the quintessential home of urban liberalism.

"The city then was truly rich," recalled historian Theodore White. "The wealthy were rich, the working people were rich, the municipality was rich."[4] White's statement was not quite accurate, but New York's economy was flourishing. The city had become a beehive of commerce and finance, communications and fashion, culture and tourism. Light manufacturing hummed in every borough, tucked into thousands of lofts, workshops, and small factories. Inflation and unemployment were low, and wages were rising steadily. New York also supported an extraordinary array of public services. No other city in the country had more than three municipal hospitals; New York had twenty-six. It also had the only city university in the United State, a famous public library system, good public schools, thousands of acres of parkland, a mass-transit network that dwarfed all others in the world, the best water anywhere, and well-regarded public housing. In later years, many would trace New York's fiscal problems to this habit of public beneficence, but during the 1950s and early 1960s the city's extensive public services seemed just part of what made New York the remarkable place it was.

At the same time, the face of the city was changing, promising both challenges and possibilities for the decades ahead. Many of the European immigrants who had arrived in huge numbers around the turn of the century had left their first neighborhoods in Manhattan for new homes in the outer boroughs; now their children were beginning to move to the suburbs. The immigrants' children were not alone. Manhattan had been losing white residents since 1910; after 1940, the white population of Brooklyn and the Bronx began to decline as well. The city was still the occupational center of the metropolitan area, but increasing numbers of workers were returning at night to homes in the suburbs.

In 1949, E. B. White reported that the Long Island Railroad had carried 40 million commuters the previous year. White had little use for such people; the commuter, he said, "has fished in Manhattan's wallet and dug out coins, but has never listened to Manhattan's breathing, never awakened to its morning, never dropped off to sleep in its night."[5] For thousands of families, however, the appeal of sleeping in Manhattan's night was outweighed by the satisfaction of finding good housing they could afford. There had been little private construction in the city between 1930 and 1945, and when new buildings began rising after the war, many of them, especially in Manhattan, actually reduced the options for poorer New Yorkers by demolishing tenements, neighborhood stores, and small manufacturing shops to make room for office-buildings and luxury apartments. Priced out of much of the urban housing market and eager for a fresh start, many New Yorkers saw the suburbs as their best bet.

Although these decisions to move to the suburbs were made individually, a host of public policy decisions shaped the context in which they were made. While urban mass transit received little state or federal aid, millions of public dollars were poured into new highways that ripped up old city neighborhoods and opened thoroughfares to new homes in the suburbs. At the same time, energy policy kept gasoline prices low; the GI Bill and Federal Housing Administration mortgages helped make the new suburban houses affordable; and national tax laws subsidized home ownership. In addition, the move from city to suburb was fostered by a practice known as redlining, under which many urban neighborhoods (particularly those that were racially diverse) were identified by banks, insurers, and federal agencies as poor risks for private housing investment.[6]

Other public policies made it more likely that the urban poor would remain where they were. For example, suburban communities usually chose not to create the kinds of services that had made New York City both a mecca and a tax-burden. By providing minimal mass transit, welfare, public health services, free medical care, or public housing, suburban towns saved their citizens tax money and, at the same time, made themselves less attractive to those who depended on such facilities. Meanwhile, housing discrimination helped ensure that black New Yorkers would be among those who stayed behind. Postwar New York City was still a work place for people of all classes, but increasingly those who actually lived there would be drawn from two groups—the prosperous, who could afford to live well in this city, and the poor, who could not afford to live anywhere else. New York's white middle class and upper working class were starting to melt away.

The story of New York during the postwar decades was one of arrivals as well as departures. As many whites left New York, blacks and Puerto Ricans arrived in record numbers. So while the city's white population declined 5 percent between 1940 and 1960, its black population increased 137 percent, passing 1 million people by 1960. Meanwhile, the city's 430,000 Puerto Ricans represented another growing minority. Like blacks from the South, many Puerto Ricans had migrated because of poverty at home and the possibility of better times "up north"; in their case, the availability of cheap fast air travel had also played a part in facilitating migration. By 1960, Puerto Ricans, blacks, and other nonwhites represented about 15 percent of the city's population, up from 5 percent in 1930 and 2 percent in 1900.[7]

New York was far from the most prejudiced of cities, and there were some indications that race relations were improving. Yet racial separation was still a pervasive fact of life, shaping the daily experience and future prospects of hundreds of thousands of New Yorkers. Occupying the city's most crowded and dilapidated housing, and confined for the most part to low-paying jobs, New Yorkers of color were excluded—in practice, if not by law—from large portions of the social, economic, and cultural life around them. Exploring Spanish Harlem, reporter Dan Wakefield was struck by how different his beloved New York skyline appeared when he imagined looking at it through the eyes of a Puerto Rican teenager hooked on heroin. Seen in this way, he wrote, "the soaring buildings seemed not so much inspiring as haughty and teasing, as if to say, 'You can see us, but you can't reach us.' It gave me a chill."[8]

This is the city that surrounded Bellevue and New York Hospital in the postwar decades,—a complicated community in the grip of extraordinary changes. Bellevue and New York Hospital shared this urban setting, but each experienced it differently because of their differing places within the city's network of power, influence, and obligation. Three aspects of postwar hospital life exemplify these differences: the way each institution designed its patient services, the way each participated in the development of its neighborhood, and the way each responded to labor activism among its employees.

Designing Patient Services

No issue could be more central to defining a hospital's urban role than that concerning what services it provides to what patients. As the city changed, so did the health needs of its citizens. Bellevue's and New York Hospital's responses to these changes during the first postwar decade were profoundly influenced by the relative power of the different constituencies within each hospital community.

Bellevue: Heartbeat of the City

More perhaps than any other hospital in New York, Bellevue was required to adapt itself daily to the life of the surrounding city and to the changing needs of the city's changing population. Surgeon William Nolen captured this aspect of the hospital when he titled an essay about his internship there: "Bellevue: No One Was Ever Turned Away."[9]

Bellevue's famed emergency service treated numerous middle- and upper-class patients—the tourist taken ill in a restaurant, the suburban matron hit by a taxicab, the Wall Street lawyer with a heart attack. Even celebrities appeared from time to time. In 1954, a group of young medical students attending an autopsy found themselves looking at the body of comedian Fred Allen, who had collapsed on the street the day before and died in the Bellevue emergency room. On another occasion, the Leopard Lady from Barnum & Bailey's Circus spent a few weeks on the dermatology ward; her stay was enlivened by a visit from the circus sword-swallower, who enchanted the house staff by agreeing to perform her act while undergoing a chest X ray.[10] The psychiatric division also treated a variety of familiar figures, from novelist Norman Mailer to the serial killer "Son of Sam." All these were exceptions, however; most of the hospital's patients were ordinary New Yorkers, and their social characteristics during the 1950s mirrored the city outside.

Located near the old immigrant districts of the Lower East Side, Bellevue still served mostly white Roman Catholics and Jews, but by the mid-1950s, nearly 20 percent of its patients were black, up from only 5 percent in the mid-1930s. Two smaller demographic groups among Bellevue's patient population gave a hint of the city's past and its future. Every year, the hospital treated several hundred elderly Chinese men, survivors of the years when immigration restrictions had prevented them from bringing their wives and children to the United States. Aging and alone, these men were ending their lives in single rooms tucked in above the shops and restaurants of Chinatown. The hospital was also serving more Puerto Rican patients than ever before. By 1955, Bellevue's Outpatient Department had signs in Spanish as well as English. Some Puerto Ricans were sick when they arrived in the city; staff at Bellevue remember malnourished and dehydrated children sometimes brought in straight from the airport. Others fell ill once they got to New York, from the combination of crowded housing, unhealthy working conditions, overwork, and the unfamiliar climate. Tuberculosis, said one physician, "went through the Puerto Ricans like wildfire."[11]

Bellevue's patients reflected New York's social conditions as well as its demography. A sizable proportion of each year's admissions were impoverished middle-aged single males from the nearby Bowery, suffering from alcoholism as well as from the other physical problems engendered by their life on the street. E. B. White's description of the Bowery suggested Bellevue's historic place in the life cycle of those who lived there; it had "plenty of gin mills, plenty of flophouses, plenty of indifference, and always, at the end of the line, Bellevue." The Bowery's role as New York City's Skid Row started to wane when the Third Avenue El came down in 1955, but new groups of patients, equally unacceptable elsewhere, were starting to appear at Bellevue. Already the hospital was treating several hundred drug addicts each year, most of them male and most addicted to heroin. As the city's drug-use patterns changed, so, too, did Bellevue's drug-related admissions—by the 1960s the emergency room was beginning to treat the victims of bad LSD trips.[12]

Everyone who came to the hospital had to live with Bellevue's poor physical conditions, but there was more to Bellevue than peeling paint, as a patient named Rebecca Morris learned during her two-month stay on one of the hospital's tuberculosis wards. Morris came to enjoy the raffish society of her fellow-patients, many of whom were black or Puerto Rican. She shared their disappointment when the whole ward dressed up for an evening of socializing with patients from the male ward downstairs, only to discover that most of the men were elderly alcoholics from the Bowery. There were other sources of entertainment on the ward, however, most notably the "numbers racket," which was run by what Morris identifies as "the Bellevue underground, a concern as private and as impressively organized as the Mafia." Ranging outward from a command post "somewhere in the depths of the hospital," the game functioned busily, she reported, among patients and nonprofessional staff throughout the hospital. On her ward, the "sputum-cup boys" were key figures in the enterprise, using their daily rounds to "exchange much more than just sputum-cups."[13]

Morris admired her fellow patients for their fortitude as well as their joie de vivre. At night, when one nurse was on duty for 200 patients, the women would care for each other, staying up to monitor the sickest ones, bringing water or the bedpan when it was needed. Something of these women's spirit is suggested by the day Morris saw one patient drawing another's gastric juices, saying as she did so: "Honey, you don't want them interns messing up your insides. They never done this before. I done fourteen last month."[14] Morris' account provides a rare picture of Bellevue from the bottom up—an institution only loosely controlled by its managers, one where even the lowliest patients and employees had more latitude in shaping daily events than would have been possible in a better organized, better staffed hospital.

"Bellevue was where poor people went, a poor person's hospital," recalls a neighborhood resident. "If you had any money, you went somewhere else. . . . You'd get a real good deal if you went there, but you had to take what was given to you." In many ways, this was true; as ordinary citizens in an overburdened public institution, Bellevue's postwar patients had to accept harried care in often dismal surroundings. Yet this comment may not do justice to the part that patients themselves played in determining what happened at the hospital. Bellevue, too, had to accept what was given to it. At other hospitals, recalls a former intern, house staff could reject any patient by writing "No beds" on the admission slip. "At Bellevue you weren't allowed to write 'No beds.'"[15] Here, unlike at many medical institutions in the city, one could count on being accepted, no matter what one's income, race, physical problems, or behavior, and no matter how many patients had already been admitted. In that sense, the hospital's work was truly shaped by patient needs.

At the same time, Bellevue also had to respond to the choices made by private hospitals. Whatever Bellevue's academic aspirations, the sick poor of the community must be cared for, and if private hospitals were accepting fewer of them, then Bellevue must accept more. If private hospitals regarded tuberculosis as a disease that no longer presented a medical challenge, then tuberculosis patients at Bellevue would sleep in the hall. If the Payne Whitney Clinic at New York Hospital had only private rooms, then the psychiatric division at Bellevue must sometimes accommodate 100 patients in a fifty-bed unit. If alcoholics and drug addicts found a chilly welcome in most private hospitals, then Bellevue staff must deal with delirium tremens and heroin withdrawal.

All in all, Bellevue's open-door policy turned the hospital into a kind of barometer of life in the surrounding city. If New York's bitter winters gave Puerto Ricans pneumonia, then Bellevue would treat pneumonia. If homeless derelicts had nowhere to bathe, then Bellevue would treat lice as well as disease. Take one look at the hospital, wrote a long-time staff member, and you know "whether the city is enjoying boom or depression, a high or low birth rate, a hard winter or a mild one—or an increase of immigrants from a specific area."[16]

Urban crises, too, put a spotlight on Bellevue's responsiveness to community needs. Throughout the 1966 transit strike, for example, hundreds of staff members—as well as the commissioner of hospitals—slept at Bellevue to keep its vital services going. The hospital's visceral connection to city events was emphasized when the jailed leader of the strike, Michael J. Quill himself, had a heart attack and was rushed to Bellevue for care. After camping out in the hospital lobby for a week, one reporter concluded: "If it's happening in New York, it's happening at Bellevue."[17]

New York Hospital: Sustaining a Vision

New York Hospital, too, was affected by the social and economic changes in the postwar city, but it had more choices than Bellevue about how to respond. In 1959, the hospital collaborated with the Hospital Council of Greater New York in a social profile of its immediate neighborhood and the sur-

Table 4.1. Comparison of Bellevue and New York Hospital, 1960

	Bellevue	New York Hospital*
Number of Beds	2,728**	1,211
General care	1,685	1,105
Psychiatric care	630	106
General care		
Average census	1,223	890
Distribution of patients		
% Private	0	14
% Semiprivate	0	33
% Wards	100	43

Sources: United Hospital Fund, NYH Annual Report.

*Does not include NYH's Bloomingdale Division, in Westchester County.

** Includes Chest Service beds.

rounding city. The council's description of the study suggested that it had been designed to learn how the hospital might serve the community better. But New York Hospital's internal discussion of the project made clear that it had been undertaken to answer two quite different questions. First, given rising family income and the spread of health insurance, was the hospital still going to be able to get the number of teaching patients it needed for its wards? Second, could it continue to attract enough paying patients? In other words, the institutional problem was not how to adapt the hospital's services to changing community needs, but to ascertain whether community changes were going to interfere with the hospital's plans to continue offering the kind of services it had offered in the past.[18]

On the question of finding enough paying patients—an urgent concern, given the declining number of middle-class residents in the city—New York Hospital briefly explored various new approaches to structuring hospital care, including the possibility of a pioneering health maintenance organization.[19] But in the end, the hospital remained committed to its established pattern of service. This does not mean that its postwar services remained static; the trustees worked tirelessly and spent millions of dollars to keep pace with technological advances. However, changes in the hospital's pattern of services were driven more by developments in medical science than by a reassessment of community needs. New York Hospital had concentrated for many years on providing specialized high-technology medicine to acutely ill inpatients, and it continued to do so throughout the postwar years.

Instead of redefining its services, New York Hospital redefined its geographical borders, reaching out more aggressively for patients beyond the neighborhood, beyond Manhattan, beyond the city limits. The hospital also worked to enhance its private service, since it was understood that private patients expected not only technical excellence, but the exclusivity and elegance of a luxury hotel. These patients were interviewed in a separate admitting office, then whisked by elevator to the twelfth floor, where they found themselves, as a medical center publication asserted, in "a separate hospital" with a view of the East River and "an environment of comfort similar to that which they enjoy in their homes."[20] The hospital's postwar medical program might be more responsive to technological advances than to changing community needs, but the physical arrangements in the private rooms were acutely responsive to patient expectations.

Downstairs on the wards, the relationship between hospital and patient was quite different. For if the private service was expected to generate revenue, one of the main functions of the wards was to furnish "clinical material" for teaching and research. In earlier years, a stay on a New York Hospital ward had represented a clear trade: the patient provided the hospital with clinical material and, in exchange, received free care. But by the early 1950s, according to hospital records, only 1 percent of the hospital's ward patients were treated entirely without charge. Nearly half the patients on the ward had hospital insurance (their inability to pay the separate doctor's fee kept them out of semiprivate care); the rest either paid for themselves as best they could or were subsidized by the city. Since these payment arrangements often produced less than the full cost of service, ward care still involved an element of charity, but the proportion was far smaller than in the past.[21]

New York Hospital's limited provision of free care did not necessarily involve turning people away. Its emergency room did refer unwanted cases to Bellevue, but, as one New York Hospital physician recalls, patients were more likely to be referred because they had "banal diseases" than because they were poor. Someone with "a real interesting fever" could count on being admitted, whatever his financial status.[22] Nevertheless, other factors helped keep the numbers of poor patients at New York Hospital lower than they were at Bellevue. For one thing, New York Hospital had withdrawn from the city ambulance service when it built the new medical center; this cut off one major source of charity patients. The postwar gentrification of the surrounding Upper East Side neighborhood also reduced the number of low-income families with easy access to New York Hospital.

Patients' own hesitance may also have lessened the demand for free care. The medical center's white walls and high towers had struck awe in the heart of many a visitor; one can imagine their effect on someone sick and fundless who is trying to get up the courage to enter the door and ask for free treatment. Anyone who knew much about the hospital was aware that charity care was the exception; this alone may well have put off some applicants. New Yorkers of color probably felt particularly unwelcome, since the great majority of ward patients at New York Hospital during this period were relatively secure white workers. Putting together all the cues, from both inside and outside the institution, it is not hard to see why, as one doctor explained, many needy citizens might have felt that it "wasn't a hospital for people like them." New York Hospital's wards contained the poorest patients in the hospital, but on the whole even they were a more prosperous group than those at Bellevue.[23]

The ward patients at New York Hospital also enjoyed pleasanter surroundings than those at Bellevue, since by this time the wards had been sectioned into four-bed rooms. There was now almost nothing to distinguish the wards physically from the semiprivate rooms. The one key difference between the two services—and it was a point of pride among the semiprivate patients—was that only the wards were used for teaching and research. In the early 1950s, however, because of the need for more revenue, New York Hospital converted many of its wards to semiprivate rooms. Then, so that there would be no loss of "clinical material," it opened half these semiprivate rooms to the teaching program. Just as on the wards, these patients would now receive much of their medical care from the house staff, and medical students would move freely in and out of their rooms for bedside instruction. With charity wards disappearing, other patient groups would have to provide clinical material for the education of tomorrow's physicians. New York Hospital's semiprivate patients might have preferred to avoid the task, but other voices spoke louder than theirs.[24]

The Medical School Connection

New York Hospital's decision to extend the teaching service to its semiprivate rooms is a clue to the growing importance of medical schools in hospital life during the first decades after World War II. These years have often been called the golden era of academic medicine, when the rapid-fire appearance of antibiotics and a dozen lifesaving vaccines made the most expansive hopes seem reasonable.

Penicillin, an antibiotic, had been discovered in 1939, and was developed with federal funding during the war to treat war wounds; it was first used against systemic infections in civilian hospitals in 1944. Another important antibacterial drug, sulfanilamide, had been available some years earlier, but penicillin's broader applications and fewer side effects made it the first "miracle drug," the forerunner of a host of antibiotic agents that transformed medical practice within a few years after the war. The vaccine for infantile paralysis (polio) was another triumph of the postwar years. Decades later, an official at New York University recaptured the drama of that era's heady achievements when he opened a closet at Bellevue and found dozens of iron-lung machines, discarded since the introduction of the polio vaccine. "Here was a room full of equipment that was the fear and dread of every parent," he said, "obsolete, all dusty and cold in a damp room. And that said it all."[25] Achievements like penicillin and the polio vaccine seemed to promise that every dollar spent on medical research would soon be translated directly into better health for the American public.

Abundant hopes were translated into abundant funding, and as dollars flowed into the new U.S. National Institute of Health, they flowed out to university researchers all over the country. One physician wistfully recalls: "If you said, 'I am a fulltime person, I want to do research,' they'd say, 'Thank you. Here's the money.'"[26] By the late 1950s, with career opportunities, unprecedented salaries, and public acclaim all pointing in the same direction, it was a rare physician indeed who chose to become a general practitioner; advanced specialized medicine came to dominate the curricula of the leading medical schools. The schools, in turn, influenced the hospitals associated with them to concentrate on the same kind of medicine.

At New York Hospital, this development caused few problems. The trustees had long ago agreed that the hospital would function on the forefront of academic medicine, and they were prepared to adjust other factors—including the semiprivate patients' reluctance to be treated by medical students—to that priority. A board committee summed up the policy in 1950, when it observed that New York Hospital could easily run without a deficit if its only purpose were patient care. "This is not our major objective. We are part of one of the great medical centers of the world."[27] Embracing this wider mission gave the medical school a strong voice within the hospital, but the New York Hospital trustees still had great power in the partnership, and to a large extent the goals sought by Cornell Medical College were consistent with their own. There would be differences of opinion—sometimes bitter ones—over specific policies, but the vision the two institutions shared gave them important common ground.

Bellevue faced a different situation, in part because it was not as free as New York Hospital to tailor its services to the demands of academic medicine, and in part because its own position was not as strong in relation to its affiliated medical schools. The schools involved were those of Columbia, Cornell, and especially New York University, which had taken over many of the other two universities' wards at Bellevue once they established their own primary teaching affiliations elsewhere (Columbia with Presbyterian Hospital and Cornell with New York Hospital). By the mid-1960s, New York University controlled three-quarters of the beds at Bellevue.[28]

Explaining New York University's close ties with Bellevue, Chancellor Harry Woodburn Chase observed privately: "Without a private hospital of our own, we are absolutely dependent on them for clinical material." Moreover, this clinical material was available under ideal conditions, since it could be used, as a later faculty report noted, "without financial responsibility for the maintenance of the patient."[29] In official statements, medical schools tended to define their work in municipal hospitals as pure public service, and there is no question that the attention of talented and ambitious physicians did benefit many city patients. Nevertheless, the schools' primary reasons for being at Bellevue were to provide their faculty with opportunities for teaching and research and to give their students opportunities for observation and practice.

As academic medicine entered its glory days in the 1950s, the gap widened between the kind of medicine that the medical schools were emphasizing and the kind that municipal hospitals like Bellevue needed to provide. Public hospitals offered a rich variety of cases for the specialist and the researcher, but they also admitted hundreds of thousands of patients each year whose disorders were unremarkable and whose most compelling health need was for consistent primary care. The new breed of academic physicians and their students was neither very interested in such patients nor even particularly well equipped to help them. Under other circumstances, those conditions might have encouraged greater separation between university medical schools and municipal hospitals; perhaps the hospitals might even have begun to train and employ their own cadre of physicians more oriented to community medicine. Instead, during the 1950s, the medical schools acquired a stronger role in the municipal hospitals than ever before.

Giving the Experts a Free Hand: The Affiliation Program

The municipal hospitals' growing dependence on medical schools had its origins in a problem faced by hospitals across the United States in the 1950s: a shortage of interns and residents. As hospitals grew larger and clinical departments more specialized, they needed more house staff; but the American Medical Association was keeping a tight lid on the number of medical school graduates, because it wanted to protect the profession's prestige and income. In the resulting competition for applicants, the winning hospitals tended to be facilities like Bellevue that had university affiliations. Institutions that lacked such connections—including most of New York's other municipal hospitals—filled in as best they could with graduates of foreign medical schools, but they faced growing criticism for the quality of their patient care and the inadequacy of their medical staffing.

In 1959, Mayor Robert F. Wagner appointed a commission headed by investment banker David Heyman to study this problem. The Heyman Commission soon concluded that if the public hospitals were to be saved, it would have to be done by the city's private medical schools and hospitals. The commission proposed that in each public facility a medical school or voluntary hospital should be paid to run the principal clinical departments. Having these private affiliates in charge would help attract top-level physicians; at the same time, the private institutions would bring to the public sector the same disinterested commitment to excellence that they were thought to pursue in their own facilities.[30]

Commission reports often vanish with the morning dew, but Mayor Wagner gave the Heyman report the most practical of endorsements: in 1961, he made Ray Trussell, who had staffed it, the new commissioner of hospitals. During the next four years, Trussell arranged affiliation contracts for thirteen municipal hospitals.

Medical staffing problems had set the stage for the affiliation program, but a further impetus came from the notorious power exerted over the municipal hospitals by the city's so-called overhead agencies—departments such as personnel, purchasing, and civil service. A generation of consultants had condemned this system; among them was the consulting firm of Booz, Allen, & Hamilton, which said that it placed "heartbreaking obstacles in the way of good and progressive administration." One purpose of the affiliation program was to evade these problems, and the new private managers were allowed a degree of freedom in fiscal and personnel matters for which any municipal hospital director would have given his soul. One typical admirer of the affiliation program explained that the municipal hospitals could not provide acceptable care on their own, since they were burdened with "restrictions and 'red tape'" and lacked "the flexibility inherent in an affiliate." Yet the flexibility granted to the affiliates was not an "inherent" property of their institutions; it was the result of a conscious choice by public officials to allow them a level of autonomy denied to the city's own managers. By ruling its own employees with an iron hand while giving private facilities considerable latitude, the city government helped set the stage for a growing private role in the public system.[31]

Bellevue was not included in the original affiliation program, since it already had an informal relationship with several medical schools, but its arrangements with New York University (NYU) were soon made virtually identical to those in the rest of the system. As a result, in addition to the commanding position that NYU had long held in relation to Bellevue's physicians, the medical school completely took over certain departments of the hospital. Did the closer affiliation produce good care? That judgment depended on whom one talked to. One community advocate maintained that the only reason NYU wanted to affiliate with Bellevue was to legitimize the exclusionist practices of its own private hospital and to spare the medical school from the "annoyance of having to respond to the medical needs of the poor while at the same time supplying NYU with the bodies of the poor in a setting, namely teaching, where it finds them useful." A more benign view was offered by Gerard Piel, who chaired a major study of the city hospitals during the mid-1960s. Piel believed that the affiliation provided Bellevue with stronger staff, better equipment, and more consistent care. Yet his commission report also noted that some NYU physicians at Bellevue showed a tendency to pursue their own interests rather than to concentrate on patient care. "The major problem is in getting the physician to the patient." Furthermore, the commission found some evidence of "selective admission practices" on the wards operated by NYU, which required the rest of the hospital to absorb the rejects.[32]

The ambiguity of the affiliate relationship reverberates in the words of Lewis Thomas, who headed NYU's medical service at Bellevue from 1958 to 1966 and then served as medical school dean until 1969. During the mid-1960s, Thomas helped spearhead New York University's effort to get the city to rehabilitate Bellevue. In an eloquent speech to Mayor John Lindsay, he paid tribute to the hospital's "unique tradition" and its pride in being able to "handle anything, at any time." Bellevue needed major reforms, he said, but "on other counts the city has on its hands a national treasure." Thomas had a gift for evoking the remarkable spirit of Bellevue, and his words were often quoted by hospital supporters. But his tributes had a subtext that merits attention as well. Why, after all, did Thomas and his colleagues regard Bellevue "with a fierce devotion which is difficult to explain?" Because, as he explained, "we do not believe there is a better place to teach medicine on earth."[33]

In that statement Thomas reminded his audience, whether he meant to or not, that NYU's interest in Bellevue was not identical to the city's. Whatever other functions Bellevue might serve, to NYU it was primarily a place to train doctors. Thomas and his colleagues were convinced that first-class medical care flowed naturally from first-class medical education. But these two activities could sometimes diverge: young physicians intent on gaining wide experience could short-change cases that seemed routine and might even find excuses to perform procedures that were not required for the patient's well-being. Although many NYU physicians cared for their Bellevue patients with skill and dedication, at the most fundamental level, their agenda was not the hospital's agenda, and there were times when the difference between the two caused difficulties.

The negative side of Bellevue's affiliation with NYU could be seen in Bellevue's outpatient service, where—as at New York Hospital—the interests of the many physicians who rotated through it had caused the department to be organized as an array of highly specialized clinics. A study in the mid-1960s revealed that nearly 90 percent of the hospital's regular outpatients were enrolled in at least two clinics each, while almost 60 percent had to attend three. Under these circumstances it was difficult for any treating physician to be familiar with a patient's full medical picture, especially since communication among the various clinics was notoriously erratic.[34]

The NYU connection not only filled Bellevue with academically inclined specialists, it also reduced the number of attending physicians with any other orientation. By the late 1960s, NYU faculty had replaced almost all the community practitioners who had dominated Bellevue's medical staff before World War II. When the city tried to obtain affiliations at the hospital for some general practitioners, the Bellevue Medical Executive Committee agreed to consider the proposal, but it noted privately with a touch of disdain that "in a teaching institution such as Bellevue is, it is hardly likely that a family physician will fit in well with the medical education programs of the students."[35] These ordinary practitioners' methods might have been somewhat old-fashioned, but their ties to the community and their interest in primary care had made a contribution to Bellevue that NYU did not replace.

Despite these drawbacks, city officials welcomed the intervention of private institutions like NYU in the public system; as one hospital commissioner explained: "Without the support of the medical schools, the municipal hospitals might as well fold up."[36] It is not difficult to understand why he and so many of his colleagues felt that way; in the troublesome task of physician recruitment, hospitals associated with medical schools did far better than those without. More broadly, modern medicine seemed to hold the key to the future, and private institutions—especially the medical schools—clearly had the inside track on modern medicine. Given the general conviction that these institutions were models of excellence, city officials made the associated, though not necessarily correct, assumption that they would be the ideal ones to reform the public system. Thousands of physicians from NYU did serve Bellevue with zeal and commitment, but to the extent that the university's voice became Bellevue's voice, the full possibilities of public care for public benefit were not always realized.

Shaping the Neighborhood

Once the city concluded that private medical institutions were the key to improving the municipal system, these institutions were in a position to exact significant public support in exchange for their participation. Most commonly, this support took the form of money; by the mid-1960s, the city was spending about $75 million per year on the affiliation program. But there were other forms of support as well. The reconstruction of Bellevue's neighborhood provides an enlightening illustration of how the city government and the hospital's major affiliate, NYU, collaborated to change the community around Bellevue. Although Bellevue's name was often invoked in the course of the proceedings, the redevelopment benefited others more than it benefited the hospital.

Similar changes were taking place uptown, around New York Hospital, during these years. Although the political and economic circumstances were different, in both neighborhoods low brownstone buildings that had stood for generations began to give way to new apartment towers and office blocks. Neither hospital brought these changes about single handed, but both were involved in the process in ways that illuminate their different networks of association and their different relationships to the urban community.

A New Look for Bellevue's Neighborhood

Well into the 1950s, the blocks west of Bellevue looked very much the way they had for generations. Tenements and rows of brownstones predominated, interspersed with small shops: butchers, delicatessens, pawnshops, cobblers, fruit stores, and barbershops. Derelicts from the bars along Third Avenue (and its southern extension, the Bowery) were much in evidence; one resident remembers "alcoholics all over the place," sleeping in doorways or curled up in the corners of the brownstone stoops. A hospital study of the late 1960s, seeking to highlight the contrasts among Manhattan neighborhoods, chose as its examples of poverty "the slums of Harlem, Gouverneur, and the Bellevue district."[37]

During the 1950s and 1960s an effort was launched to eradicate the slums around Bellevue. Though the needs of the hospital and its staff were frequently cited as a rationale, the initiative came from the NYU medical school, recently established in a new medical center just north of Bellevue, between

First Avenue and the river from 30th Street to 34th. The center trustees were eager to upgrade the surrounding neighborhood, to benefit both the medical school and its own private facility, University Hospital (later Tisch Hospital). Other medical centers including New York Hospital–Cornell were pursuing similar goals during these years, but not being in as desirable a district as New York Hospital–Cornell, NYU could not rely on private investment alone. So it turned to the government to help subsidize the process. As early as the mid-1940s, with plans for the medical center still on the drawing board, NYU leaders made it clear that if they were going to build their medical complex, the city must do its part by wiping away the slums on the west side of First Avenue.

After several years with no action, NYU decided to take matters into its own hands. In 1952, Winthrop Rockefeller, chair of the NYU Medical Center board, lent the city $25,000 to finance a survey of the area between 30th Street and 33rd, from First Avenue to Second Avenue. Robert Moses, then chair of the city's Slum Clearance Committee, gave the project his enthusiastic support, and within less than two years the Municipal Planning Commission obligingly characterized those three blocks as "substandard and unsanitary." The city then obtained a large federal grant toward the cost of acquiring them and a corporation was formed to develop the property. Many delays followed, but the site was ultimately leveled and, in 1963, a new apartment complex opened opposite NYU. The first exposed-concrete apartment building in New York, Kips Bay Plaza was an austere twenty-one-story block designed by the noted architect I. M. Pei, built around a central garden that was screened from public view. It housed about 300 fewer families than had originally oc-cupied these blocks, and in any case, few middle-income families could afford to rent an apartment there, let alone the many poorer households that had been displaced by the project.[38]

When the NYU Medical Center had launched the initial study of the Kips Bay site in 1952, it also commissioned a survey of the seven blocks south of that, opposite Bellevue. The goal, as Center Director Edwin Salmon explained to Moses, was to recommend improvements that would ensure "the future pro-tection and proper redevelopment of this area." Another memorandum from Salmon to Winthrop Rockefeller helped clarify who needed the protection. NYU, Salmon explained, had initiated "large-scale and costly improvements . . . with little or no protection from inconsistent or objectionable uses of ad-jacent areas." The blocks opposite Bellevue were "unplanned, substandard, congested and subject to continued deterioration unless remedial steps are proposed." The slum was in the eye of the beholder. The area in question housed about 2,100 families and 300 small businesses. Although the neighbor-hood was far from elegant, its residents insisted that it was stable and comfort-able and that rehabilitation rather than demolition could solve any problems that existed. Taking a more activist stance than their neighbors to the north, they formed a preservation committee in the summer of 1959 and organized a series of protest meetings, some of which drew as many as a thousand people.[39]

The reaction of Robert Moses demonstrated both his indifference to their arguments and the powerful network of social and political connections that the neighborhood activists were confronting. Two days after hearing from the preservation committee's lawyer, Moses wrote to Mrs. John J. McCloy, president of the board of managers of the Bellevue nursing school, explaining: "We are having trouble with some of the people presently living in Bellevue South." The nursing school trustees supported the urban renewal project because it included plans for additional nurses' housing. These trustees, most of whom were women, were important to Moses, not only because they could speak for Bellevue but also because they were married to some of the most powerful men in New York. Mrs. McCloy's husband, for instance, was a leading Wall Street lawyer, a former president of the World Bank and, at the time, chairman of the board of Chase Manhattan Bank. Moses urged Mrs. McCloy to have another board member—Mrs. Nelson Rockefeller—speak to her husband, the governor of New York State, on the project's behalf, and he suggested that members of the board should also get in touch with Mayor Wagner. "He is a little inclined to be sympathetic to the 'old-timers' in the district."[40]

Moses need not have worried about the influence of the "old-timers." Although neighborhood protests continued for another year, Bellevue South went forward unimpeded. Before the end of 1960, the blocks from 23rd Street to 30th Street between First and Second Avenues, had officially been designated as a second urban-renewal area. The Slum Clearance Committee was replaced by a new agency, the city Housing & Redevelopment Board (HRB), but though the HRB pledged an end to Moses's "bull-dozer approach," the demolition opposite Bellevue continued very much as Moses had planned it. Of 253 buildings, all but twenty-eight were demolished and replaced by seventeen apartment towers. Three hundred neighborhood businesses disappeared as well. George Baderian had lived over his candy store on the corner of 23rd Street since 1911. "It is wrong what they are doing to this neighborhood," he told a reporter. "I spent my life here. . . . When I leave here, I die." Asked about another business that had been displaced by a last-minute boundary change, a city planner shrugged his shoulders: "Hell, there are no guarantees about anything in this life."[41]

The new Bellevue South was no rich man's enclave. About 10 percent of its apartments were public housing, and the rest were subsidized for moderate- and middle-income tenants; even the most expensive units rented for considerably less than the average rent at Kips Bay Plaza. Yet the social cost was high, particularly if one looks not just at Bellevue South but at the whole sweep between First and Second Avenues, from 23rd Street to 33rd. Overall, for an expenditure of $160 million, much of it public money, the project had dislocated nearly 10,000 individuals and wiped out a small-scale but healthy neighborhood economy. A diverse and accessible urban neighborhood had been replaced by towers and empty plazas, designed in a fashion that was already drawing criticism from many city planners by the time it opened. The district had been losing population before these projects began, but it is difficult to imagine that any gradual evolution of the neighborhood could have been as wrenching as that brought about by this wholesale clearance. Indeed, the character today of nearby blocks that were not redeveloped—a combination of brownstones, older apartment buildings, some high-rises, and many small businesses—suggests that neighborhood stability could have been achieved at far lower social and economic cost.[42]

During these years, hospitals all over the United States were taking similar steps to control and gentrify their surroundings, but many of them were private institutions with relatively loose ties to their immediate neighborhoods. How did it happen that a public hospital like Bellevue should have been involved in a similar undertaking? The answer is that Bellevue itself played a relatively small part in the process. It acquired no new property during this period, and most of the lobbying that went on was undertaken by people associated with NYU. If one thinks of Bellevue Hospital primarily as an appendage of NYU, a training-ground for future doctors and nurses, then the urban renewal effort could be considered a success. By the late 1960s, from First Avenue to Second, 23rd Street to 33rd, hardly a building remained of the slums that had offended center leaders in the past. Kips Bay Plaza gave NYU a handsome neighbor immediately to the west, while the cheaper new housing opposite Bellevue provided affordable apartments for at least some of the staff from both the hospital and the medical center.

Bellevue's primary purpose was not to accommodate medical professionals, however; it was to serve the poor. This mission was hardly served by sweeping away so many prospective patients. Yet city officials generally supported Bellevue South. Some shared the belief, articulated by Mayor O'Dwyer in 1949, that demolishing "large groups of obsolete and rundown buildings" was the key to urban stability.[43] Some welcomed the chance to create better housing for nurses and house staff. Others focused primarily on keeping NYU satisfied; if slum clearance along First Avenue was essential to keeping the medical school at Bellevue, it seemed a price worth paying.

Probably no one in that neighborhood had ever found Bellevue appealing. The high wall, the iron gate, the grim facade—none of these could be called welcoming. One man who lived nearby during the 1950s recalls the complex as an "ominous presence . . . cold, very cold."[44] Yet for years, besides being a significant care provider to the city as a whole, Bellevue had given medical treatment and employment to hundreds of people who lived nearby. After the 1960s, this important community connection was diminished—not through the hospital's own policies, but through the wholesale clearance initiated by NYU and the city government in Bellevue's name.

A New Look for New York Hospital's Neighborhood

In the development of Bellevue's neighborhood, as in numerous other situations, dozens of interacting groups helped determine what happened. At New York Hospital, the development of the surrounding blocks was much more influenced by the hospital leaders' own vision of what their institution needed in order to achieve its purposes.

When New York Hospital arrived on East 68th Street in 1932, the neighborhood was the last ungentrified section of the Upper East Side, bounded on the east by a shabby industrialized riverfront and on the west by the noise and soot of the Second and Third Avenue Elevated (El) lines. Neighborhood photographs taken as late as the 1940s show a patchwork of old-law tenements with fire escapes tacked onto their facades, clotheslines arching over backyards, ethnic shops on the corners, and children playing in the streets. A social survey on one nearby block in 1945 found that only five of 95 household heads had gone beyond high school, and only about half the families spoke English at home. Half of the families had lived on the block for more than ten years.[45]

Even as this community was being recorded, however, it was beginning to disappear. Two landmark events in 1940 helped facilitate the process: the demolition of the Second Avenue El, and the completion of the East River Drive from 49th Street to 92nd, which revitalized the riverfront with parks and promenades. Little changed during the war, but once peace returned, only two more tasks remained in order to clear the way for luxury development: the demolition of the Third Avenue El—completed in 1955—and the removal of the neighborhood's tenements. By the early 1950s, as new investment poured into the blocks west of New York Hospital, hundreds of older buildings were swept away, along with the people who lived in them. "As the values went up, they started moving them out," recalls a hospital staff member. "There was just no space for them." In the future, the Upper East Side would belong, in Theodore White's words, to "the rain-makers and climate-makers."[46]

Gentrification of the surrounding neighborhood presented New York Hospital with certain difficulties. First, future land acquisitions could become prohibitively expensive if values continued to rise. Recognizing this danger early, the trustees moved rapidly to purchase the blocks nearest the hospital, using them as rental property until they were needed for institutional purposes. The upgrading of the neighborhood also caused a second problem: fewer and fewer hospital employees could afford to live near by. For this reason, much of the extra property that the hospital acquired was ultimately used to build subsidized apartments for nurses, interns, and residents. By 1970, New York Hospital's real estate holdings had become so large that its board of governors hired the former president of Rockefeller Center to manage them, noting that "the Center has become a vast landowner and landlord."[47]

Representatives from New York Hospital spent many hours conferring with their institutional neighbors (Cornell Medical College, Rockefeller University, and Memorial–Sloan Kettering) on how to shape their district, "guiding it along lines desired by those now having a great interest in this area." The York Avenue institutions wanted, as New York Hospital's Annual Report explained, to create a "unique urban health campus community" that would provide an "optimal environment for the conduct of their programs."[48] In New York Hospital's case improving the tone of the surrounding blocks would make the hospital attractive to physicians, while private and semiprivate patients—many of whom came from the suburbs—would be reassured by a neighborhood of quiet streets and elegant apartment houses.

Many of the New York Hospital trustees had personal reasons, too, for encouraging the gentrification of the medical center's neighborhood. The great majority of them lived on the Upper East Side and, many, like Vincent Astor, had business ties with banks, insurance firms, and investment companies that stood to gain from rising property values. More broadly, their privileged and cosmopolitan lives gave them little context for appreciating—or perhaps even noticing—the working-class neighborhood that was disappearing from their gates. During these years the dominant figure on the New York Hospital board was John Hay Whitney, the son of the center's founding donor, Payne Whitney. Jock Whitney had come into the family fortune when his father died in 1928; he then made a second fortune by investing the first one. He also excelled in polo, horse-breeding, and golf, had one of the finest private art collections in the country, and maintained six residences, including a townhouse in New York, a 500-acre estate on Long Island, and an apartment in London. Throughout the 1950s and 1960s the board usually contained at least four or five of Whitney's relatives, associates, and subordinates; his biographer had a point when he called the hospital a "Whitney fiefdom."[49] Most of the other trustees were investment bankers or corporate lawyers; all except the one Jewish member were listed in the Social Register. Nothing captures better the rarefied air breathed by the board than the fact that in 1960 three of the trustees were on leave simultaneously—serving as U.S. ambassadors to France, Belgium, and Great Britain.

Given their backgrounds, it is perhaps not surprising that Whitney and his fellow trustees tended to see the blocks surrounding the hospital more as a setting for serving the nation (and even the world) than as a community with its own health needs and priorities. That orientation might have caused political problems in a different kind of neighborhood. Columbia-Presbyterian, for instance, began during these years to encounter aggressive community criticism over the inadequacy of its services to nearby Harlem. The revitalization of the Upper East Side, however, surrounded New York Hospital with neighbors who could afford to buy health care anywhere. Their presence imposed little obligation on the hospital, leaving it free to pursue its own scientific and educational goals.

New York Hospital could probably not have prevented the upgrading of its neighborhood if it had wanted to. Nevertheless, the hospital trustees did participate in shaping their surroundings—conferring frequently with their institutional neighbors, acquiring enough nearby land to meet expansion needs for nearly forty years, and building a cordon of affordable housing around the hospital for the staff they considered most essential. History and real estate played their parts, but the trustees exploited both so as to support their own vision of New York Hospital's place in the city.

The Hospitals, Seen from the Street

The developments around Bellevue and New York Hospital were influenced by different events and financed in different ways; yet by the late 1960s, each hospital had become the hub of a district dominated by large medical institutions.

Bellevue had always been an imposing presence in the neighborhood, fill-ing the blocks between First Avenue and the East River from 26th to 28th Streets. As McKim, Mead & White's plan took shape between the wars, the hospital complex grew even bigger, expanding from two blocks to four. Then after World War II, New York University's new medical center moved in just to the north, stretching all the way to 34th Street. Meanwhile, to Bellevue's south, the hospital nursing school expanded to fill the whole block from 26th Street to 25th, and a new Veterans Administration Hospital was constructed south of that, from 24th Street to 23rd. By the late 1960s, medical institutions ran in an unbroken line along the east side of First Avenue from 34th Street to 23rd. The stretch of York Avenue around New York Hospital developed in a similar way, and indeed came to be known as "Hospital Row."

This pattern was not unique to medical institutions. Many contemporary urban planners encouraged the clustering of buildings by function, seeing it as a rational sorting out of urban land use. Other single-purpose develop-ments of the time included the apartment-house complex of Peter Cooper Vil-lage and Stuyvesant Town and the performance halls of Lincoln Center. For the insitutions involved, there are considerable advantages in such proximity. In the case of Bellevue or New York Hospital, professional staff could move easily from one facility to the next; medical and nursing students could rotate through the different buildings without traveling very far; and scientific, support, and administrative services could be shared.

From a community point of view, however, giving over a neighborhood to such large buildings with such similar uses raised certain problems. These are best understood by considering Jane Jacobs's argument for a very different kind of urban development. In *The Death and Life of Great American Cities,* Jacobs maintains that an ideal neighborhood should contain a wide variety of apartments, shops, offices, services, and even factories. These buildings should operate on different schedules, she says, and should attract numerous pedestrians of different ages and classes. Crisscrossing the neighborhood on a thousand different errands, pedestrians help keep the streets lively and inter-esting. They create a fertile economic environment for neighborhood com-merce, and, by their very presence, provide the neighborhood with the best form of urban security, which Jacobs calls "eyes on the street."[50]

One enemy of neighborhood vitality, according to Jacobs, is "the curse of border vacuums." Noting the blight or stagnancy that often surrounds such apparently dissimilar places as waterfronts, university campuses, civic cen-ters, hospitals, and large parks, Jacobs concludes that all these developments represent dead ends—either literally, in the sense of the waterfront, or opera-tionally, in the sense that they do not invite entry by those who have no con-cerns there. Traffic into these areas may be limited to certain groups, certain times of day, certain entrances. In any case, the easy coming and going of pedestrians is blocked, and with it, the ebb and flow of street life that helps keep a neighborhood lively and safe.[51]

By the late 1960s, the pattern of development around Bellevue and New

York Hospital looked more like Jacobs's idea of a border vacuum than like her ideal neighborhood. In both districts, just as she described, the east side of the street for eight or ten blocks was effectively closed to people having no business in the institutions located there. Many thousands of people visited these buildings, but most of the pedestrian traffic occurred during the day, and all of it was channeled into a few entrances instead of being dispersed up and down the street. After dark, only the change of shift at midnight generated much activity. Increasingly, too, visitors and staff arrived and departed by car. Finally, each facility had absorbed one or more city streets into its complex, creating the long featureless superblocks that, according to Jacobs, discourage casual pedestrians.

Since facilities like parks and hospitals serve important urban functions, Jacobs recommends that the areas around them be made particularly dense and diverse to foster the street-life that such facilities tend to discourage. Around Bellevue and New York Hospital, however, the trend of development was in precisely the opposite direction. The changes on First Avenue opposite Bellevue illustrate the pattern. All the way from 23rd Street to 33rd on the west side of the avenue, where breweries, workshops, restaurants, garages, and small stores had once proliferated, large office buildings and apartment towers dominated the scene, with very few shops on their ground floors. The new buildings contained many people, but they had a deadening effect on pedestrian traffic, partly because a number were set in open plazas that created formidable barriers of their own. Their entrances tended to channel people along a few paths instead of encouraging active use all along the street. By the late 1960s, hardly a place remained on this stretch of First Avenue where a casual passerby could eat or shop or buy a cup of coffee. The sidewalks in this neighborhood had once provided a stage for the diverse economic and social life of the neighborhood. Now they had become simply thoroughfares—barren spaces to pass through on the way to somewhere else.

Like the rest of the neighborhood, First Avenue had been made more modern and more orderly; so had York Avenue around New York Hospital. Did this make those districts more appropriate surroundings for their respective hospitals? That depended on the institutions' goals. For New York Hospital, with its academic mission and its many private patients, the new character of its neighborhood brought far more benefits than problems. But for Bellevue, whose primary mission was to serve the city's poor, the changes were a more serious matter. There stood the hospital, tied visually and organizationally to NYU, looking out on a neighborhood that had been reshaped according to the priorities of the medical school and a generation of planners and developers. No one who spent time in Bellevue's lobby or emergency room could question that this institution was still intimately connected to the surrounding city. Yet, whatever message these interior spaces conveyed, the changing face of First Avenue communicated the tension between Bellevue's position as part of an academic medical complex and its obligations to the broader community of poor New Yorkers.

Dealing with the Unions

During these years still another group joined the chorus of voices seeking to be heard at Bellevue, at New York Hospital, and at many other hospitals: the workers. While labor unions asserted themselves with new vigor in the public system, they also launched the most intense campaigns that New York City had yet seen to organize the private hospitals. Workers had been complaining about conditions in New York hospitals for many years, but social and political changes in the city and in the nation—including the rising aspirations of a new generation of black and Hispanic workers—helped ensure that this time labor's voice would be heard more loudly than ever before.

The way that Bellevue and New York Hospital responded to these organizing campaigns provides further insight into the larger issue addressed in this chapter—the responsiveness of each hospital to the various demands of the community. At Bellevue, where unions had been active since the 1930s, events took one course; at New York Hospital, where unions had hardly made a dent, they took another. But neither hospital was left untouched. The story begins with a telephone ringing in Detroit.

Labor Tries the Door at New York Hospital

On December 15, 1958, the attorney for New York Hospital was summoned out of a meeting in Detroit to take a phone call from New York. Henry Pratt, the hospital director, was on the line, reporting that six organizers from Local 1199 were standing on the corner of 68th Street handing out leaflets.[52] This union had won a major victory a week earlier, when the trustees of Montefiore Hospital in the Bronx had agreed to a union election—the first ever held in a New York City hospital. Since then, leaders of other voluntaries had condemned Montefiore for giving 1199 its first foothold. Now the invaders were at the gates of New York Hospital.

A pharmacists' union, the Retail Drugstore Clerks, had established Local 1199 to organize hospital workers, and it was testing the waters all over the city, planning to concentrate its campaign on the six or seven institutions that seemed most approachable. New York Hospital did not offer promising territory, being a huge hospital led by powerful trustees unlikely to bend to union pressure. Nor did its workers show much interest in the campaign, perhaps in part because it was among the best paying of the city's voluntary hospitals. In any case, in February 1959, when Local 1199 announced the seven facilities it planned to target, New York Hospital was not on the list.[53]

New York Hospital's leaders were delighted to be spared 1199's attentions, but by this time they were already preoccupied with a new challenger: the Teamsters. This union, which had several thousand members in the municipal hospitals, had always believed that private medical institutions could not be organized. Montefiore's settlement with Local 1199, however, reopened the question, and they felt compelled to defend their status as the city's premier hospital union. Looking around for a high-profile institution that would dramatize their arrival on the scene, they chose New York Hospital.

As 1199's representatives disappeared from New York Hospital's street corner in the winter of 1959, Teamster organizers took their place. There they stood for months, six days a week, twice a day, handing out leaflets. The hospital's leaders followed the campaign with meticulous care. Every day, a memorandum listing the number, gender, and race of the organizers on duty went from the hospital's security officers to the personnel department, from there to Pratt, and from Pratt to the hospital attorney. Pratt also appeared before the board of governors to discuss the "acute seriousness" of the situation. With the trustees' support he issued a series of letters to hospital employees, stressing the advantages of working at New York Hospital, the constraints on the hospital budget, and the dangers of unionization. Unions lead to strikes, he explained, and strikes can kill. "It is unthinkable that the lives of our patients should be jeopardized by the act of a union leader."[54]

The first test of the Teamsters' strength at New York Hospital came on March 25, when thirty-five pickets (many of them Bellevue employees, according to Pratt) appeared in front of the hospital wearing placards reading: "New York Hospital unfair to organized labor." There they remained for about twelve hours, turning away several delivery trucks. The next day, the picketers were gone, but Teamster organizers continued to appear with their leaflets. Hospital security officers kept close track of them and evicted those who made their way into the hospital building. Whenever the union held a meeting of hospital staff, Pratt would send a "responsible executive" to monitor the proceedings from across the street. Inside the hospital, workers who showed signs of union sympathies were promptly identified; Pratt later assured a colleague that "several of the more active union members are no longer employed here."[55]

In the fall of 1959, ten months after they had first appeared, the Teamsters ended their drive at New York Hospital. A number of factors internal to the union probably helped influence the withdrawal, but the Teamsters must also have been discouraged by the lack of support they had received from the hospital work force. During the union's first major effort, the demonstration on March 25, every hospital employee had crossed the picket line and gone to work. The summer of 1959 brought only modest improvement. Teamster insiders later estimated that they never attracted more than 11 percent of the New York Hospital workforce.[56]

Why did the hospital's employees not show more interest in the union? Job satisfaction can hardly have been the reason, since the turnover rate in nonprofessional jobs at the hospital during this period was about 50 percent per year. One factor may have been the hospital's own response to the union threat. In rapid succession during 1959, the board of governors raised its minimum wage, expanded overtime allowances, improved workers' insurance coverage, and instituted a new grievance procedure. This cloudburst of benefits might well have convinced employees that they would gain more by letting the hospital woo them away from the union than by signing up with it.[57]

Perhaps it made a difference, as well, that the Teamsters often seemed less interested in organizing the hospital than in destroying their rival Local 1199, which they attacked in a typical flier as "leeches masquerading under the word Union." At a time when workers in voluntary hospitals were still uncertain about union action and when 1199's success at Montefiore struck many as a hopeful beginning, the Teamsters' insistence that the "drugstore clerks'" achievements were worthless may actually have eroded potential union support at New York Hospital. In addition, the Teamsters may have placed too much emphasis on the power of the "Teamster juggernaut" to inflict its will through strikes.[58] Many hospital employees were proud of their work, dedicated to their patients, and profoundly ambivalent about the possibility of going on strike. For them, the Teamsters' belligerent tone may not have been the best approach to building a union. In any case, the Teamsters built no union at New York Hospital.

In the end, the "drugstore clerks" of Local 1199 concerned New York Hospital's leaders more than the Teamsters did. All through the spring of 1959, the hospital divided its attention between battling the Teamsters and making sure that the seven other hospitals targeted by Local 1199 would not capitulate, as Montefiore had. In April, Local 1199 called a strike. Mayor Wagner later recalled how strenuously "observer" facilities like New York Hospital worked to stiffen the resistance of those hospitals directly involved. "New York Hospital, Columbia-Presbyterian—boy, those fellows were conservative! The struck hospitals were not acting on their own."[59] With these stalwarts behind them, the voluntaries gave hardly an inch, and after forty-six days, the union settled for almost exactly what it had been offered in the first place: some improvement in wages and grievance procedures, but no union recognition.

Local 1199 had lost the battle, and yet it had won the war. In using the full extent of their wealth and influence to beat down their impoverished employees, the hospital trustees had undermined the very image of disinterested public service that they had worked for decades to establish. "This is the most clear-cut social issue since the revolt of the gladiators," exclaimed one observer. A reporter noted the incongruity of hearing men with impeccable philanthropic credentials sound like Henry Ford at his most reactionary. "They are men who build gymnasiums for underprivileged kids," he wrote, "and then pay their parents $32 a week and scream bloody murder when they try to join a union." When even a justice of the New York State Supreme Court told hospital leaders that their attitude was "an echo of the nineteenth century," it was clear that the tough settlement of June 1959 would not be the end of the story.[60]

June 1959 was not the end of the story. Local 1199 grew steadily and, in 1963, it was able to win passage of a state law requiring private hospitals to engage in collective bargaining with their employees. The next year Pratt notified his employees that the State Labor Board had set an election date "to determine whether or not you want to pay union dues and hand yourself over to union control." By this time there was a new contender at New York Hospital: Local 144 of the Service Employees Union. The hospital immediately launched another all-out campaign against this foe—issuing repeated mailings, conferring with supervisors, and surreptitiously monitoring meetings both at union headquarters and at employees' homes. Pratt's efforts were successful and, in November 1964, Local 144 went down to defeat, 1,064 votes to 340.[61]

There were no more major union campaigns at New York Hospital. Local 144 soon retreated to its original base in the proprietary hospitals, leaving Local 1199 in command of the voluntaries. When even the mighty Presbyterian Hospital was unionized in 1970, New York Hospital became the only major private hospital in the city without a union contract. Thus, using a combination of carrot and stick—of improving benefits while relentlessly opposing every union initiative—its leaders had kept its enemies at bay. In terms of wages and benefits, New York Hospital's workers probably gained as much as anyone did from the union movement. Every time Local 1199 won another raise and New York Hospital leaped to match it, every time the hospital adjusted its personnel policies to deflect a new organizing drive, the union was shaping hospital policy as surely as if every employee had been a member. But the other function of a union went unrealized: to provide an alternative voice within the institutional structure. Those in charge at New York Hospital had no intention of responding to that kind of participation by their workers.

Bellevue: An Ally Downtown

To see in full flower the kind of system that New York Hospital's managers feared, we have only to look at the experience in the public hospitals during the same years. The election of Robert F. Wagner as Mayor in 1953 brought to power a man who—unlike the New York Hospital trustees—prided himself on his good relations with labor. He had a family tradition to uphold; he was the son of Senator Robert Wagner (D., New York), who had spearheaded the passage of the National Labor Relations Act in 1935. Like his father, Mayor Wagner was convinced that responsible unions could smooth employee relations by providing an organized structure for grievances and suggestions. Also, he was well aware that the unions provided at least one channel to the votes and campaign support of the huge city work force. Accordingly, in July 1954 Wagner issued an order permitting municipal employees to be represented by unions in their dealings with the city.

Labor made only modest gains under the new rules. Union representatives could help individual workers with grievances and salary appeals, but they could neither speak for whole departments nor negotiate contracts. Some workers called the process "collective begging," to emphasize its difference from collective bargaining. Even the strongest union in the city hospitals, the Teamsters, could do relatively little for its members. Weaker still was the Teamsters' rival: District Council 37 (DC 37), the city division of the American Federation of State, County and Municipal Workers (AFSCME). With fewer than 500 members in the municipal hospitals, DC 37 had, as one organizer recalled, "no growth, no staff for the local, very few shop stewards."[62]

In 1957, just in time for his reelection campaign, Mayor Wagner took a second step and created a formal system for collective bargaining. Energized by the new rules, DC 37 began to gain on the Teamsters. An aide remembers being pursued tirelessly by an organizer from the union. "He kept chasing us and asking us to join, until finally I said, 'I'm tired of you. Give me that green card.'" Reaching beyond the limitations of city bargaining, DC 37 courted the hospitals' primarily black employees with a round of social events, including fund-raising projects for black colleges and charity organizations and celebrations for the independence of each new African country. By 1959, DC 37's hospital unit (Local 420) had a membership of some 6,000, compared to the Teamsters' 7,000.[63] (It was about this time that the Teamsters, presumably feeling the heat, abandoned their drive to organize New York Hospital and turned their attention back to the municipal hospitals.)

Union organizers at municipal hospitals still faced many restrictions in their bargaining with the city, but the opportunities they enjoyed were immeasurably greater than those at New York Hospital. In the public hospitals, as one union official recalled, "There was no Mayor who said you shouldn't, no Commissioner who said I won't."[64] Backed by official city policy, collecting dues via paycheck, getting time off for union duties, posting their notices on hospital bulletin boards, and holding meetings on hospital premises, these union workers were in a far stronger position than they would have been at New York Hospital. Yet it is worth noting how little Bellevue's own administration had to do with establishing these conditions. Bellevue's director seemed quite sympathetic to the union, but the policies that really mattered were not being made at the hospital; they were coming from City Hall—and they reflected the mayor's own values and political needs far more than the priorities of Bellevue Hospital. Bellevue would benefit in a number of ways from the unions' rising power, but decision-makers elsewhere would set the stage for that rise.

In 1965, DC 37 got a new leader: Victor Gotbaum. The new man had a master's degree in international relations, but he had also spent several years with AFSCME on the streets of Chicago and his style was as tough as any Teamster's. Gotbaum's first undertaking in New York was a welfare workers' strike, which ended victoriously in February. The union had hardly finished celebrating, however, when it faced a new challenge. The Teamsters chose that moment to call for a union election in the municipal hospitals. For years, both DC 37 and the Teamsters had known that sooner or later they would face each other for exclusive control of the hospitals. Now the test was at hand, and the Teamsters seemed to have every advantage; they were much larger and wealthier, and city officials were thought to prefer dealing with them because, despite their confrontational demeanor in public, they tended to be more accommodating in actual negotiations. DC 37 had been preoccupied for months with the welfare strike. Now, with a depleted treasury and an exhausted staff, the union would have to make up all the lost ground, and more besides, to win a majority.

"We were fifteen to one underdogs when they called for the election," recalled Gotbaum. "Nobody thought we could win." Yet he observed, "the stakes were very, very high." Four groups comprising 20,000 hospital employees would be voting in the election: clerical staff, messengers, cooks, and—by far the largest group—aides, a catch-all category incorporating 16,000 unskilled workers in housekeeping, food service, nursing, and several other departments. Because the New York City Department of Hospitals was so big, the union that won a majority in any one of those groups would have a majority citywide, and thus become its sole bargaining agent, eligible for the first time to negotiate on major issues—salaries, promotions, and pensions.[65]

DC 37 did everything it could to delay the election past the April date originally requested. When all procedural dodges had been exhausted, the AFSCME president prevailed on George Meany, head of the now merged labor organization AFL-CIO, to telephone the mayor and ask for a postponement. (The Teamsters union had no claim on Meany's loyalty, since it had been expelled from the AFL-CIO in 1957, after revelations of corruption among its top officials.) Wagner is generally thought to have hoped the Teamsters would win the election, but like virtually all other observers, he apparently believed they were so far ahead that he could gain some political capital without hurting the front-runners by doing Meany a favor. In any case, Meany got his favor, and the election was put off to December 1965.[66]

DC 37 then launched its campaign, spearheaded by a remarkable organizer, Lillian Roberts, whom Gotbaum describes with pride as a "ghetto alley-cat." Raised in the Chicago housing projects, Roberts started work at eighteen as a hospital aide because she could not afford to go to nursing school. She joined AFSCME, became an organizer, and ultimately came to New York to work on the welfare strike. When she was named head of DC 37's Hospital Division in spring 1965, she rapidly assembled a team of full-time organizers from people already working in the municipal system. Ella Woodley, for example, had been an aide at Bellevue for many years and, though she belonged to the union, had never been active. The arrival of Lillian Roberts made all the difference. "I'm telling you, she saw potential," says Woodley. "I started getting involved; it's a bug that never leaves you. . . . She made me inspired. I believed, I tell you, I believed, I believed."[67]

Roberts assembled a team of about sixty workers who threw themselves into the campaign, backed up by a blizzard of spot radio announcements, pamphlets, special brochures, biweekly bulletins, and leaflets. Woodley remembers working feverishly "all shifts, day and night." The campaign, she says, "was like in the air, everywhere." Every Friday, Roberts would hold a staff meeting at Bellevue. "She definitely didn't particularly care for negativity," recalls Woodley. "There was nothing that couldn't be done." While Roberts worked the hospitals, Gotbaum reached out to the community, winning support from the city's Central Labor Council and half a dozen individual unions, including Local 1199. Like New York Hospital, DC 37 had the advantage of going up against the unpopular Teamsters. The vote in the New York City hospitals was one of the largest elections ever held involving the Teamsters; Gotbaum was instructed to keep an open line to AFL-CIO headquarters on election night so that the results could be monitored as they came in.[68]

On the day of the election, the polls near every city hospital opened early in the morning so the night shift could vote before going home. Lillian Roberts knew the Teamsters were strong at Bellevue "and they used a lot of muscle there. . . . So I thought, 'I better hang close to Bellevue.'" All day, workers came and went from the polling place across First Avenue. When she spotted anyone starting to go home without voting, Roberts says, she would tell them: "Please, this is your future and your time and you have to. You must. If you never do anything else, this is for you." And then the Bellevue workers "did their thing. I was never so happy in my life. . . . When I saw what happened in Bellevue, I knew we had won the election."[69]

Roberts was right. With nearly three-quarters of the eligible workers voting, DC 37 had won the right to represent three of the four contested employee groups, covering nearly 20,000 workers. Only a unit of 400 cooks had gone for the Teamsters. The vote had been close—with about 12,000 people voting in the largest group (the aides), DC 37 had won by only 300 votes citywide, and by only seventeen votes at Bellevue. Nearly a year more would pass—spent in appeals, delays, legal arguments, and finally strike threats—before DC 37 was finally certified. But in November 1966, Mayor Wagner's successor, the newly elected John V. Lindsay, signed the city's first contract with DC 37. The union then had a majority in the Department of Hospitals, as well as a majority of nonuniformed workers citywide. New members flooded in, and, by 1967, the union had become the exclusive bargaining agent for nearly 85,000 city workers.[70]

For hospital employees, DC 37's victory meant raises, better benefits, and a new training program devised by Roberts that helped aides progress into positions as nurses and technicians. The DC 37 victory also meant that Victor Gotbaum, a man whose primary political base was in the municipal hospitals, moved into a central role in city policymaking. Mayor Lindsay preferred dealing with a few strong unions and, as bargaining units were consolidated over the next few years, DC 37 gained more and more members. The union further strengthened its position when it provided Lindsay with badly needed support during his 1969 reelection campaign. By the time Lindsay's second term began, Gotbaum had moved into a position that one observer described as "No. 1 in the emerging power structure at City Hall."[71]

The impact of DC 37's victory on the quality of patient care is much more difficult to asses. About the time the union won its first contract, Bellevue underwent one of those periodic spasms of public exposure that has characterized its history since the nineteenth century. In the hurricane of exposés and self-exoneration that followed, it became almost impossible to assess whether conditions at Bellevue had actually changed for the worse, for the better, or had stayed very much the same. One of DC 37's principal contributions was to support these exposés. Gotbaum issued news stories, pamphlets, and fiery press releases that described the grim conditions that hospital workers and patients faced each day. At the same time, he worked behind the scenes to stimulate broader investigations of the hospital system by outside agencies. Thus, the union provided Bellevue's workers and patients with an advocate and ally that was not available in the more autocratic structure of New York Hospital. Bellevue's obligation to respond to outside groups had sometimes created problems, but it also made it possible for DC 37 to take an important role in addressing some of those problems.

Designing clinical services, rehabilitating neighborhoods, and responding to hospital unions might seem to be unrelated subjects. Yet watching how Bellevue and New York Hospital operated within each of these spheres during the 1950s and 1960s has helped to illuminate how differently private and public hospitals functioned. Enjoying the autonomy of a private institution, New York Hospital was able to define a rather narrow clinical mission and pursue it single mindedly, to promote the development of its neighborhood in ways best suited to its goals, and to block the entry of unions into its work force. Bellevue exerted far less control over its own destiny. Its clinical services reflected an ongoing tug-of-war between the academic interests of its university affiliates and the daily demands of a million needy New Yorkers. Its immediate neighborhood was transformed in less than a decade, but though these changes were made in Bellevue's name, they were influenced very little by Bellevue's managers, and many of them served university, municipal, and investors' interests more than the hospital's. As for labor relations, the hospital found an important ally in DC 37, but the union's victory grew out of decisions made at City Hall, not at Bellevue; moreover, labor's strong position, once established, added still another voice to the cacophonous Bellevue chorus.

Bellevue had a central mission—to provide medical services to the poor—but that mission was continually complicated by the needs and demands of a thousand competing voices. The medical schools wanted teaching and research opportunities; the city wanted a stronger tax base; the employees wanted a say in their work life. Politicians wanted patronage; homeless people wanted a clean bed; reporters wanted news; private hospitals wanted a place to send rejected patients; the community wanted a supportive neighborhood institution; the mayor wanted to be reelected. Everyone wanted something, and everyone was in a position to demand that Bellevue play a part in bringing it about. In some ways, the responsiveness required of Bellevue prevented it from being the hospital it sought to be. In other ways, its responsiveness forced it to be much more. "Bellevue is more than a city hospital; it is the very life beat and death rattle of the city," wrote the *Daily News*. "Bellevue is the city's people, fighting for their lives."[72]

5

The Limits of Reform

1965–1970

We have observed Bellevue's responsiveness to the pressures from its immediate environment—from its patients, its neighborhood, and its workers. Between 1965 and 1970 Bellevue also found itself responding to two events of broader scope: the first was the launching of Medicare and Medicaid; the second was the upheaval within the public hospital system that culminated in the creation of the New York City Health & Hospitals Corporation. Each of these two health-reform initiatives was expected to improve Bellevue's fortunes dramatically; neither of them did so. Exploring the reasons why sheds light on the programs themselves; it also illuminates an important chapter in the evolution of New York's public hospital system.

The federal government's Medicare/Medicaid program and the municipal government's Health & Hospitals Corporation (HHC) were both inspired by a recognition that some social groups were receiving less good health care than others. Each of these initiatives was intended to rectify that imbalance. But besides having certain common origins and goals, the two programs had a common limitation: both were shaped by a profound reluctance to interfere with the autonomy of private health providers. Despite government's growing role in paying for private care, these programs placed little pressure on private hospitals to adapt their services to public priorities. This shared characteristic facilitated the launching of the two initiatives, but it also caused problems that would reveal themselves with increasing clarity in the years ahead.

The idea that Medicare/Medicaid and HHC might help equalize the level of health care in New York City made these two programs of vital importance to the municipal hospitals, because by the mid-1960s, the public system had fallen into disrepair. The postwar construction effort had lasted only a few years, and it had barely dented the unmet needs that had accumulated during the Depression and the war. In addition, the public hospitals were feeling the political effects of serving a changing patient population. Being the city's provider of last resort had had one political meaning when a sizable proportion of New Yorkers needed such a service. But health insurance had enabled thousands of working-class and middle-class New Yorkers to move to the private sector for their health care. Those left behind to use the public hospitals, besides being fewer in number, tended to be the poorest and least well organized of the former patients; as a group they had considerably less clout than the masses of working-class citizens who had depended on the system in the past. Thus the municipal hospitals' deteriorating physical condition reflected a broader trend: the waning political significance of the patients they served.

Despite this trend, other tendencies of the era made it seem possible that the decline of the municipal hospitals might be reversed in the future. During the mid-1960s, questions of social justice moved to the center of the public agenda, both locally and nationally. In a political climate enlivened by the civil rights movement, President Lyndon B. Johnson's War on Poverty, and the promises of the Johnson administration's Great Society, new attention was paid to the many forms of inequality in American society. Health care was only one such area, but it was a vital one. In this area New York City offered a vivid case study, because its public hospital system made visible the needs and inequalities that remained out of sight in many communities. The contrast between the city's beleaguered public hospitals and its august private medical centers symbolized a more fundamental gulf between the life chances of poor and minority New Yorkers and those of more prosperous citizens. Both Medicare/Medicaid and the city's Health & Health Hospitals Corporation were expected to lessen that gulf.

Medicare/Medicaid, passed in 1965, established a vast system of federal and state reimbursement for health services to the poor, the disabled, and the elderly. The program might have been designed differently, with the money going to expand public medical programs. Instead, like the school voucher experiments undertaken in later years, Medicaid/Medicare let each consumer obtain services where they chose, thus determining for themselves whether public dollars would go to public or private institutions. If, as was widely expected, most recipients chose the private sector, then public dollars would follow them there. This massive transfer of public funds to private providers might have raised concerns about accountability, but documents of the time suggest that the planners were more concerned with designing the program so that private providers would want to participate. As a result, few safeguards were built in to ensure that services would be provided in a way that was responsive to public priorities in terms of cost, quality, and appropriateness.

The design for New York's HHC reflected a similar reluctance to impose constraints on private medical institutions. HHC owed its life to a series of exposés about conditions in the municipal hospitals. For a time, serious thought was given to undertaking a sweeping reorganization, under which both public and private hospitals would be drawn into a single system of public obligation for the public funding they received. In the end, however, the planners chose to limit their organizational reforms to the municipal hospitals. Creating a new corporation to manage the public hospitals did bring some administrative improvements, but since many of the public system's problems derived from its unequal relationship with the private sector, a reform design that left that relationship untouched could not, by itself, ensure a single standard of health care in New York City.

New York was not unusual in adopting programs that deferred to private medicine. Medicare/Medicaid was a national program, and the policies under which it operated in New York were essentially the same as those established elsewhere, except that New York's policies were more generous. As for the creation of HHC, the unusual feature was not the city's final decision to leave the private hospitals alone, but the fact that it briefly considered doing otherwise. Ultimately in New York, as in most communities, the consensus prevailed that private hospitals should be left free to excel according to their own goals, while the public system backed them up by undertaking the tasks they chose not to perform.

This continuing stratification of New York City's hospital network was reflected in the experiences of both Bellevue and New York Hospital in the late 1960s. Once again, Bellevue had to respond to a range of social demands, whereas New York Hospital was able to participate in those aspects of reform that served its institutional goals while remaining aloof from those that did not. Tying the experiences of the two hospitals together during these years were two major changes: the advent of Medicare's millions and a new conviction that something had to be done about the public hospitals.

Trouble in the Municipal Hospitals

When New York City began writing affiliation contracts with private medical schools and hospitals, many believed that this initiative alone would address most of the flaws in the public hospital system. Early reports were generally optimistic, but during the mid-1960s a change in the political atmosphere began to intensify public concern about the state of the municipal hospitals, not only for their own sake but as an example of what was happening to the city.

"A Furor of Investigations"

As Mayor Robert Wagner entered the final years of his third and last term, many New Yorkers felt that his unflappable urbanity had degenerated into something more mechanical; he seemed to have run out of ideas. At the same time, the tone of public life was becoming more contentious. Most of the city's problems were difficulties of long standing, but in the assertive climate of the mid-1960s, discontent with every feature of urban life seemed to bubble to the surface. The *Herald-Tribune* captured the general mood when it began its series on the city: "New York is the greatest city in the world—and everything is wrong with it."[1] Declining to run again in 1965, Wagner was succeeded on the Democratic ticket by Abraham Beame, whose background as a machine politician only underlined the bankruptcy of the city's dominant party. The handsome young Republican candidate, John V. Lindsay, made an irresistible contrast, as he campaigned in shirt-sleeves under journalist Murray Kempton's appealing tribute: "He's fresh and everyone else is tired." In January 1966, Lindsay took office as the city's first Republican mayor since Fiorello LaGuardia.

Instead of calming the waters, Lindsay's arrival simply heated up the controversies that had been building during Wagner's final years. Every group of New Yorkers seemed to have a grievance and none, it appeared, could be resolved without diminishing the position of another group. National events added to the sense of crisis: President Johnson's War on Poverty satisfied some aspirations but aroused a host of new ones; divisions over the escalating war in Vietnam spread into every corner of American life; and black Americans demanded their rights with increasing desperation. Street fighting had already erupted in Harlem and in Bedford-Stuyvesant in 1963 and 1964. As Los Angeles, Detroit, Newark, and a score of other cities burst into rioting and flame in the years that followed, many New Yorkers wondered when they too could expect, in James Baldwin's ominous words, "the fire next time." Taking New York's troubles as a symbol of urban problems across the nation, *US News and World Report* provided a gloomy answer to its own question: "Does New York City Have a Future?"[2]

Any catalog of the city's ills reserved a place toward the top of the list for the state of the municipal hospitals. Candidate Lindsay had highlighted their "shocking condition" during his 1965 campaign, and as 1966 became 1967, one exposé followed the next. The *New York Times,* the *Daily News,* and the New York *Post* did studies exposing the dire state of the municipal hospitals. So did the deputy mayor, the city comptroller, a task force of city administrators, the New York Academy of Medicine, a joint committee of the State Legislature, the Institute for Policy Studies, the Systems Development Corporation, the Blue Ribbon Panel appointed by Governor Nelson A. Rockefeller, the State Department of Health, the State Commission of Investigation, and a special citizens' panel appointed by Mayor Lindsay. There was, as one Bellevue employee observed, "a furor of investigations." The findings were almost universally bad. A typical account in the New York *Post* praised the municipal government for the scale of its ambition, observing that "no other city in the nation makes a comparable investment in its citizens' health." Yet, it said, "by now it is no news that the hospitals which our city runs are a mess."[3]

Whatever their proposed solutions, the investigators all tended to identify the same problems. First, virtually every panel agreed that the hospitals' fundamental difficulty was, as the governor's Blue Ribbon Panel reported, "chronic underfinancing over a period of many years." Coping with shortages had long been a way of life for public hospital staff. Physicians had become accustomed to never having enough gloves or dressings. Cornell medical students were found to be keeping Bellevue supplied with syringes and blood-pressure units by smuggling extras out of New York Hospital. The radiology department was so understaffed that interns maintained the only way to get X-ray reports promptly was to climb in the department windows after hours and collect them oneself. Hospital aides described their ongoing battles to get enough sheets and towels for their patients.[4] Case by case, experiences like these had become part of public hospital lore, recounted with a certain gallows humor. Together, they revealed a system under desperate financial strain.

Besides the public hospitals' budget problems, the rigidity of the city's oversight process drew universal criticism. One report showed that it had taken a hospital nine months and eighteen authorizations to hire one X-ray technician. "They say we don't make decisions and we're low caliber," complained a Bellevue administrator, "but they won't even let us buy pencils." Such constraints, as everyone observed, made the hospitals obsessively accountable for each penny of expenditures without enhancing—or even exerting much control over—the quality of their performance. As one manager observed: "We are administering a government of 300,000 employees with techniques designed to prevent graft by the Tweed Ring."[5]

The third problem identified by all investigators was the wretched physical condition of the hospitals. "This committee will never forget," said a state senator, "the sight of patients sleeping in the hallways of the hospitals of the richest city in the world." Another legislator asserted: "There is not one single hospital plant in the system which can be considered up-to-date with adequate facilities comparable to a modern university affiliated teaching center." Bellevue's history of stop-and-start construction was typical of the conditions uncovered. In 1944, the city had approved a plan for major renovations at the hospital. No action followed, and gradually even Bellevue's newer buildings fell into disrepair, deteriorating from half a century of heavy use and stingy care. Preventive maintenance was virtually discontinued because of a lack of staff and supplies. A British physician who visited the hospital in the 1950s was said to have "just rubbed his eyes when he saw the filth, the ceilings falling down, and everything so dilapidated." Learning to function in the crumbling facility had become so much a part of daily life that at one retirement dinner, the honoree was presented with a bronze model of one of the hospital's arthritic elevators, complete with its usual sign: "Press down for up." In 1958, it was agreed that the old complex was too far gone to save; instead, a single new tower would be erected to house the entire hospital. Some preliminary excavations were started in the early 1960s, but then the money ran out again, and grass began to grow back over the construction site.[6] As one report after another made clear, Bellevue's declining physical plant symbolized the city's neglect of the whole public system.

The Department of Hospitals had faced criticism before, but the investigations of the 1960s introduced a new element into the debate; it raised questions for the first time about the role of the municipal hospitals' private affiliates. The leaders of these institutions had always explained the soaring cost of the affiliation program as the necessary price for adequate medical care, but by 1966 another participant was on the scene—one qualified to speak knowledgeably about hospital affairs from a different perspective. The new voice was that of District Council 37 (DC 37), freshly certified as the bargaining agent for most Department of Hospital workers. Largely because of the union, the studies of the municipal system in 1966 and 1967 took a different course from their predecessors: they began to explore the extent to which the affiliated private institutions had exacerbated the city hospitals' problems. Since the affiliation contracts had the potential to take away jobs held by city employees, DC 37 had its own reasons for stressing this point. Nevertheless, the union enhanced the debate by forcing onto the agenda the question of private institutions' accountability for public funds.

DC 37 also made an important contribution by drawing outsiders into the discussion. Medicare/Medicaid, which had just been passed, gave the state government a financial interest in hospital care throughout New York, since it was obligated to pay a share of all Medicare/Medicaid services. Building on this and on the union's own political friendships, DC 37 established contact with the State Legislature's committee on Public Health and Medicare. The chair was Seymour Thaler, a Democratic state senator from Queens, whose father, a garment finisher, had been a shop steward in the International Ladies Garment Workers Union. Described by the *New York Times* as a "man of instant indignation. . . a high-voltage, leather-lunged loner," Thaler had a talent for expressing his committee's findings in blistering and highly quotable form. When, for instance, he accused the city and the private medical establishment of "a deliberately conceived conspiracy" to destroy the municipal system, he drew massive press coverage.[7] This heightened the pressure on other groups to sharpen their own investigations, both to satisfy their informational needs and to put their own particular spin on any implications of guilt that might emerge.

The Affiliation Contracts under Attack

Past exposés of the municipal hospitals, which had generally been organized by the medical staff or their supporters, had tended to highlight the dedication of the system's physicians, struggling for their patients' welfare against the uncaring politicians and a heartless bureaucracy. Approaching the issue from a different perspective, Thaler raised new questions about the physicians' selflessness. He was one of the first, for example, to suggest noisily in public that municipal hospital patients were being subjected to unneeded procedures in the interests of training and research. Among many other charges, he claimed that surgeons at Bellevue sometimes operated on psychiatric patients for practice and that hundreds of unnecessary liver biopsies had been performed on Bellevue's alcoholic patients. Department officials immediately denied the accusations and denounced the accuser, but within a week the commissioner acknowledged that some experiments had indeed been conducted without patient consent. "Sometimes people just don't think of it," he explained. "Within a big system like this, there's bound to be irregularity."[8]

Even if the questionable practices uncovered by Thaler were exceptions, the fact that senior physicians had tolerated them suggested a lack of empathy and respect for patients that was at variance with the claims that had been used to justify the affiliation contracts. Physicians had been portrayed as the saviors of the system, yet Thaler's findings suggested that too many of them cared more about research than they did about their patients. In 1957, Dickinson Richards had asked an audience of medical colleagues: "Can you wonder if some of us look with a somewhat jaundiced eye on plans for new medical research that include not a thought in the world for the immediate care of the patient?"[9] Perhaps Richards had not always lived up to that high standard, but, by the late 1960s, few physicians associated with the city's affiliates even seemed to be articulating it.

Revelations such as those made by Thaler created a new environment for the debate about the affiliation contracts. Even if one sympathized with the concerns of science-minded physicians and ambitious young interns, their behavior hardly represented the superb and selfless patient care that the affiliates had promised to deliver. Furthermore, once Thaler set the ball rolling, people began to raise administrative questions about the contracts as well. The affiliation program, it became clear, was characterized by grand expenditures and minimal accountability. In his initial presentation to the Board of Estimate, Commissioner Trussell had estimated that the program might cost "a few million." By 1966, it was costing about $75 million per year—nearly a quarter of the department budget.[10]

Despite the size of the city's investment, it was obvious that the affiliation program had not improved the hospitals as much as had been hoped. The private institutions involved had generally been able to obtain new staff, supplies, and equipment for the departments they ran. But these improvements had frequently created within each municipal hospital the same kind of inequality that had long characterized the citywide system—high professional salaries and plenty of resources for the departments controlled by private institutions, while publicly run areas down the hall faced continued shortages and deterioration. Investigators began to discover that equipment purchased for municipal hospitals had instead found its way into affiliated institutions. They also identified physicians being paid by the city who rarely appeared on city premises. Some claimed the program's excesses were inevitable, given the city's flaccid monitoring; one observer commented: "If you just put a pile of money on the table and tell them to take it, naturally they'll take it."[11] But even this rationale undermined the idea that the affiliates could be trusted to bring disinterested excellence into the municipal system.

The Impact at Bellevue

Every study panel in the 1960s made an obligatory visit to Bellevue, followed by a stop in the press room to deplore what they had found. The result was, in the words of the director of nursing, a series of "calumnious and calamitous headlines." Bellevue's most dramatic moment in the spotlight came in September 1966, when Thaler and his committee made their first visit. The next morning Thaler told the press: "What we saw last night at Bellevue Hospital was horrifying. The conditions at Bellevue are a blot on the conscience of the State of New York." The hospital's problems, he said, "have often been described in the press. They must be seen to be believed." He concluded: "Bellevue is a crumbling ruin and a disgrace to every administration of this City that permitted Bellevue Hospital to fall into a state of decay that would rival the conditions in the worst slum building in New York City."[12]

About the same time, a former Bellevue employee named Frank Leonard also came forward. He had worked for several years as an attendant in the psychiatric division and he had nothing good to say about it; he described a barbaric world in which staffing shortages were so acute that employees found "brutality becomes a necessity," either to protect themselves or to vent their frustration. The employees' reaction was only human, Leonard said, but the patients were suffering. "People ought to understand the consequences of maintaining a place like Bellevue." The *World–Journal Tribune* chimed in with its own account of the psychiatric division, strikingly headlined, "A Night at Bellevue: They Scream Behind Bars."[13]

Bellevue's problems were hardly news to its three medical schools. Columbia was troubled by the bad conditions at Bellevue, though it was prepared to remain at the hospital. Cornell Medical College, however, had been quietly trying to extricate itself for years. In 1956, it had nearly won an agreement for a new city hospital to be built across the street from its own medical center. When that fell through, Cornell's chief of service at Bellevue had helped to lobby the city for improvements at the hospital. That produced only halting progress, however, and the Department of Hospitals' decision to concentrate on strengthening its weakest facilities had left Bellevue more neglected than ever. Well before the exposés of 1966, Cornell had concluded, as the president of the medical center intimated to his colleagues, that "city neglect of the physical plant and the shortage of personnel at Bellevue had reached dangerous levels" and that Cornell should get out if it could. The stumbling-block, he said, was the board's conviction that "such withdrawal nearly inevitably would be interpreted in a bad light" and might be seen as "abandonment of a community responsibility."[14]

Bellevue was peripheral to the Cornell and Columbia medical schools, since each had a distinguished teaching hospital within its own medical center. By contrast, New York University had no other major affiliation and was therefore far more dependent on Bellevue. (On one occasion, when NYU had complained about conditions at Bellevue, a hospital commissioner had been heard to observe: "Fuck 'em. They have nowhere else to go."[15]) But even NYU could be pushed too far. In 1966, a university official told a reporter: "Word has gone out that Bellevue is in serious trouble. We're starting to have trouble recruiting residents and interns." That fall, NYU told the city that it would break off its relationship with the hospital unless rapid improvements were made in staffing and equipment. Within days, the city's head of health services announced: "Something drastic has to be done about Bellevue."[16] Two weeks later, Thaler's denunciation of conditions at the hospital hammered the message home.

Public Dollars, Private Goals: Medicare and Medicaid

It was in this supercharged atmosphere—with six separate studies of the municipal system in full cry, with NYU demanding changes at Bellevue, and with Cornell eyeing the door, that New York State received federal approval for its Medicare/Medicaid plan. This program, which provided public financing for health care, had two parts. The first, Medicare, covered the elderly and disabled of all incomes and was to be administered by the federal government. The second, Medicaid, covered the poor and was to be administered by each state according to its own standards. The details varied by state, but essentially the federal government would pay at least half the cost of health care for all those eligible for either Medicare or Medicaid.

From the beginning, New York City's experience with Medicare/Medicaid was unlike that of most American communities. The most important difference was the program's relationship to what had existed before. In many parts of the United States, Medicare/Medicaid made health care accessible to millions who had been unable to afford it in the past. But in New York City, access to health care was already close to universal, because of the large array of private teaching hospitals, the extensive public subsidies to private institutions for the care of the poor, and the huge municipal system of public hospitals and clinics.

New York City's most distinctive feature was its level of medical subsidies for the nonwelfare poor. Many communities made some kind of provision for the most destitute, through private charity and/or tax monies; but New York was unique in that it recognized that one could be well out of poverty and yet still be "medically indigent"—that is, unable to pay for health care. Each year, the municipal hospitals treated tens of thousands of New Yorkers who would not have qualified for free care in any other city in the country. Indeed, a study made shortly before Medicare/Medicaid took effect found that about 40 percent of New York's hospital patients met the municipal standard for "medically indigency."[17] The city's generous eligibility criteria expressed a much broader idea: that free health care was not just a charitable arrangement for the very poor, but a need and right of many ordinary citizens.

Under federal guidelines, nearly all disabled and elderly persons were eligible for Medicare. The states, however, set their own eligibility criteria for the means-tested Medicaid program; and in the process of doing so, each one expressed its own approach to health services for the poor. New York State's Medicaid guidelines, published in April 1966, approved free care for all families with incomes below $6,000. This standard represented the highest income ceiling for Medicaid in the country, $2,100 above the next highest state (California). Yet it did not break new ground. It simply applied New York City's existing criteria for free care to the new program.[18]

The generosity of this standard had particular implications for New York City, because of another factor that made its Medicare/Medicaid program unique. Almost everywhere else in the country, the responsibility for paying the state's share of the program was spread among all taxpayers. But in New York State, owing to the power of the suburban and rural Republicans in the State Legislature, responsibility for paying half the state's share was passed down to the local level. This meant that the greatest financial burden was carried by the communities with the highest Medicare/Medicaid costs—those with the largest numbers of poor, elderly, and disabled citizens, most notably New York City. As a result, in later years, when the cost of health care began to soar, the impact on New York City's budget was much greater than that experienced by other urban areas.

In 1966, these problems lay in the future, and few city officials foresaw them. Joseph Terenzio, director of the private Brooklyn Hospital, expressed a widely shared optimism when he accepted Mayor Lindsay's offer to be commissioner of hospitals, a position he had turned down when Mayor Wagner had offered it to him a year earlier. Terenzio explained: "Because of Medicare, the chronic underfinancing of municipal hospitals will come to an end."[19]

Medicare and Medicaid at Bellevue

The director of Bellevue welcomed Medicare and Medicaid like a long-sought sail on the horizon. These programs, he predicted, would "virtually eliminate all classifications of medical indigency." They would enable many needy patients to obtain care in the private sector, thus reducing the burden on public hospitals; at the same time, public hospitals could count on new revenue for serving those patients who remained. Reinforcing that hopeful view, the mayor soon announced plans for an extensive renovation of Bellevue's older buildings. For decades, the city had used the promise of future reconstruction as a reason not to maintain or improve the existing plant. Now, thanks to Medicare and Medicaid, Bellevue could count on full reimbursement for most of the patients it served. This expectation, together with the publicity about bad conditions at the hospital and NYU's threat to withdraw, had created a new political climate.[20]

Medicare/Medicaid also made possible organizational changes that had been considered in the past but never acted upon. Bellevue's patient population had been dropping for a decade, as antibiotics shortened hospital stays, tuberculosis cases diminished, and the lure of the suburbs plus the pressure of urban renewal reduced the population of the surrounding area. On an average day in 1965, the hospital was serving just over 2,000 patients—about 25 percent less than it had in 1950. As this trend continued, Bellevue would soon have too few patients to accommodate the teaching needs of three medical schools. Accordingly, the city's health services administrator asked both Cornell and Columbia to consider withdrawing from the hospital. The president of New York Hospital-Cornell Medical Center accepted the suggestion with alacrity, noting privately that it was "opportune." Columbia moved more reluctantly, but ultimately it agreed to establish itself at Harlem Hospital. By the fall of 1967, both Columbia and Cornell had left Bellevue, ending a tradition that went back nearly a century. The city then wrote its first formal contract covering Bellevue's affiliation with New York University.[21].

Overall, Bellevue experienced a series of dramatic changes during the first few years of Medicare/Medicaid: the sudden approval of the rehabilitation project, the end of Cornell and Columbia's tenure, and the consolidation of NYU's power at the hospital. More drama lay ahead, however, because even as these events were occurring, Medicaid itself was undergoing major changes.

Originally, seeing Medicaid as a bonanza for the financing of health services to the poor, New York City launched a blitz of radio announcements, subway ads, and news stories urging eligible New Yorkers to enroll. By 1967, more than 2 million people—about a quarter of the city population—had done so. Of these, less than half were on welfare; the rest were "medically indigent" according to New York State criteria. Yet even as new applicants began flooding in, the generosity of the criteria evoked a backlash in the State Legislature, particularly when it became clear that nearly half the people in the state were now technically eligible for Medicaid.[22]

What caused concern in Albany caused outrage in Washington. Many members of Congress were shocked at New York's high income ceiling for Medicaid—nearly two and a half times the national minimum wage. Accustomed to a lower cost of living and a less expansive tradition of social welfare, those legislators resented the fact that federal taxes would have to cover half the cost of New York's program—a program so inclusive that a state with less than one-tenth of the national population accounted for one-third of the country's Medicaid patients.[23] Two years had elapsed since the hopeful summer of 1965, when Medicaid had been passed as part of President Lyndon Johnson's crusade to end American poverty forever; by the fall of 1967, Johnson's plans for the Great Society were in disarray—starved by the growing cost of the war in Vietnam, weakened by the president's own waning political fortunes, and discredited by the riots of three summers.

In this charged political climate, New York State's Medicaid policy struck many legislators as a typical liberal scheme, one that was impractically extravagant and based on the sacrifice of others—in this case, the taxpayers of the forty-nine other states who would have to help foot the bill. The reaction was swift. In November 1967, Congress cut the federal share for nonwelfare Medicaid patients from 50 percent to 25 percent. Caught with a $150 million shortfall, New York State followed suit a few months later, excluding from the program most adults under 65 unless they were on welfare. More cuts followed and, by 1970, nearly 1 million New York City residents had been dropped from the Medicaid rolls. During the next few years, the number of New Yorkers on welfare rose sharply, and the proportion of those eligible who actually went on welfare increased from 60 percent to 90 percent. Among them, no doubt, were many of the medically indigent families that had been excluded from Medicaid from 1968 to 1970.[24]

Despite the cutbacks, Medicare and Medicaid provided a passport for thousands of patients to leave the municipal hospital system. Meanwhile, those who remained in the public system faced new obstacles to the free care they had received in the past. For example, a new state law required that, for the first time in their history, the city's municipal clinics must charge for their services. In 1967, the fee was set at $8 per visit; within a year, it had risen to $16. Even patients eligible for Medicare or Medicaid had to pay 20 percent of the clinic fee. Some charges were waived, but the need to plead poverty created a tone that had not characterized the city's public clinics in the past.[25]

Clinic patients at private hospitals encountered the same rising fees and copayment requirements as those at public facilities, which may help to explain why both public and private hospitals reported a net decline in outpatient services between 1965 and 1970. One study concluded: "It is hard to determine where these patients have gone for care." In fact, growing numbers of poor New Yorkers were simply doing without medical treatment until they were acutely ill. Then, once they were sick enough for emergency care, Medicare or Medicaid would pay the whole cost. At Bellevue, while every other form of service, including outpatient visits, declined, visits to the emergency room increased almost 40 percent between 1967 and 1970.[26]

As Medicare/Medicaid altered the pattern of hospital services, so it altered the city's pattern of spending for those services. In the private hospitals, every dollar's worth of inpatient care that was provided to a Medicare or Medicaid patient automatically earned the facility a dollar of reimbursement—50¢ from the federal government, 25¢ from the state, and 25¢ from the city. This arrangement made the city an involuntary partner in the private hospitals' escalating costs. In 1960, payments to private medical institutions had represented only one-sixth of the municipal government's expenditures for hospital care; by the early 1970s, they had risen to more than one half.[27] As each year went by, therefore, the city found itself spending more and more of its health dollars for services that it neither administered nor controlled.

The municipal hospitals were serving Medicare and Medicaid patients too, but these hospitals received only a part of the federal and state revenue they earned; the rest went instead to the municipal general fund. Nor did they receive the quarter share of the Medicare/Medicaid reimbursement that the city itself was expected to contribute, since the city maintained that its annual subsidy to the Department of Hospitals was payment enough. Total costs for the Department of Hospitals did increase, but much more slowly than those of the private hospitals. For example, between 1967 and 1970, while New York Hospital's budget rose by more than one-third in real dollars, the department budget increased by only about one-fifth. At the same time, the city's own subsidy to the hospitals began to decline in real dollars. This was not unreasonable, considering that New York had been investing its own money in the system for generations, but it meant that instead of dramatically improving conditions in the public hospitals, the principal effect of Medicare/Medicaid was to sustain them at something like their customary level, while reducing their cost to the city.[28]

In the beginning, Medicare/Medicaid had seemed to be the salvation of the public hospitals, easing their workload while enriching their budgets. Although it brought vital support to many medical institutions in the rest of the country, in New York City it did considerably more for private hospitals than for public ones.

Medicare and Medicaid at New York Hospital

At New York Hospital, unlike at Bellevue, Medicare/Medicaid was initially viewed with some ambivalence. On the positive side, the new program did promise more revenue. This chance of new funds came at a good time, since New York Hospital was continuing to match every wage rise that Local 1199 won in the unionized hospitals. The increased revenue also helped cover the rising costs of new medical technologies. Despite these benefits, hospital leaders were concerned that the new program would further erode the supply of "clinical material" for teaching. A hospital committee estimated that under the new program, more than half the ward patients would be able to afford private or semiprivate care. In his annual report for 1966, New York Hospital's board president called Medicare one of several "formidable challenges" that similar medical centers were facing. He warned that the hospital's current balance of teaching, research, and patient care required thoughtful maintenance "and even defense, for many influences tend to distort it," most notably "drastic changes" like Medicaid and Medicare.[29]

Fiscally, Medicaid/Medicare began well, moving New York Hospital from a net deficit in 1965 to a surplus in 1967, the first full year of payments. But the honeymoon ended almost before it began. In its 1968 backlash against soaring health costs, the State Legislature imposed a freeze on Medicaid reimbursement rates for hospitals. The New York Hospital president reported late that year that "the interest of the federal, state and local governments" had encouraged the board to approve a significant raise in wages. In addition (lending credence to the idea that the hospital had discouraged charity patients in the past), he noted that ever since Medicaid took effect, the hospital had accepted large numbers of the poor. But the freeze on reimbursement had sharply diminished the revenue expected to pay for those commitments. "The high hopes of 1965 have paled," he wrote, "in the realization that our national resources are inadequate to meet our needs."[30]

Then came a court decision, riding to the rescue. In 1969, a federal judge disallowed the rate freeze. Under the terms of the national legislation, he said, New York State's Medicaid program must reimburse hospitals for all "reasonable costs," just as Medicare did. This decision confirmed the arrival of a new era in health finance. For years, hospital expenditures in New York City had been subject to a variety of controls. The only significant public grants that private hospitals had received to cover their daily running expenses were the city payments for their services to the poor. Although these had become more generous over the years, they still required individual certification for each patient covered, they had remained below full cost, and every increase in the rate required action by both the Board of Estimate and the City Council. As for health insurance, at least some pressure was exerted by the fact that higher Blue Cross rates to the hospitals had to be financed by higher consumer premiums, which required approval by the State Insurance Board. Under the new system, by contrast, there was no review process; all "reasonable and customary" costs were to be reimbursed, and Medicare added an extra 12 percent to cover research, repairs, and depreciation.[31]

The old controls on hospital spending were hardly made of iron, but the fact that they had had some impact becomes clear when one sees what happened once Medicare/Medicaid swept them away. The reaction of one private hospital trustee exemplifies the new atmosphere. Learning of the favorable court decision during a bargaining session with Local 1199, he turned to the union representative and said, only half in jest: "Ask for anything you want!" Wages went up, as did all hospital expenditures. In 1966, New York Hospital's president had warned that the growing role of government in hospital finance could be dangerous, since regulatory bodies, pushed by "unenlightened public opinion," might put "an artificial ceiling" on hospital rates. At least in the short run, he need not have worried. Between 1966 and 1969, the cost per inpatient day in New York City hospitals rose twice as fast as during the four years before Medicare/Medicaid began. New York Hospital's budget, after rising at about $2 million per year during the early 1960s, began to increase by $6 to $7 million per year after 1967. Tax dollars paid for a growing share of those escalating costs; by 1969, more than half the private hospitals' revenues came from public sources, primarily Medicare and Medicaid.[32]

Changing Patterns of Patient Care

Medicare/Medicaid did not trigger a dramatic expansion of New York Hospital's services; in fact, the hospital's total admissions actually declined between 1965 and 1970. Other private institutions in the city added patients, but the numbers were not very large, and much of the increase was offset by losses in patient numbers from the public hospitals. The net result was that the number of general care patients served in all New York hospitals increased by only 4 percent between 1965 and 1970—less than the increase during the five previous years. When patients of all types (not just general care) are considered, the total number served actually declined between 1965 and 1970 (see Table 5.1.).

Table 5.1. Average hospital censuses in New York City hospitals, 1965–1970

Average Daily Census	General Care Patients	Other Types of Patients	All Patients
Municipal hospitals			
1965	7,606	6,890	14,496
1970	6,999	5,147	12,146
% Change, 1965–1970	-8	-25	-16
Voluntary hospitals[1]			
1965	19,138	4,209	23,347
1970	20,392	3,815	24,207
% Change, 1965–1970	+7	-9	+4
All hospitals[2]			
1965	30,231	11,267	41,498
1970	31,376	9,286	40,662
% Change, 1965–1970	+4	-18	-2

Source: *Hospitals and Related Facilities of Southern New York* (New York: Health & Hospital Planning Council of Southern New York, 1966, 1971).

[1]Private not-for-profit hospitals

[2]Total includes beds in proprietary (private for-profit) hospitals but not in state and federal hospitals

The greatest workload changes during the early years of Medicare/Medicaid occurred not in general care but in specialized services, such as mental illness, tuberculosis, and chronic care. In those areas, hospital populations decreased dramatically. Various factors contributed to the decline, including the availability of new psychotropic medications and the declining prevalence of tuberculosis, but Medicare/Medicaid reimbursement also played an important part by financing nursing home care for long-term patients and community treatment for the mentally ill. Because public hospitals had previously cared for most such patients, they experienced the greatest change. Between 1965 and 1970, the number of chronic and mentally ill patients in municipal institutions dropped by 25 percent—more than three times the decline in general care (see Table 5.1).

The impact of these changes on the status of the municipal hospitals in the city can be seen most clearly if one looks at a longer time period: from 1955 to 1975. The public system's total bed count and its share of total beds in the city both declined somewhat during the first ten years of this period, but after Medicare/Medicaid began, there was a second and much sharper drop. By 1975, the municipal hospitals had nearly 7,500 fewer beds than they had had in 1955, and these accounted for just 28 percent of the beds in the city, down from almost 40 percent in 1955 (see Table 5.2).

The private hospitals, too, served a declining number of tuberculosis and mental patients during these years, but in the field of general care, the private hospitals gained while the public ones lost. Moreover, because the private hospitals were still free to choose which services they would provide to which patients, the exodus to the private sector did not represent a cross-section of the municipal caseload—more white patients than black found a welcome in the private system, more Medicare than Medicaid, more acutely ill than chronic, more expectant mothers than drug addicts, more sober employed than homeless derelicts. Like the spread of hospital insurance, the arrival of Medicare and Medicaid had further narrowed the circle of New Yorkers who had to depend on public care, leaving behind, once again, the people with the least choices and least resources.

For private hospitals, the greatest change during the early years of Medicare/Medicaid was the declining number of ward patients. A year or so before the program went into effect, a young surgeon at Presbyterian Hospital had candidly described the crucial role that such patients played in educating physicians: "They are ignorant and unquestioning, and have come

Table 5.2. Changes in the number and distribution of hospital beds in New York City, 1955–1975

Change in number of beds:		1955–1965	1965–1975
Municipal hospitals			
% General care		-1	-17
% Other services		-20	-47
% Total beds		-10	-31
Voluntary hospitals[1]			
%General care		+9	+9
%Other services		-21	-42
%Total beds		+3	+1
Municipal hospitals' *share of total beds in city:*	*1955*	*1965*	*1975*
%General care	28	26	21
%Other services	62	65	61
%Total beds[2]	39	35	28

Source: *Hospitals and Related Facilities of Southern New York* (New York: Health & Hospital Planning Council of Southern New York, 1955, 1965, 1970)

[1]Private not-for-profit hospitals.

[2]Total includes beds in proprietary hospitals but not in state and federal hospitals.

from pretty backward places; they have a profound faith in the medical profession. . . . We can turn their minds and their bodies inside out because they come to us as charity patients." In these patients, he explained, "you have a vein of raw material that will never get worked out."[33] By the late 1960s, this "vein of raw material" was indeed getting "worked out," as Medicare/Medicaid enabled greater numbers of patients to pay for their care.

New York Hospital had started using some of its semi-private beds for teaching in the early 1950s, when neighborhood changes and the spread of hospital insurance brought the first decline in ward patients. As Medicare/Medicaid triggered an even sharper decline, the hospital took the final step, extending the teaching program to the rest of the semiprivate service and even to the private rooms. No one lost sight of the greater freedom the physicians enjoyed on the wards, however, and at this point New York Hospital–Cornell Medical Center began to appreciate what it had lost in withdrawing from Bellevue: access to hundreds of teaching patients, with only minimal administrative responsibility for their care.

From time to time during the late 1960s, representatives of the medical center continued to discuss the possibility of other municipal affiliations. Metropolitan Hospital, only a mile and a half uptown, looked like a possibility until, through a story in the *New York Times,* leaders at the medical center learned about the hospital's many problems, including the fact—apparently new to them—that municipal hospitals were required to admit all patients who applied. "If this is true," wrote one center official to another, "we should go pretty slow" before affiliating with Metropolitan. It would be difficult to maintain "our high standards of work . . . if at the same time we can't control the volume of patients at Metropolitan." If the center decided to go ahead with the affiliation, he said, "we should see if we can relieve ourselves from the provisions of the law by an effective operating understanding with the New York City Department of Hospitals."[34]

Then, in the spring of 1968, the center decided to suspend discussion of a public affiliation for a time, because the ongoing exposés of the municipal system appeared to be setting the stage for a major reorganization. Neither the affiliation contracts nor Medicare/Medicaid had resolved the public hospitals' difficulties as promised, but perhaps reorganization would be the answer.

A Modest Reform:
The Health & Hospitals Corporation

Two concurrent events had given new intensity to the discussions about improving the municipal hospitals: the searing reports on the hospitals' condition and the expectation that funding from Medicare/Medicaid would cover the cost of doing better. When Medicare/Medicaid first appeared, many public officials assumed that its greatest contribution would be to reduce the city hospitals' workload to manageable proportions. In contrast, some private medical leaders thought the new program might sweep the city system away altogether. One such visionary was Martin Cherkasky, head of Montefiore Hospital, a private facility. Cherkasky had built his own medical kingdom in the Bronx, where Montefiore and its affiliated medical school, Albert Einstein, dominated the provision of health care. Pressing for an even grander integration in the future, Cherkasky maintained that the existing duplication between public and private institutions was "inefficient, it is insanity." The city should have only one system of hospitals, and it was clear to him which should prevail: the private one.[35]

The idea that private institutions could provide a larger share—if not all—of New York's hospital care had been raised off and on for years, most frequently during the voluntaries' annual plea for higher reimbursement rates. At such times, spokesmen from the private hospitals often contended that if the city would subsidize their full cost for serving the poor, the voluntaries could accommodate more fundless patients, reducing the need for public beds. Yet the argument must have been at least partly rhetorical, since municipal hospital expansion projects were generally supported by all the organizations that tended to speak for voluntary interests, like the United Hospital Fund, the Hospital Council of Greater New York, and the Greater New York Hospital Association.

In fact, the private hospitals had good financial reasons for wanting the public system to remain in place. Before Medicare/Medicaid, many voluntaries functioned on very tight budgets. Even if the entire city hospital budget had been converted to subsidies, it might not have covered the cost of accepting responsibility for the municipal system's aging buildings and troublesome patients. The existing distribution of duties suited many private institutions very well, leaving them free to pursue their own priorities while the public system took responsibility for the patients they felt unable or unwilling to serve.

The chief anesthetist at Bellevue, also a member of the staff at NYU's private facility, University Hospital, presented with tactless clarity the different and complementary missions of the municipal hospital and the private medical center: "The city concept is that you have to take care of everybody, with no resources. The medical center concept is that you take care of nobody unless you want to, and bring everything to bear on it."[44] Even the commissioner of hospitals in the early 1950s, Marcus Kogel, embraced this residual role for the city system, explaining that city institutions served as "the instrument which makes it possible for the great voluntaries to be what they are—magnificent models of hospital practice."[36] Many private hospital leaders agreed with Kogel that the municipal hospitals were essential to their own institutions' freedom of action.

This conviction gave the leaders of private hospitals a stake in the well-being of the public system, and the affiliation program intensified their concern. No affiliate, however insulated, could remain untouched by its municipal twin's problems. Aside from the daily inconveniences, the affiliates were publicly identified with the municipal hospitals in which they worked. Reporters writing banner headlines were not likely to check contract details before including an affiliate in the blame for any scandals that emerged. The affiliation program had tried to construct within each public hospital an alternate universe, free from city constraints; instead, the program had helped broaden the constituency for improving those parts of the public system that the affiliates could not control.

Looking for a Savior

By the late 1960s, it had become clear that simply choosing new city officials could not solve the municipal hospitals' problems. During these years, every one of the top jobs affecting the hospital system changed hands, but the difficulties remained. Mayor Lindsay, for one, had not turned out to be the quintessential urban problem solver for whom many had hoped. His periodic tours through the city hospitals painfully revealed both his humanity and his powerlessness. Most mayors had declined to expose themselves in this way; Lindsay, to his credit, took the tours. Yet, confronted with flaking paint falling on patients lined up on stretchers in the corridors of Harlem Hospital, all he could do was burst out to his companion: "For God's sake, can't we cut through the red-tape and get these problems solved?"[37] The answer, apparently, was no.

In an effort to streamline municipal health care, Lindsay in 1966 created the position of health services administrator (HSA), with responsibility for both the Health Department and the Department of Hospitals. The first administrator, Howard Brown, soon found himself enmeshed in quarrels and turf disputes, unable to achieve any of the grand reforms he had envisioned. Brown's problems were aggravated by his own inner turmoil about keeping his homosexuality a secret. The fear of discovery haunted his term as HSA and helped precipitate his resignation less than eighteen months after taking office. Brown's personal problems were only part of the story, however, as was suggested by the fact that once he left, Lindsay had to offer the job to thirty-three people before he could find someone who would accept it. He did find a new administrator, and—after that man soon departed—another, but by then it was clear that no HSA was going to save the municipal hospitals.[38]

If the health services administrator was not to be the savior, neither was the hospitals commissioner, now one step down in the city hierarchy. Joseph Terenzio entered the commissionership in 1966 with some optimism, since his arrival coincided with the days of Medicare's rosiest promise. Terenzio was an attorney and the first nonphysician in the job; he was also the first commissioner who had had professional training in hospital administration. But as it turned out, management skill was not enough. Or perhaps Terenzio's experience, which had been entirely in private institutions, was not transferable to the thorny ground of municipal hospitals.

Like Lindsay, like Brown, Terenzio often articulated eloquently the problems that public hospitals faced. But the fact that neither he nor his superiors seemed able to achieve significant change confirmed in many minds the need for a fundamental restructuring of the city hospital system.

The arrival of Medicare/Medicaid helped reopen the question of whether the private hospitals should take responsibility for the city system. The single level of care that Medicare/Medicaid was designed to promote was hardly consistent with the obvious inequalities between public and private hospitals; also, the financial problems associated with a takeover would be reduced if most of the costs were covered by government funding. In 1967, the Public Health Committee of the New York Academy of Medicine declared: "There no longer is any social or medical reason for the continuance of the Municipal Hospital System of New York City. Since it may be presumed that there will be no more medical indigency, the reason for the Municipal Hospital system will be removed." The State Joint Legislative Committee on the Problems of Public Health and Medicare concurred: "The era of the charitable patient is over. . . . Segregation of patients for economic criteria is more likely to be eliminated if, in fact, the municipal hospitals lose their specific identity and are merged into the voluntary system."[39]

The proposal to create a single standard of hospital care by turning the city hospitals over to private management addressed two major issues identified by the myriad investigations of 1966 and 1967: the abysmal condition of the municipal institutions and the city's poor record in remedying the problems. It left untouched, however, the third major issue raised by the study findings: the question of whether the private institutions could reliably carry out this public role. As nearly every study made clear, the private affiliates had been rather casual about their use of public funds. Furthermore, if New Yorkers no longer had a functioning public hospital system, the private hospitals would have to abandon their practice of excluding patients for financial, medical, educational, or administrative reasons. Would they make this change? Perhaps Frank Van Dyke of the Columbia School of Public Health was correct when he said: "The voluntaries cannot be trusted to run the whole show."[40]

Even those who wanted to keep the public hospitals in the hands of city government recognized the need to lessen the gulf between the quality of public and private care. Some proposed that, instead of abdicating to the voluntary hospitals, the city should challenge them by accepting private patients just as they did. Although this idea had been discussed in the past, it had received little recent attention; at a time when the city hospitals were having trouble getting sheets for their beds and toilet paper for their bathrooms, they were in no position to start competing for the carriage trade. Medicare's promise of consistent revenue, however, had revived the possibility. In 1966, the city's health services administrator, Howard Brown, proposed that the municipal hospitals be reorganized to serve New Yorkers of every income level. Proclaiming that "the money is at hand to rebuild our city system," Brown argued that the city should use its Medicare and Medicaid revenues to transform its hospitals from havens for rejects into community facilities serving all incomes and classes of patients. Middle-class patients (being, as Brown said, "better complainers") would stimulate the staff to do their best work, while serving patients of all classes would remove the stigma that had so long tainted public medicine. "All evidence shows," he said, "that economically segregated poor-law hospitals will not work." Both public and private hospitals would continue to exist in Brown's scenario, but they should be as similar as possible in plant and clientele.[41]

Brown's effort to broaden the municipal hospitals' role aroused little enthusiasm in influential circles. For a time, it seemed more likely that the hospitals might be converted instead to private management, as Cherkasky had proposed. But the question of accountability remained and it was exacerbated by the way the new funding mechanisms worked. In the past, any private institution that administered a public hospital would have been paid for its services through the city budget process, and therefore would have been subject to any monitoring the city decided to impose. Now most of the private hospitals' public revenue would come to them automatically, through Medicare and Medicaid, however well or poorly they responded to municipal policy. Under these conditions, the city would have little leverage for requiring the private managers of municipal facilities to adapt their services to public priorities. Community boards could be created to advise individual hospitals, but who would speak to the system as a whole?

New Visions for the Public System

Of the many investigations during 1966 and 1967, two addressed the question of accountability with particular care. The men directing them could not have been more different. The first study was conducted by a young Texan named Robb Burlage, working under the sponsorship of the Institute for Policy Studies, a liberal think tank in Washington, D.C. Burlage had come of age in the civil rights movement and had been present at the creation of the New Left, having attended the historic Port Huron meeting in 1962 that gave birth to Students for a Democratic Society. By age and by inclination, Burlage belonged to a circle of young professionals who were trying to use their occupational credentials to foster social change. During the 1960s, in New York as in many cities, this commitment led a growing number of young doctors, nurses, and other health-care providers to make common cause with the patients they served by cooperating with neighborhood groups in periodic demonstrations, sit-ins, and protests. The title of one memoir from the period captures the insurgents' mood: *White Coat, Clenched Fist*.[42] Policy analysts, like Burlage, played their own part in this movement, contributing their skills to the rising critique of established medicine.

Another study of New York City hospitals was carried out by the Piel Commission, a group appointed by Mayor Lindsay and named for its chair, Gerard Piel. As a young man just after World War II, Piel had purchased the nearly defunct *Scientific American* magazine with two friends and turned it into a profitable and internationally respected publication. The recipient of innumerable prizes and honorary degrees, Piel sat on the boards of the

American Museum of Natural History, Radcliffe College, the American Civil Liberties Union, and Harvard University. Piel's establishment credentials were mirrored by the members of his commission. Five of the seven served on the boards of private hospitals or insurance companies and four worked on Wall Street.[43]

Given the political and generational gulf between Burlage's world and that of Piel, one would not expect that they would see the municipal hospitals' problems in the same way. Nevertheless, their proposed solutions had one important common theme: both were convinced that in order to ensure a single standard of health care in New York, there must be a single, publicly controlled conduit for the public money spent on that care.

Burlage's study was published first, in the spring of 1967. Taking the flawed affiliation program as evidence that delegating further power to the private sector would only compound the problem, Burlage proposed the creation of a Metropolitan Health Services Commission—a public authority with power over all health-care expenditures and construction in the region. It would administer some health services and purchase others from private providers, like voluntary hospitals. Besides the hospitals, Burlage envisioned an array of neighborhood health centers, an emphasis on health workers' ties to the communities they served, and a network of strong community boards. He believed that this design would combine centralized power with decentralized participation and ensure a direct connection between public funds and public priorities.[44]

The Piel Commission submitted its report a few months later in 1967. It began by documenting the poor state of the public hospitals and it asserted that by maintaining them in this condition, the city was perpetuating an "invidious double standard of private and welfare medicine" that was "demeaning to all concerned." Furthermore, with the affiliates' growing responsibility for clinical care in the municipal facilities, the city's role had dwindled to just one function, which Piel later characterized as "running lousy hotels." It would be better for the city to abandon this thankless task, said the commission, let the voluntaries take over the hospitals entirely, and give New Yorkers a single system of care.[45]

Thus far, the Piel report resembled a number of its predecessors, with its litany of municipal malfeasance and its recommendation for a private takeover. But unlike most earlier panels except Burlage's, the Piel Commission also concluded that some publicly controlled structure should be established to hold the private hospitals accountable. Looking at the growing flood of public dollars for health care, Piel and his colleagues made, as he later explained, "this real Galilean discovery that the way to do it was to get public policy put onto public money." If the city could "get a whiphand" over the federal, state, and city dollars going to New York's private hospitals, then it could use that fiscal power to ensure that their services met public priorities. "The whole crime with all this money that's gone into medicine," explained Piel, "is that none of it has gone to enforce public policy or express it. The whole idea was to capture that money."[46]

To serve as the control point for public dollars, the Piel Commission recommended the creation of a "quasi-public" Health Services Corporation within city government. The city would be divided into health-care regions, each one centered on a medical school, with private hospitals required to provide all needed services to residents of their districts. This Health Services Corporation would oversee the system, using its control of all public dollars to ensure that standards were met and that the mix of services offered met community needs. Piel's plan differed from Burlage's in a number of respects, but its central point was the same: a single public entity must preside over the spending of public dollars for health care, so that all providers who received those dollars would be held accountable for responding to public priorities.

No Radical Reform

Burlage's report was read in municipal and health-care circles and helped to inform the thinking of the Piel Commission, which was still at work at the time, but it did not generate much comment among the general public. The Piel report, in contrast, reached a wide audience when it appeared in late 1967, owing in part to front page coverage and warm editorial support from the *New York Times*. Mayor Lindsay, however, greeted the report coolly and showed little interest in acting on its recommendations. In retrospect, several observers have argued that even if Lindsay had embraced the commission's proposals, he could not have imposed local control over Medicare/ Medicaid spending as the report suggested, given the historic power struggle between the city and the state, and the federal government's reluctance to set a precedent it would have had to follow nationally. In any case, Lindsay did not try. And without control of the Medicare millions, a health corporation could not play the strong role that the Piel Commission had recommended, let alone the broader function that Burlage had envisioned.[47]

The possibility of handing the public hospitals over to private management as Cherkasky had proposed resurfaced briefly, but this idea had not evoked much enthusiasm among the voluntaries themselves. More important, the public employees' unions strongly opposed it. The leaders of these unions were afraid of losing the ground they had only recently gained in the city hospitals, and they made clear that they would fight a private takeover. Thus, with significant obstacles facing the only three serious proposals for citywide restructuring (Burlage's, Piel's, and Cherkasky's), the reform fever of 1966 to 1968 ended with a tacit agreement to leave the relations between the city's public and private hospitals untouched. Only the Department of Hospitals would be reorganized.

The reorganization method chosen was to convert the Department of Hospitals into a semiautonomous public-benefit corporation. For more than a century, reformers in many U.S. cities had been devising such bodies to insulate municipal functions from politics and corruption. In New York City, for example, good-government groups had helped create the board that supervised the construction of Central Park in the 1850s, the Metropolitan Board of Health in 1866; and the board that administered Bellevue and its allied hospitals from 1902 to 1928. In this type of protected environment, it was thought, disinterested citizens could serve the public without fear or favor, sheltered from the winds of popular opinion and political pressure.

Starting in the Progressive Era, the same good-government advocates also won a host of procedural reforms, from civil service to purchasing protocols, that were designed to restrain government corruption. As these changes accumulated, the process of doing municipal business grew increasingly complicated. By the 1960s, the resulting cobweb of approvals and signoffs—which extended far beyond anything required of private institutions—had come to be seen as intrinsic to public management, an inherent weakness of government programs. Much of this elaborate structure had been erected at earlier reformers' behest. Yet, once erected, it was cited by other reformers as a reason why programs should be removed from public control.

For example, when the dean of the New York University medical school wanted to emphasize the need to "cut red-tape that has impaired patient care" at Bellevue, he contrasted the hospital's inefficiency with the smooth running of NYU's own University Hospital. At this facility, he said, one could let a contract without having to seek either bids or higher level approvals. Instead, the chief of service "merely picked up a telephone, informed a hospital official of the need, and the purchase was made forthwith."[48] Few citizens would have approved so casual a system in any public institution. Yet the government's lack of such flexibility had come to be seen as a fundamental flaw in the public way of doing business. So it was argued that an independent health corporation could work more effectively than the Department of Hospitals by avoiding the excessive bureaucracy of municipal operations—in effect, by being less responsive to the ordinary burdens and requirements of popular government.

Meanwhile, carrying disengagement one step farther, NYU was exploring the possibility of separating Bellevue from the rest of the Department of Hospitals. Early in 1967, soon after it was announced that Columbia and Cornell would be leaving Bellevue, NYU began to explore the possibility of taking over Bellevue under a fifty-year lease. That fall the *New York Times* broke the news that "the city's oldest, proudest, and most investigated hospital" might become, in effect, a private institution. State Senator Seymour Thaler responded with fury. "Without public hearings or public awareness," he raged, "the city apparently has decided to go out of the hospital business. . . . Through all the long, lean years we sustained the municipal hospital system, but now, with Medicare and Medicaid paying most of the bills, we're getting rid of our hospitals."[49]

Victor Gotbaum added muscle to Thaler's condemnation, asserting that if the lease of Bellevue went through, DC 37's members "would walk off our jobs—it's that simple." The union would close down not only Bellevue, but all the municipal hospitals. Gotbaum described NYU's proposal as part of a "concerted campaign to downgrade and destroy the entire city hospital system so that it can be turned over piecemeal and at bargain basement prices to the voluntary hospitals." The best institutions would be unloaded, he warned, while the rest would be allowed to deteriorate until they were condemned. The accusation that the Bellevue proposal was part of a larger plan drew a flurry of denials from Health Services Administrator Brown, NYU, the United Hospital Fund, and the Greater New York Hospital Association. But City Comptroller Mario Procaccino confirmed that several other municipal hospitals besides Bellevue were being considered for long-term leases.[50]

Once Gotbaum blew the whistle, the plan to turn Bellevue over to NYU was abandoned almost immediately. Mayor Lindsay might have chosen to go ahead anyway; certainly he could have won support from some medical interests, and many reform groups would probably have backed the plan as well. But the timing was wrong. Midway through his first term, Lindsay's base of support was narrowing. His active commitment to improving conditions for African-Americans had won him both local and national recognition, helping to keep New York cool while other cities were exploding. But these policies had eroded his support among many working-class and lower middle-class white voters. When Lindsay proposed creating a Civilian Review Board to handle allegations of police brutality, it was overwhelmingly defeated in a referendum in the fall of 1966. That negative vote symbolized a broader rejection—of poverty programs, affirmative action hiring, desegregation drives, and all the other liberal initiatives that many middle-class whites believed were eroding the social, political, and economic position they had built for themselves in the city.

Lindsay read the rejection of the Civilian Review Board accurately, and knew that he would need new allies if he wanted to win a second term in 1969. Discarding the somewhat self-righteous tone he had taken toward the municipal unions during his first campaign, he reached out to labor, enacting a series of regulations designed to give a few large unions enhanced power. Victor Gotbaum, as head of one of the largest municipal unions, moved to a central position in city policymaking. In this political context, a plan for Bellevue that was opposed by Gotbaum could not happen. Within a few weeks of Gotbaum's blast against the long-term lease proposal, the city dropped all discussion of the idea. A few weeks after that, Mayor Lindsay submitted to Albany a request for emergency funds to renovate several municipal hospitals.[51] The city, it appeared, was still in the hospital business.

NYU had not quite given up on its plans for Bellevue; for months the medical center continued to study the Bellevue project, with the help of a research grant obtained for the purpose. But even as NYU pursued these possibilities, and as municipal officials weighed other proposals, events outran them. In the spring of 1968, the city received the last major report on the municipal hospitals, this one from the New York State Commission of Investigation. It was the worst of all.

The report condemned the city for running a hospital system characterized by "deterioration and dirty buildings, obsolete equipment, and endless red tape, waste, and inefficiency." It also asserted: "We refuse to believe that this great city with all the resources of fiscal power and governmental authority at its command is unable to protect the lives and health of its citizens." Criticisms like this had been made before, but the commission gave their comments new teeth by ending with an ultimatum: if the city could not fix its hospitals within a few months, it would have to turn them over to some organization that could. Seizing the moment, DC 37 chimed in with its own ultimatum, threatening to take the city to court unless conditions improved.[52] Time had run out; the city would have to take some action.

The Health & Hospitals Corporation Is Born

Of all the ideas for reforming the city's health-care system that had been proposed between 1966 and 1968, only a hospitals corporation appeared politically feasible. Mayor Lindsay was not enthusiastic about the idea, but no other proposal was both radical enough in appearance to satisfy system critics and moderate enough in substance to avoid conflict with the myriad interests involved.[53] Though no announcement was made at the time, Lindsay immediately appointed a task force to develop the necessary legislation, including in it representatives from all the groups that had the power to block the proposal: the unions, the Piel Commission, the medical community, the Bureau of the Budget, and the Department of Hospitals.

Working through the summer and fall of 1968, the task force arrived at a compromise that codified the consensus that had been emerging during the year. First, the proposed plan would not touch the private hospitals. Second, employees of the new corporation would remain city employees, so the unions' standing would remain unchanged. Third, top officials of the Department of Hospitals would retain their status in the new corporation. In short, three forces that had played a major role in shaping conditions within the present department—the private hospitals, the unions, and the existing management—would maintain their roles unaltered in the new structure.[54]

By the time the state legislation creating the Health & Hospitals Corporation was passed, state and federal cuts in Medicaid had made the new corporation's financial future look much less hopeful, but this darker outlook aroused little comment. After having been assaulted for years with the inadequacies of the present system, major protagonists as well as members of the general public were inclined to accept anything feasible that represented a change. Gotbaum undoubtedly spoke for many when he observed: "It couldn't be worse than it was. . . . You had nowhere to go but up."[55]

In May 1969, the public-benefit Health & Hospitals Corporation (HHC) was established as a semiautonomous unit within the New York City government. Fourteen months later, on July 1, 1970, HHC took ownership of all municipal hospitals. Although the new corporation operated under the aegis of the city's Health Services Agency, it had more latitude than an ordinary city department, being empowered to float its own construction bonds, select its own contractors, receive its own grants and gifts, set up its own personnel procedures (under civil service guidelines), and administer its own budget. The members of the HHC board were also empowered to select their own chief executive, the corporation president, who would serve at their pleasure.[56]

Despite these provisions, the hand of City Hall rested more heavily on HHC than a list of the corporation's new powers might have suggested. Only a portion of the corporation's revenue came from the city tax levy; but through the alchemy of political compromise, the independent body envisioned by Piel and Burlage had evolved into a city agency in which the comptroller, the City Planning Commission, and especially the mayor still played major roles. Indeed, much of the crucial work in designing the new corporation's structure and procedures was carried out by representatives of the very agencies that HHC had been established to circumvent; predictably enough, they built in many of the same checks and balances that had bedeviled the old Department of Hospitals. As for the mayor, he had the power to appoint every member of the board except the chief executive—five city officials who served ex-officio and ten direct appointments. (Five of the mayor's ten direct appointments were to be nominated by the City Council, but the mayor could withhold his approval until the Council offered names to his liking.) This structure meant that any new mayor would immediately control five seats on the board through his selection of the city officials; in addition, two of the directly appointed seats expired each year, giving even a first-term mayor a majority of the board by the end of his second year in office. Finally, the mayor's power to control the board gave him the power to choose the HHC's chief executive.[57]

Between 1968 and 1970, the campaign to improve the municipal hospitals had been shaped by a series of important decisions: to include a significant role for the mayor, the comptroller, and the City Planning Commission; to keep the union's power unchanged; to maintain the same top administrators; and to build in many of the same bureaucratic checks and balances. In the end, HHC looked much more like the old Department of Hospitals than like the pioneering public-private agency that Piel had envisioned. "I've always denied paternity of that corporation," said Piel in later years.[58]

Most critically, the decision not to alter in any way the relationship between the city's public and private hospitals ensured that the creation of HHC would represent modest reform rather than revolution. Every investigative panel confirmed the accuracy of former Commissioner Ray Trussell's blunt statement to the Joint Legislative Committee: "The city hospitals have traditionally been the recipients of all the unwanted, difficult situations that develop in the community, and particularly of people who do not have money. . . . One of the reasons for the municipal hospitals is to take care of the patients nobody wants."[59]

Given this unequal balance of responsibilities and resources, the decision to confine the restructuring of hospital care to the municipal hospitals virtually guaranteed that it would have only limited impact. As a way of improving the quality of hospital care for poor New Yorkers, the creation of HHC was the city's most significant effort at hospital reform in forty years; but it was a pale shadow of what was needed. In the end, the limitations of HHC were both the result and the symbol of a more fundamental pattern—the city's reluctance to require the same responsiveness from private institutions that it did from public ones. No U.S. city invested more in its public hospitals than New York did, yet these facilities continued to serve a residual role, filling in the gaps of the private system rather than fulfilling a comprehensive mission in the area of community medicine.

The introduction of Medicare/Medicaid during the same period reinforced the pattern. In many communities that had done less for their poor residents in the past, the new programs dramatically increased access to health care. But in New York City, the experience was different. Medicare/Medicaid enabled many of the elderly and some of the poor to move from the stigmatized public sector to the private—a sphere that probably represented to them the institutional mainstream. But by leaving the private hospitals free to choose whom they would serve, while counting on the public system to respond to all those in need, New York City's Medicare/Medicaid program also reinforced the old distinction between the worthy and unworthy poor—emphasizing for a new generation the identity of the public hospitals as the place for society's rejects—for all those whose race, behavior, insurance status, or diagnoses made them unacceptable elsewhere. The new reforms might ease that role, but they would not challenge it.

Just before his resignation, Health Services Administrator Howard Brown, who had always opposed a private takeover, reversed himself and suggested that perhaps the private hospitals should be put in charge of the municipal system after all. Asked about the morality of abandoning the city's tradition of helping the poor, he said sharply: "There are two traditions. One is the tradition of helping the indigent, to which I have devoted the recent part of my life. The other tradition is falling plaster, lack of paint, a shortage of nursing, and overcrowding."[60] As Brown observed, the city had sustained the first of these traditions by creating the huge municipal system, with its extraordinary responsiveness to the needs of the people of New York. Yet the second tradition had persisted as well, ensuring that the public hospitals would continue to struggle, never quite matching the city's best intentions.

6

Holding the Fort
After 1970

One night at Bellevue in the 1980s, an emergency room nurse going off duty summed up her shift for a colleague: "There was one old regular who calls himself Eighth Street Eddie and a weeping Haitian couple and a Chinese man with abdominal pain and a prisoner in handcuffs—looking really furious—being guarded by two policemen. And other regulars—Berenice, who has sickle-cell anemia, and several homeless. . . . It wasn't an unusual night at all."[1]

In many respects, this round-up could have come from any night in the hospital's history. Perhaps in 1910 the weeping couple would have been Italian instead of Haitian, and perhaps the chronic disease would have been tuberculosis instead of sickle-cell anemia. But the main elements in the account would have been familiar to Bellevue staff from any era: the ethnic and clinical diversity, and the presence of patients like prisoners and the homeless, who would rarely be found in more selective hospitals. In this sense, the social values embodied in Bellevue's emergency room during the final years of the twentieth century were the same as those that had animated the hospital throughout its history.

What gave Bellevue's traditional role new significance during these years was its increasing divergence from what was going on in the world outside the hospital. Bellevue had always had to scramble for resources, but starting in the 1970s a series of economic and political changes in American society began to erode the whole concept of public support for the kind of community commitment that institutions like Bellevue represented. In this environment, the determination to reduce government expenditures took on philosophical as well as financial meaning, while a reverence for the marketplace came to dominate public discourse. By the 1990s, the force of these trends, interwoven with an aggressive effort to control the cost of health care, had set the stage for a debate that would put into question the very survival of the municipal system.

Like every hospital in the United States, Bellevue struggled to adapt to the changing demands of these years, but perhaps its most significant achievement was the ways in which it did *not* change. Simply by continuing to fulfill its historic mission in a changed environment, Bellevue performed an essential function during difficult times: it kept the needs of the city visible. Because of Bellevue, problems that might otherwise have sunk out of sight remained in public view. At the same time, the necessity for community solutions to those problems was made plain every time an ambulance screamed up to the emergency room door or a penniless woman obtained the prenatal care she needed in a Bellevue clinic. In an era when public pronouncements placed increasing emphasis on the necessity for each individual to make it on his own, Bellevue stood as visible testimony to the power and value of civic obligations.

Counting Costs

During the final decades of the twentieth century, New York City began to lose its place as ebullient pacesetter for the nation. Economic problems brought a halt to the city's long tradition of easy spending. In health care, sharp questions were raised about the cost and value of modern medicine—most notably the kind of highly specialized care in which New York had excelled for so many years. Meanwhile, a souring of the political mood left the city psychologically disinclined to launch the bold public initiatives that in the past had helped make New York the very symbol of urban possibility.

New Economic Problems

Changes in the economy led the way. After more than thirty years of almost uninterrupted growth, a recession hit the United States in 1974. And while the nation's economy slumped, New York City's took a nose-dive. This precipitated a financial crisis that had been building for a number of years, as the city continued its free-handed spending despite a weakening tax base, a decline in federal assistance, and a mounting burden of expensive short-term debt. Throughout Mayor John Lindsay's last term (1970–1973), as well as the first term of his successor, Abraham Beame, each year's budget was balanced only by a combination of bookkeeping wizardry, massive borrowing, and the rosiest possible projections of future revenue.

Analysts after the fact have identified all the harbingers of fiscal disaster that should have been recognized; but at the time, New York's cycle of borrowing and spending was supported by a wide cross-section of city constituencies, including political officials, the real estate community, the recipients (both rich and poor) of city services, many economic forecasters, several hundred thousand municipal employees, and the lending institutions themselves (who profited from the city's borrowing and encouraged it until nearly the end). As an example of the seductive politics underlying the city's finances, much of New York's short-term borrowing during this period went to help developers of middle-income housing get long-term mortgages. This was an obligation undertaken by no other municipality in the country, but it was favored by potential tenants, construction unions, lending institutions, real estate interests, insurance companies, and a host of others. Each program had its defenders, and so the borrowing continued. By 1974, the city's short-term debt stood at $3.4 billion.

The New York State Urban Development Corporation (UDC) had also invested heavily in moderate-cost housing mortgages. When UDC defaulted, late in 1974, its collapse exposed the fragility of the city's own fiscal arrangements. This precipitated the crisis and one morning in the summer of 1975, Wall Street bankers refused to lend the city any more money, leaving it unable to make the debt payments that were just coming due. The effects were rapid and painful. New York's finances were taken over by a new state agency, the Emergency Financial Control Board (EFCB), which instituted a policy of retrenchment. In the preceding seven years, New York's spending had risen 30 percent in real dollars; over the next seven years, it fell by 33 percent.[2] City wages were frozen, many thousands of municipal employees were laid off, the subway fare was increased, and students at the City University were required to pay tuition for the first time in its history.

Under other circumstances, the strongest municipal union, DC 37, might have been on the barricades, protesting those cuts. But DC 37's leader, Victor Gotbaum, was convinced that if the city went into receivership, municipal employees would lose everything they had won through collective bargaining, perhaps including collective bargaining itself. Therefore, as chairman of the new Municipal Labor Coalition, Gotbaum persuaded DC 37 and the other public employee unions to invest nearly $4 billion of their pension funds in city bonds—one-fifth of the total money raised to bail out the city. He and his fellow union leaders then persuaded their members to accept a succession of wage freezes, pay deferrals, and staff cuts worth millions of dollars. During the years that followed, most job actions took place not when union officials led their workers out but when rank-and-file members balked at concessions to which their leaders had agreed.[3]

In New York City, as in the nation, hard times provided a rationale for spending cuts that many already favored. During the 1960s, municipal workers and their clients had used their combined numbers, the liberal mood of the period, and even the fear of civic unrest to expand the city's network of health and social services. By the mid-1970s a backlash was building. Thus when bankruptcy threatened New York, many embraced the idea that excessive generosity toward municipal workers had brought on the crisis. Those managing the city's finances agreed that concessions to business must be maintained and even expanded in order to restore the city economy, but municipal workers would have to tighten their belts and city residents would have to do without the array of public services that for generations had added spaciousness to the life of ordinary New Yorkers.

In this climate, even reasonable claims by city workers came to be seen as impractical luxuries. As Raymond Horton, director of the Citizens Budget Commission, observed: "What are the consequences of paying the hospital workers the desirable wage, assuming you could ever find out what the desirable wage is, given the city's limited ability to pay?" Others viewed the new arrangements more regretfully, but accepted them nonetheless. Senator William Proxmire said to New York Mayor Edward Koch during a Senate hearing: "It is cruel that it has to come out of the hide of the workers, but that's the way it is."[4]

By 1979, New York City had crawled back to solvency, thanks to its austerity budgets and the sacrifices of many lower income New Yorkers; that year the city was able to reenter the credit markets on its own for the first time in four years. Yet what Eric Lichten has termed "the politics of austerity" lived on into the 1980s and 1990s, subjecting social programs to periodic cuts and reductions in service even after overall spending began to rise again.

New Questions about Health Care

While New York's municipal hospitals were adjusting to the austerities of the fiscal crisis and its aftermath, they were also dealing—as were all U.S. hospitals—with the emergence of a new skepticism about health care. This skepticism arose partly from a practical concern over dollars and cents: between 1960 and 1980, national expenditures on hospital care soared from $27 billion to $248 billion, while the share of the Gross National Product spent on health care rose from 5.3 percent to 9.4 percent.[5] But money was not the only concern; many Americans had also begun to express doubts about the very nature of the health services that they were buying at such expense.

For half a century, efforts to improve health care had concentrated on extending the benefits of modern medicine to more people. Throughout these years, academic hospitals had been promoted as the ideal, admired both for their research and for their highly technical services. During the 1970s, however, critics began to suggest that this style of medicine was leaving important needs unmet. Why should hospitals only five blocks apart have the same expensive diagnostic machines, while two-year-olds went without their immunization shots? Why should there still be such marked differences in infant mortality and life expectancy between the rich and the poor—and between blacks and whites? Were the spiraling expenditures improving people's health or were they simply supporting more handsomely the army of providers that had grown up to sell them services?

Scholars and journalists vied with each other to identify and explain the failings of modern medicine, while a flood of books and articles publicized examples of questionable ethics, discriminatory treatment, medical mistakes, unserved populations, and unaddressed public-health needs. In the movies, the benign image of Dr. Kildare making a house call was replaced by the heartless, chaotic, and ultimately lethal institution portrayed in the George C. Scott movie, *The Hospital*.

Many still believed that American medicine was the best in the world, but they knew that its cost was rising faster than inflation, and much faster than the increase in services. Nor were individual citizens the only ones concerned. Employers were finding it increasingly difficult to cover the cost of the health benefits they had promised their workers, and unions were having to fight harder and sacrifice more to protect and extend those benefits. Government had the greatest interest of all; the very programs that had fed the cost-explosion—Medicare and Medicaid—had turned the government into the country's largest purchaser of health services.

By the 1970s, public officials were taking the lead in trying to bring health costs under control. One of their first targets was construction. New York State pioneered by establishing the first system in the country under which hospitals were required to obtain a "certificate of need" (CON) from a regional planning group before proceeding with new construction. In fact, the CON process was only modestly successful in controlling health costs. Construction reviews gradually became more stringent, but many hospitals simply shifted their expansion funds to the acquisition of new machinery. Costs continued to rise.

Attacking on another front, New York was also the first state to establish a comprehensive system for regulating the price of hospital care. Instead of reimbursing hospitals for all the costs they reported, New York began requiring its private insurers, as well as Medicaid and, later, Medicare, to base each hospital's reimbursement rate on the costs that the hospital had reported in previous years. This represented a change from the "all reasonable costs" formula of the past, and many hospitals had a difficult time during the initial years of the program. In New York City, deficits in the municipal hospitals lurched upward, and more than two dozen small voluntary or proprietary facilities closed. Gradually, however, under the political pressure exerted by hospital leaders, hospital workers' unions, and other interested groups, the rates became more generous. In particular, teaching facilities were allowed to exempt many of the factors that kept their costs high, while a series of state pools was established to reimburse hospitals for patients who did not or could not pay their bills. Costs grew more slowly than before, but they continued to rise.[6]

In fact, the way that hospitals were reimbursed gave them little incentive to use their resources sparingly. Even in New York State, the longer a patient stayed and the more ancillary services were received, the more the hospital could charge. To rebalance the incentives, the federal government introduced a new plan in the 1980s called the Prospective Payment System (PPS). PPS changed the rules, providing hospitals with a lump sum for each patient's stay, based on the patient's diagnosis and a variety of other factors. If a hospital could treat a patient for less than the standard payment, it would make money; if the treatment cost more, it would lose money. Thus, at least in theory, the new system encouraged short stays and an economical use of resources. Once again, New York City hospitals found the initial transition difficult, in part because the program reached the state in the late 1980s, just as the crack-cocaine epidemic brought a sudden surge in length of stay. This crisis soon passed, however. The payment levels were gradually made more generous, and urban teaching facilities were paid billions of dollars extra to cover their additional costs in training future physicians and serving large numbers of high-need patients. These add-ons served important social goals, but they also helped undermine the effort to keep health costs low.[7]

Overall, the cost-control efforts by state and federal authorities between 1970 and 1990 had only modest success in slowing the rate at which America's health expenditures were growing. Nevertheless, they did impose periods of acute uncertainty on many hospitals, and they set the stage for the sterner challenges of the 1990s.

New Political Strains

Events like the fiscal crisis and the pressure to control hospital costs did not occur in a vacuum. In New York, they were both mirrored and intensified by changes in the political mood of the city. Even before the city's budget problems, it had become clear that the unkept promises of the 1960s would not be fulfilled at any time in the near future. In order to build and nurture great public initiatives, citizens have to have trust in the future, trust in each other, and trust in their government. After 1970, in New York as in many other American communities, that kind of trust was on the wane.

During those years, every civic transaction in New York City seemed to become a battle, pitting community residents against City Hall, neighborhood against neighborhood, and borough against borough. Middle-class whites counted their grievances, convinced that their interests were being sacrificed to those of poor blacks and rich whites. Yet New Yorkers of color were equally dissatisfied. Initiatives described as massive concessions often struck them as token efforts that were abandoned or diluted as soon as they encountered opposition from the white majority. At the same time, government reductions affected minority residents disproportionately, depriving them not only of services but also of the city jobs they had only recently attained. For many New Yorkers, nonwhite as well as white, the city seemed to have become a vista of broken promises, polarized neighborhoods, and declining economic prospects.

New Yorkers were not alone in these feelings; the pessimism of the 1970s touched many American communities. President Lyndon Johnson had left Washington in disgrace, his promises for an "unconditional war on poverty" largely unfulfilled, the civil rights movement had shattered, the Watergate scandal drove President Richard Nixon from the White House, and the Vietnam War ended in debacle.[8] Shaken by these turbulent years, Americans began to look with increasing skepticism at government promises of any kind. In particular, many middle-class whites concluded that whatever the government had done for poor and minority citizens had been done at their expense. The economic slowdown of the 1970s legitimized such feelings, creating a climate in which restrictions on social spending, including health programs, came to be accepted as a necessary response to fiscal constraints. As a result, many programs that had hung on all through the Nixon administration suffered their first major cutbacks under a Democratic president, Jimmy Carter.

Even the economic recovery of the 1980s and 1990s brought little sense of social solidarity. During those years, public discourse moved from anxiety to complacency, stressing the benefits received by the more fortunate members of society while overlooking the increasingly unequal distribution of those benefits. In an approach best articulated by Republican President Ronald Reagan but perpetuated in various ways by his successors, the marketplace came to be seen as the solution to most social and economic problems, and the need for personal responsibility among the poor was given more attention than the need for social responsibility among the many. In that environment, the disillusionment of the 1970s evolved into something harsher: a sense of contempt, not only for government programs, but for the people who depended on them.

New York remained among the most liberal of U.S. cities, but the strains dividing the country throughout the late twentieth century also had an impact there. For more than a century, New York's array of public institutions, including its municipal hospital system, had been a point of civic pride, part of what defined the city's place in the world. Those institutions continued to exist after 1970; no other American community could match their size and scope. But their civic context had changed. For decades to come, the challenge they would face would not be to set expansive new goals but to hold onto as much as possible of what had been built in previous years.

Living with Limits

From the 1970s onward, the intersection of changes in the economy, in health care, and in politics affected every hospital in New York City. For public facilities like Bellevue, the changing political mood and the city's fiscal crisis dominated the horizon. Private facilities like New York Hospital, on the other hand, were more preoccupied with government's entry into rate-regulation. Every facility had to grapple with resource limitations in one way or another, but the different impact of those trends on Bellevue and New York Hospital confirmed and even sharpened the longstanding differences between public and private hospitals.

Hard Times for Public Hospitals

From the day of its founding in 1970, the New York City Health & Hospitals Corporation was dogged by administrative, financial, and political turmoil.

Management problems abounded, the deficit kept rising, and HHC seemed to be a prism for all the polarized politics of the city. At one particularly acrimonious meeting, hostilities between board members and the public grew so heated that six people were taken to the emergency room and four more were arrested. The atmosphere had barely cooled when the fiscal crisis began, setting off a new wave of chaos and uncertainty. "The Health & Hospitals Corporation," observed one analyst, "has spent its life in troubled seas."[9]

Shaky leadership at HHC over the years both reflected and exacerbated the agency's problems. Some HHC presidents served with distinction, but several resigned under charges of corruption, and many others seemed to owe their arrivals and departures more to the changing winds of city politics than to the needs of the agency they headed. The demoralizing process came close to parody when one HHC appointee flew in from Denver, used the phrase "nigger in the wood-pile" in one of his first speeches, and was gone by the end of the week. An agency headed by this succession of short-term presidents was in a weak position to defend its interests in the municipal corridors of power.[10]

Mayor Edward Koch (1978–1989), a Democrat, believed that HHC caused most of its own troubles. He took a highly critical stance toward the agency during his first two years in office, reiterating that its poor management and extensive services for the uninsured were "bankrupting the city." He began by trying to draw Governor Hugh Carey into joint sponsorship of a plan to close a number of New York's thirteen public acute-care hospitals. The wily Carey kept his distance, however, and when Koch's outspoken health adviser, Dr. Martin Cherkasky, announced that the mayor was planning to close down half the public system, a firestorm erupted. Cherkasky was eased out of office within a year, but his comments appear to have been more ill timed and ill phrased than ill informed.[11]

In 1979, Mayor Koch announced the closing of four public hospitals. Two, Cumberland and Greenpoint, had already been slated for closure, since they were being replaced by a more modern hospital, Woodhull. But a lacerating public debate, pulsing with racial implications, arose over the other two hospitals on Koch's list, Sydenham and Metropolitan, both in or near Harlem. Ultimately, Sydenham, Cumberland, and Greenpoint were closed as planned. Metropolitan, much the largest facility, only escaped the ax after one of Koch's top black officials resigned in protest, the NAACP filed a class-action suit, neighborhood groups deluged City Hall with complaints, labor leaders from DC 37 organized massive demonstrations, and the federal government contributed $17 million to help keep it open. The bitter, racially charged battle left its mark. According to one observer, the episode helped prepare the ground for Koch's loss to David Dinkins, New York's first black mayor, in 1989. On another level, the situation provided a sharp reminder that, whatever their troubles, the public hospitals occupied a more important place in the life of the city than Koch had understood. If these facilities no longer commanded a broad political constituency, they were still wanted and needed by enough groups to make it politically awkward for any office holder to eliminate them completely.[12]

After that first bruising battle, Koch talked no more of hospital closings; instead, he concentrated on reforming HHC administratively. The agency improved its fiscal management and significantly increased its third-party collections, thus permitting the city to reduce the real dollar value of its annual subsidy during a period when the Corporation's costs—along with all national health costs—were continuing to rise (see Figure 6.1). There were drawbacks to Koch's reforms, however. By changing HHC from what he described as "the turf of minority politicians" to an agency dominated by his own allies, he tied it more closely than ever to City Hall. Also, the darker side of HHC's growing dependence on third-party reimbursement was suggested when three clerks at Bellevue reported that they had been forced by their supervisors to alter data on hundreds of patients so that Medicaid, rather than city taxes, would pay for their care.[13]

In 1989, David Dinkins defeated Koch's bid for reelection. Under other circumstances the new mayor might have lived up to the hopes of the many poor, minority, and liberal voters who helped elect him. But the city's deficit had started to climb again in Koch's final years, and Dinkins spent most of his term trying to bring it down again. He launched few new social initiatives, and the city subsidy to HHC was cut substantially. Yet even though, as Figure 6.1 makes clear, the city contribution now represented only a fraction of

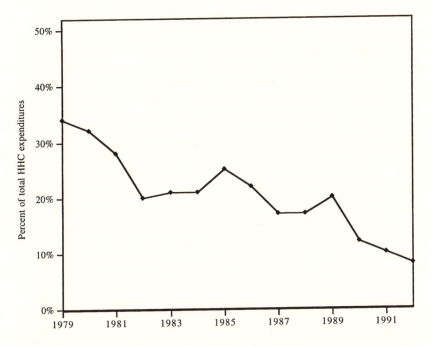

Figure 6.1 Tax-levy support received by the NYC Health & Hospitals Corporation, as percent of total HHC expenditures, 1979–1992. Source: United Hospital Fund.

HHC's total budget, the municipal government continued to hold a whiphand over its finances, frequently diverting the Corporation's own revenues to other city purposes.

Growing complaints about HHC's fiscal impotence finally led Mayor Dinkins to approve a new agreement, giving the agency more autonomy. "We are not going to treat the Health & Hospitals Corporation like a financial colony anymore," said the city's budget director, promising that the city would no longer "balance our budget on their backs." Disputes continued, however. Within days of the agreement, a law suit won by a coalition of municipal unions forced the city to pass on to HHC $38 million from the state's bad debt and charity pools—money that had been specifically allocated to municipal hospitals but which the city had diverted to the general fund.[14]

By the time Dinkins left office in 1992, New York was contributing less than 10 percent of the HHC budget, as compared to more than 33 percent in 1979 (see Figure 6.1). Some reduction was inevitable, given the city's difficulties and HHC's improved collections, but the cuts of the early 1990s slashed deep, throwing the municipal hospitals back into the kind of turmoil they had experienced during the fiscal crisis. In 1992, the City Hospital Visiting Committee reported that because of "draconian budget cuts, demoralized staff, and soaring service demands," care in the municipal hospitals was "the worst in recent memory."[15]

Bellevue: Old Problems in a New Building

At Bellevue, the city's financial crisis in 1975 hit just shortly after the hospital finally moved into its new building—the one proposed by Mayor LaGuardia in 1945, under construction since 1964, and described as near completion by every mayor since then. On the day of the dedication ceremony, Mayor Lindsay presented the annual Mayor's Award for Excellence of Service not to a city dignitary but to the entire hospital staff. Bellevue's director, Bernard Weinstein, gave an ecstatic speech, hailing the fact that at last the hospital's "physical surroundings will match its staff's ambitions for patient service."[16]

Was Bellevue really on the point of a major transformation? A dissenting view was already on record, offered by William Nolen, a surgeon who had interned at the hospital. In 1969, hearing of the plans for the new building, Nolen had published a fond but salty tribute to Bellevue, affirming his conviction that her spirit would successfully withstand modernization. "I have faith in Bellevue," he wrote.

> She resists improvements as her bacteria resist antibiotics and in the end, virulent, she survives. So let the city fathers move in with their millions of dollars. Let them build new buildings, hire more help, buy more syringes, do their damnedest to destroy her personality and make her a replica of every other white, cold, sterile and efficient citadel of healing. She will resist that standardization. And I am willing to wager that when the last new building has been built, the last technician hired, the last dollar spent, there will still be no scissors on Ward M5.[17]

Nolen's prediction proved more accurate than Weinstein's. A staff nurse later recalled that when the new building opened, "many of us felt we were nearing the promised land." But then came the fiscal crisis and within months the hospital was forced to lay off more than 1,000 employees. Soon afterward, the hospital director left Bellevue for a position in Westchester County. He was a loss to the city, observed Victor Gotbaum in later years, "the kind of guy you'd like to have stay around. How the hell was he going to stay around? . . . I think he really wanted to do the job, but then he found out it was almost impossible." Meanwhile, the cuts continued.[18]

Even after the city's fiscal crisis was officially over, the politics of austerity lingered on, creating an atmosphere at the hospital that would have been familiar to any former patient or employee. Staff shortages continued, and leadership problems aggravated the hospital's other difficulties. From the early 1980s on, few directors lasted more than a year or two. For some employees, there was a kind of zesty pride in battling the odds to give good care. Others found the process enormously disheartening. One Bellevue plumber was said to comfort himself with the knowledge that the hospital basement lay below the water level in the river; he always said that if things got too bad, he knew exactly which valves to open to float the whole place out to sea.[19]

In 1986, Bellevue marked the 250th year since the opening of its ancestor, the city Almshouse. The anniversary evoked an outpouring of recognition and nostalgia for the hospital, including a special show at the Museum of the City of New York and a U.S. postal stamp issued in Bellevue's honor. Despite the festivities surrounding the anniversary, however, daily life at the hospital continued to be shadowed by the struggle to care for a patient population composed disproportionately of what one visitor called "the impaired, the homeless, and other non revenue-generating patients." Among these patients was a new group just emerging: people with AIDS. By the time of Bellevue's anniversary, AIDS had become the hospital's single most common medical diagnosis and Bellevue was treating more AIDS patients than any other hospital in the country. At a time when considerations of cost and revenue seemed to dominate public policy, Bellevue stood out for its continued commitment to such patients. Yet as resources shrank and needs increased, the hospital found it increasingly difficult to carry out its mission.[20]

In 1989, all these problems seemed to come together in the death of a thirty-three-year-old staff physician named Kathryn Hinnant. One week into the new year, Hinnant was found murdered in her office on the fourth floor of Bellevue's new building. Five months pregnant, she had come in on a Saturday afternoon to catch up on some work while the hospital was quiet. At 5 A.M. the next day, her husband found her body, raped and strangled, on her office floor. Bellevue was no stranger to violent death; indeed, the very day that Hinnant died, one of the hospital's psychiatric patients had hanged himself. But as far as anyone could remember, no employee had ever been killed at Bellevue.[21]

Three days later, the police arrested a twenty-three-year-old vagrant named Steven Smith for the murder. Smith had been admitted to the hospital a month before, after claiming that he had tried to kill himself by drinking rat poison. He had been discharged after a week, however, without ever reaching the psychiatric division. Since his release, he had been living on Bellevue's deserted twenty-second floor, sleeping on a cot behind some storage boxes and moving freely about the hospital during the day wearing a stolen lab coat and stethoscope. Smith had been caught stealing hypodermics only a week before the murder, but after being released pending trial, he had returned to his hideout in the hospital.[22]

To Bruce Vladeck, president of the United Hospital Fund, the grim circumstances of Hinnant's death—and Steven Smith's life—suggested conditions in Dickensian London, with the poor living in degradation while an indifferent middle-class turned its back. "The tragedy is," he said, "we know how to do better; we just can't get our act together and do it."[23] The gulf between New York City's haves and have-nots grew still sharper at the end of the 1980s, when a sudden decline in the nation's economy hit the city with particular force, causing the worst recession since the 1930s. By 1990, the U.S. Census Bureau reported that the only part of the United States with greater income disparity than Manhattan was a hamlet in Hawaii near a former leper colony. On the one hand, New York's residents included some of the most privileged people in the world. On the other, one-fifth of the city's population (and one-quarter of its children) were living in poverty, while almost 1 million people were receiving public assistance. The crack-cocaine epidemic was ravaging a generation of young people, and—for the first time since the Depression— the city had a homeless population numbering in the tens of thousands.

Bellevue held up a mirror to the city's social and economic problems. By 1990, homeless people constituted a significant proportion of the hospital's caseload; the typical length of stay for a Bellevue inpatient was 20 percent longer than the city average, primarily because so many of the patients had nowhere to go when they were discharged. The drug wars reverberated through Bellevue as well, sending gunshot victims to its emergency room and AIDS patients to its ward. People discharged from state mental institutions cycled in and out of the hospital's psychiatric wards, and every night the emergency room dealt with ailments that used to be treated by the long-vanished family doctor.

Although Bellevue had finally moved into a well-equipped modern building and was widely recognized for its trauma services and microsurgery, its core responsibility remained something much more basic: to care for the people who had nowhere else to turn. Because of this mission, Bellevue represented a kind of last-bet home for every New Yorker, in the mordant sense of poet Robert Frost's definition: "Home is where, when you have to go there, they have to take you in."[24] This was a less expansive role than the hospital staff had hoped for when the new building was dedicated. Yet, in a retrenchment-minded era, Bellevue continued to perform an important civic function, not only because of the care that it provided but also because it ensured that the need for that care remained in public view.

New York Hospital: Functioning in a New Environment

New York Hospital occupied the same borough of the same city as Bellevue and, like Bellevue, it was a large teaching hospital. It was even jolted by the traumatic death of a young woman during the late 1980s, just as Bellevue was. Nevertheless, its development between 1970 and 1990 was quite different from Bellevue's. Exploring that difference makes clear how separate the worlds of public and private hospitals remained, even in a period when private hospitals received much of their revenues from public sources.

In 1971, New York Hospital was honored with a commemorative U.S. postage stamp (just like Bellevue)—this one celebrating the 200th anniversary of the year the hospital had received its first charter from King George III of England. The decade that followed should, in theory, have been far less troubling for New York Hospital than for Bellevue. The political changes in the city made less difference to a private hospital, and the municipal government's financial travails barely touched it. By this time, nearly half the city's health expenditures were going to private providers, but when the fiscal crisis forced the city to reduce its health-care spending, all the cuts came out of municipal services. Thus New York Hospital and its fellow voluntaries remained comfortably insulated from the public sector's financial difficulties.[25]

Despite this advantage, New York Hospital's annual reports during the 1970s issued frequent warnings of a "deepening financial crisis" caused by "underfunding of our programs by governmental and other private sources." The basis for this distress was the state's decision to regulate hospital rates. New York Hospital leaders were convinced that without special consideration, hospitals like theirs would be forced to choose between sinking to "a level of mediocrity" and going bankrupt. They reiterated that they must be granted more revenue; cutting costs was not an option, since that would inevitably compromise the quality of medicine. (The kind of medicine they had in mind was made clear in the hospital's annual report, where a two-page discussion of New York Hospital's financial problems was illustrated with a picture of the most expensive procedure imaginable: a heart-transplant operation.)[26]

Besides causing financial problems, the government's entry into rate regulation was experienced by New York Hospital's leaders as an institutional threat. Indeed, one of the things that made those years disturbing for the hospital trustees was the fact that they were encountering for the first time an experience that Bellevue had faced throughout its history—the sense of being, as the New York Hospital president said, at the mercy of "social, political and economic conditions which are beyond its management or its control."[27] Well into the 1980s, the hospital's annual reports reverberated with complaints about "non-medical problems created by outside forces" and descriptions of the new policies as "unilateral," "unfathomable," "bizarre and unfair," "unrealistic," and "politically-motivated."

As Figure 6.2 makes clear, New York Hospital's expenditures continued to

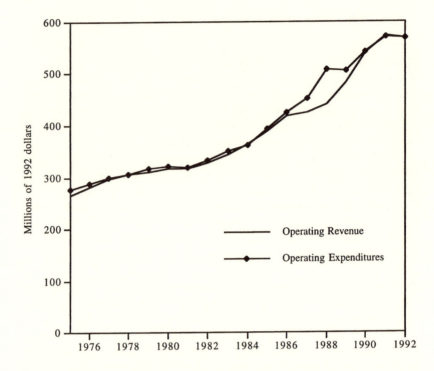

Figure 6.2 New York Hospital operating revenue and expenditures, 1975–1992, in constant dollars. Source: New York Hospital.

rise; but the facility also increased its revenue, by reaching out to patients from the surrounding suburbs and by adding a variety of new specialized services, including the city's first Burn Center. As a result, throughout most of the 1970s, the hospital's operating deficit remained at a manageable level.[28] When the shah of Iran came to the United States in 1979 in order to be treated for cancer at New York Hospital, his choice confirmed the fact that the challenges of the previous decade had not forced the hospital to compromise its standing as a world-class medical institution.

The financial health of New York Hospital continued to improve as the state's rate-setting arrangements grew more generous and in 1984 the hospital was able once again to report a small operating surplus. Yet it is important to note that the hospital had managed to stabilize its finances not so much by reducing its expenditures as by increasing the amount of money it took in. As a result, the strategy did not do much for the drive to cut health costs. Nevertheless, it did a good deal for the hospital, and as hospital director David Thompson prepared to retire in 1986, he could take pride in the financial health of the institution he was leaving.

Just a year later, Thompson's successor, David Skinner, found himself presiding over an institution wracked with turmoil and in desperate financial trouble. In only twelve months the operating deficit had soared from $4 million to $22 million; the following year it would hit $57 million. What had altered the situation so radically, and in so short a period? At the time, New York Hospital's leaders attributed their problems to the recent introduction of the PPS reimbursement system, but the calamity at this hospital was far out of proportion to what happened at other facilities.[29] Clearly some other force was at work besides a change in reimbursement policy.

There is a more convincing explanation for New York Hospital's troubles and it can be traced to a night in 1984, when an eighteen-year-old girl named Libby Zion was brought by her parents to the emergency room, complaining of a fever and an earache. Not long after her admission, the girl's fever shot up to 108°F, and within hours she was dead. Her father was an articulate and well-connected attorney who had previously worked as a reporter for the *New York Times*. Convinced that the house staff's inattention and inexperience had killed his daughter, he set out to punish everyone responsible. Besides suing the hospital and three members of the house staff, he launched a media compaign that brought the case enormous publicity.[30]

In January 1987, a grand jury gave added weight to Zion's accusations. While declining to indict the young house physicians, the jury report asserted that their "woefully" inadequate care and repeated mistakes may have killed the patient. The State Health Department took up the case next; it fined the hospital for providing inadequate care and required it to submit weekly reports on the quality of its services. Two years later, the state adopted sweeping new regulations limiting the hours that house staff could work and requiring that they be better supervised. These rules evoked heated controversy in medical circles, and every dispute over the new rules helped keep alive in people's minds the association between New York Hospital and the death of Libby Zion.[31]

Just as the fine for the Zion case was being levied in 1987, the celebrated pop artist Andy Warhol died at New York Hospital, less than twenty-four hours after undergoing routine gall bladder surgery. While the cause of death was unclear, both medical and nursing errors were mentioned as possibilities, and the hospital's name reappeared in the newspapers in the worst context possible. The *New York Times Magazine* both confirmed and accentuated New York Hospital's difficulties in January 1988 with an article entitled "A Great Hospital In Crisis."[32] For more than a century, New York Hospital had nurtured its public image, rarely appearing in the press except when it initiated and controlled the story. Now every reporter in town had something to say about a time-honored institution that had fallen on hard times. Even the harshest critics did not say that New York Hospital was a terrible place; they argued simply that it should be excellent all the time instead of most of the time. But great medical centers build their public following on trust, not on probability statistics, and after the events of 1987, fewer people were inclined to trust New York Hospital. Between 1986 and 1988, admissions dropped sharply, while the deficit went through the roof.

This was the predicament that the new director, David Skinner, inherited when he arrived to take charge of New York Hospital in the summer of 1987. A thoracic surgeon with a reputation for strong-mindedness, Skinner threw himself into his new assignment, reining in the hospital's spending and at the same time pressing the medical staff to shorten patient stays and increase the volume of services provided by their respective departments. It is a measure of how much pressure the hospital felt in the wake of the Zion and Warhol deaths—and how little it had felt before—that it introduced more cost-related changes in the first few years of Skinner's tenure than in the previous twenty years of state and federal rate regulation.

Skinner's innovations provoked a near mutiny among the physicians and some talk of a law suit from Cornell Medical College; but by then, Skinner had taken decisive charge of the hospital, while reducing the operating deficit from $57 million to less than $1 million. Moreover, he had won permission from the state to proceed with a long-delayed plan to erect an entire new building for the hospital on a platform above the nearby East River Drive. With these achievements in his favor, no dissatisfaction among the medical staff was likely to dislodge him. The board of governors supported their man, Cornell settled its dispute with the hospital, the medical school dean accepted a position in his native Texas, and Skinner pressed on with his program.

Changes within the center might avert disaster, but if New York Hospital was to remain a medical leader, it must generate new sources of patients, preferably ones able to pay their bills. By 1990, New York City's total population was smaller than it had been in 1940, and the ethnic pattern was changing, with fewer whites and more black, Hispanic, and Asian residents. These changes meant, among other things, that hospital patients who could pay their own way were growing harder to find. New York's great medical centers had always competed for such patients, particularly in Manhattan, where six of the city's ten largest hospitals and four of its seven medical schools were located. Now, with costs rising and the supply of paying patients dwindling, the competition had become more intense. Even before the terrible conjunction of the Zion and Warhol cases, New York Hospital had been on the lookout for new sources of patients.

Reaching beyond the contested territory of Manhattan, New York Hospital established agreements with a number of suburban hospitals; the outcome was that by 1983, more than a quarter of New York Hospital's patients were coming from outside the city. Then, in the early 1990s, Skinner established what came to be called the New York Hospital Care Network, a much more formal system connecting nearly a dozen nursing homes, hospitals, and clinics in and around the city. Within a few years, most major Manhattan hospitals had followed his lead and were scrambling to establish their own networks. "Everyone is talking with everyone else," said the president of Columbia-Presbyterian. "You walk into a hospital and think it's perfect for you and then you find out Dr. Skinner from New York Hospital was there yesterday and Dr. Rowe from Mount Sinai is coming tomorrow."[33]

New York Hospital had come a long way from the gloom of 1971 and the cataclysm of 1987. Medical services were now paid for in a very different way, and the development of the network had launched the hospital into a brand new relationship with the world outside its walls. Yet certain essentials had hardly changed at all. Despite reformers' cries for a new approach to medicine, despite New York State's efforts to make health care less expensive, New York Hospital was still using its formidable talent and resources to pursue exactly the same priorities that it had chosen in the 1920s: research, education, and the provision of highly technical, very expensive, medical care. The cases that did not fit these priorities could be handled by its affiliates. And the patients no private institution wished to serve could go—as they always had—to public hospitals like Bellevue.

Comparing Resources

By 1990, New York Hospital and the other great private teaching hospitals, along with their affiliated institutions, accounted for a greater share of the city's hospital beds than ever before.[34] Holding their ground through two decades of cost-control efforts and reformers' complaints, the academic giants had accommodated external demands when necessary, yet they had barely swerved from their longstanding commitment to high-level, high-cost medicine. They had prevailed, at least in part, because of their excellence; but they had also benefited from a variety of privileges enjoyed by private hospitals that were not available to the public system. Taking New York Hospital as an example, what were some of the resources that helped this institution survive not only the external challenges of the 1970s and 1980s but also the debacle of the Zion and Warhol deaths?

Perhaps New York Hospital's greatest resource was its considerable freedom of operation, even in a regulated era. Although private hospitals were bound by numerous laws and codes, they did not have to obey the many additional requirements placed on municipal facilities by civil service rules, city regulations, and guidelines from the Department of Hospitals central office. New York Hospital also had geographical freedom; it was not obligated—as Bellevue was—to serve a particular district. Instead, it could recruit the kinds of patients it wished to serve from as far afield as it chose. In addition, it had more freedom than Bellevue to adapt the nature of its services to the pattern of available funding. For example, the two hospitals treated about the same number of inpatients, but in outpatient care, where reimbursement was lower and the proportion of uninsured patients far higher, New York Hospital served about half as many people as Bellevue did.

As for inpatient services, New York Hospital had considerably more control over its patient selection than Bellevue did. For fifty years (starting when the medical center opened on 68th Street), New York Hospital had not even participated in the city's ambulance network. Once it rejoined the system in 1983, it necessarily received a more diverse array of patients, but it was not legally required to admit them, even if they were emergency cases. Federal law simply stipulated that emergency patients must *either* be cared for (without necessarily being admitted) until they were medically stable *or* be safely transferred to a more appropriate facility. Hospitals were generally free to define for themselves what constituted an "emergency patient," a "medically stable" condition, and a "safe transfer." As for a "more appropriate facility," every public hospital in New York had stories of transfers they had received from private emergency rooms that appeared to have been driven more by a lack of insurance than by a need for particular medical services.[35]

New York Hospital admitted many poor and minority patients, and once they entered the hospital they received the same food, room assignments, and personal services as any other semiprivate patient. But it could limit the number it accepted; indeed, until 1991, the hospital's admission policy specifically stipulated that patients without insurance must pay a deposit on admission.[36] If the hospital did not always enforce that provision, it was free do so when it chose. It could also limit the number of patients it accepted with long-term physical or social problems that might interfere with treatment or prolong their hospital stay.

The experience of Bellevue and New York Hospital with the AIDS epidemic provides a good example of the link between program quality and the hospitals' control over admissions. In 1989, when Bellevue was treating about 150 AIDS patients per day, New York Hospital averaged only forty-five; its AIDS population had been even lower until it obtained federal, state, and private funding to establish a special AIDS program. When it did, the services it developed were probably preferable from the patients' point of view to anything Bellevue could offer. But maintaining a program of such quality depended on the hospital's freedom to accept only a specific number of patients and to limit its admissions to the patients with the most appropriate clinical symptoms. Bellevue, meanwhile, continued to admit every person with AIDS who needed care.[37]

In this respect and in many others, public hospitals like Bellevue were denied the advantages that helped the city's leading private hospitals make their way through the 1970s and 1980s. Indeed, some of those advantages—like the capacity to limit admissions—actually depended on the fact that the public system was held to a different standard. Yet in spite of these disparities, Bellevue managed, just like New York Hospital, to come through two difficult decades with its mission intact. This makes it important to consider what resources the municipal system was able to draw upon that helped sustain it through those years.

First, the public hospitals had the advantage of doing a job that no one else seemed to want to perform, at least on the same scale: caring for the city's poorest and least appealing patients. Through the years, city officials frequently complained about the cost of this task, and most of them tried to streamline the way it was carried out, but rarely did they or anyone else argue that it was unnecessary. During the 1980s, in particular, the public hospitals demonstrated their importance to the city by taking a leading role in dealing with the devastating interaction of AIDS, homelessness, crack-cocaine addiction, and the reappearance of tuberculosis. The municipal system's historic dominance in the provision of last-resort care may have seemed like a dubious distinction, but it gave the hospitals a significant position in the life of the city, not only because the patients themselves needed help but because addressing their problems was directly linked to the health and security of the whole community.

The municipal hospitals had another asset, though it was not always acknowledged: the racial dimension of their work. Everyone knew that the public system treated far more than its share of the city's minority residents, and in an era when many social programs were being cut, when racial polarization intensified, and when racial politics could turn ugly with amazing speed, maintaining the public hospitals became one important symbol of the city's concern for New Yorkers of color. The uproar over Mayor Koch's hospital closings in 1980; the arrival of Vice-President Walter Mondale to announce that Metropolitan Hospital would be saved (within months of an election in which President Jimmy Carter very much needed to carry New York); and Mayor Dinkins's subsequent refusal to even discuss closing more public hospitals—all testified to the political meaning of the public system, a meaning intensified by its racial undertones. The various groups that fought hospital budget cuts were frequently condemned for politicizing a topic that, in theory, concerned only beds and budgets, but decisions about hospitals—especially public ones—have rarely concerned only beds and budgets. Among the public system's resources was its significance as a political symbol, assuring the city's least privileged citizens that their needs still counted for something in the life of the community.

Another asset that sustained the public system was its role as a workplace. Through the years, the municipal hospitals provided jobs for hundreds of thousands of New Yorkers, representing all skill levels and every ethnic group. The municipal unions, particularly DC 37, provided an important voice for those workers and for the hospitals in which they worked. The unions were weakened by the city's financial troubles during the 1970s and 1980s, by their own acquiescence in the austerity policies that followed, and by their internal leadership problems. In addition, their commitment to existing staffing arrangements probably made it somewhat more difficult for HHC to adapt to changing methods of health care. But in an era of budget cuts and attrition, DC 37's insistence that the municipal hospitals must be preserved, its financial support for community groups fighting the same fight, its advocacy at the national level (through its parent union) for New York's municipal hospitals, and the various law suits that it initiated against the city on behalf of HHC—all combined to make the hospital workers and their representatives a significant asset for the public system.

The municipal system had one more vital resource: the size and quality of its emergency services. Most of the Level I Trauma Centers in New York City were located in public hospitals, and besides providing a vital urban service, these centers had another important characteristic—they were the one part of the public system that was used by New Yorkers of every class. This meant that while middle- and upper-class citizens were having their broken legs set, their heart attacks attended to, or their overdoses stabilized, they were also able to see close up the panoply of problems that beset their city and the essential role that the public hospitals played in coping with those problems.

Bellevue's Emergency Department, in particular, was widely recognized as New York's front line of defense against sudden trouble—the place policemen and firemen insisted on being taken when they were hurt, the place designated to care for the president of the United States if he was injured while visiting the city, the primary responder for any major urban disaster, from fires to roof collapses to toxic leaks. With a large staff of emergency medicine specialists, social workers on duty around the clock, interpreters on call for more than two dozen languages, and central Poison Control responsibility for the whole city, Bellevue's Emergency Department was generally understood to be a service that any New Yorker might depend on for his or her life. It is an indicator of this fact that during the darkest days of the 1990s recession, Bellevue obtained permission to undertake a multimillion dollar rebuilding of its Emergency Department. Besides benefiting the patients, the public hospitals' role in trauma care benefited the hospitals themselves, by highlighting their role in serving the whole community.

The rebuilding of Bellevue's Emergency Department in the midst of budget cuts and retrenchment suggests the continuing resilience of New York's public hospital system. Drawing upon very different resources from the city's private hospitals, and pursuing a very different mission, Bellevue and its fellow institutions had managed to survive the trying times of the 1970s and 1980s. But it was too early to declare victory. The most striking trends of the period—the efforts to control health costs, the cuts in social spending, and the waning enthusiasm for public institutions—had only been introductory chapters in an unfolding story. During the 1990s, Bellevue would be tested by far more radical versions of the same trends; and in the face of those changes, Bellevue would be challenged as never before to justify its continued existence as a public hospital.

A Revolution in Health Care

The new era began with a drive to reform American health care. In 1993 the United States came very close to adopting a national program for universal health insurance. Health costs had continued to mount despite the efforts of two decades, while the proportion of the population covered by health insurance was dropping. Health-care reform seemed to have the support of a wide range of Americans, from legislators to sweatshop workers, from corporation presidents to the unemployed. When then Arkansas Governor Bill Clinton featured the issue in his winning presidential campaign, emphasized it in his first State of the Union speech, and then named a task force headed by his wife, Hillary Rodham Clinton, to draft the necessary legislation, many observers believed that a national health program would be enacted within the year.

The Rise of Managed Care

The Clinton plan, as it emerged, called for the creation of large "health alliances," each of which would provide or purchase a full range of health services for its subscribers. Every American would join one of these alliances, with public funds subsidizing the enrollment of the poor. Because subscribers would pay a flat rate per year, the alliances would have a financial incentive to arrange efficient low-cost care. At the same time, standing as middlemen between health-care providers and thousands of subscribers, the alliances could force the providers to charge reasonable rates and force consumers to use health services efficiently. This approach, often called "managed care," was not unlike the service already offered by health maintenance organizations (HMOs). Some HMOs, it was assumed, might become alliances; so might some insurance companies or large employers. So might leading medical centers, if they developed enough affiliations with other kinds of medical institutions; indeed, New York Hospital's new network seemed well positioned to function as an alliance.

Within a year of President Clinton's inauguration, health reform was dead. The president's effort to launch several major initiatives at the same time helped torpedo his proposal, as did problems with the program design, an antipathy in some circles to the role that government would play in overseeing the system, and several serious political errors by Mrs. Clinton and some of her colleagues. In addition, advocates of the plan faced the perennial difficulty of converting consensus on a problem into consensus on a solution. As the debate proceeded, dozens of influential groups, from Medicare recipients to insurance companies, weighed in with their criticisms. Three concerns were articulated most loudly: first, that the new plan might erode the quality of American health care; second, that it might force "rationing" of the care available; and third, that patients might lose the right to choose their own physicians. In the end, many people seemed to have decided that it was safer to keep the system they had, whatever its flaws, than to risk entering a new arrangement that might be worse.

But even as this debate was going on, the system that people had decided to keep was changing. While managed care was being attacked in Washington, D.C., it was being embraced by the organizations that paid for most of America's private health expenditures: employers, insurance companies, and health maintenance organizations. Seeking to limit the use (and therefore the cost) of the medical services they covered, major health-care payers began to impose their own limits on consumer choice. In effect, they were engaging in most of the cost-cutting strategies that Clinton had envisioned, while remaining free of the federal regulations that his plan had also included to ensure social equity. By the time health-care reform was finally pronounced dead in 1994, this private-sector implementation of managed care was reshaping the pattern of medicine throughout the country.

Managed care grew more slowly in New York State than in other parts of the country, but, by 1995, about one-quarter of the people in the state were enrolled in HMOs, while most other insurers were altering their policies along managed-care lines. Increasingly, patients were required to be screened by "gate-keeper" primary physicians before consulting specialists, to obtain second opinions before many kinds of surgery, and to receive their care in outpatient settings whenever possible. Insurers also limited the circle of hospitals and physicians whose services they covered, and they required those providers to lower their fees in exchange for being included in the circle. The distance that health-care financing had traveled from the free-spending style of the past was made clear when one HMO official casually referred to "the best-case scenario, where no services are provided."[38]

As managed care expanded in the United States, hospitals that treated acute conditions were among the institutions most profoundly affected, both because their services were expensive and because they accounted for such a large proportion of health-care expenditures. One hospital official, who said he had begun his career as a "cost-unconscious physician," summarized the change: "Now, with managed care, cost is considered in every decision."[39] Patient stays grew shorter, and hundreds of procedures were moved from hospital rooms to clinics or doctors' offices. In the ensuing competition for the inpatient business that remained, large purchasers of health care were able to enforce steep discounts in exchange for the thousands of referrals they controlled.

The emerging rules for institutional success were neatly summarized in a *New York Times* headline: "Hospitals' New Creed: Less Is Best."[40] In this environment, the characteristics that had long distinguished New York's leading hospitals suddenly became handicaps. For generations, they had specialized in providing not less but *more*—more attention, more services, more technology, and more specialists. They also cost more to run, because of their extensive educational programs. The city had long taken pride in the fact that 15 percent of all the physicians in the country received their training in New York hospitals. But large payers questioned whether the nation really needed the army of specialists that these medical centers took such pride in producing. And even if it did, why should the payers increase their own expenses by subsidizing this training?

Hospital care for the uninsured faced similar challenges. The state pools that had provided extra subsidies for charity care and medical education squeaked through to renewal in 1996, though with reduced funds. The same legislative session, however, brought a more significant change: the end of New York State's twenty-five-year experiment with rate regulation. Now each hospital had to negotiate the best rates it could with each of its major payers. Since the state pools had never covered the full cost of charity care, hospitals had been accustomed to distribute the rest of the burden to their paying patients. But the tough bargaining that went with managed care left little room for such strategies. Undoubtedly the poor should receive care, the insurers argued, but why should their subscribers pay for it? The very effectiveness of market competition in reducing health-care costs lay in its capacity to eliminate "extra" expenses like subsidies for the uninsured. Market forces were designed to produce efficiency, not charity.

Pressed to compete for every dollar, many private hospitals concluded that charity was a luxury they could no longer afford. Some spokespeople suggested that it was unreasonable even to expect them to do so. "I know of no requirement that restaurants are required to feed the hungry," said Sister Jane Frances Brady, president of St. Joseph's Medical Center in New Jersey. "I know of no requirement that Macy's is required to clothe the naked. . . . But the hospitals are required to provide any kind of care to all comers, and we feel that it is an impossible situation."[41]

No Help from Government

As the private hospitals' tradition of providing at least some charity care began to give way, government assistance for the poor took on new importance. "Providing health care for those in need is not a hospital problem," explained the leader of one private medical center. "It is a statewide social problem, and therefore the state's responsibility."[42] But even as the demand for public support was increasing, the willingness to provide it was melting away. In 1993, the New York mayoralty was won by Rudolph Giuliani, the first Republican to hold the office since John Lindsay. The next year the Republican Party won control of both houses of the U.S. Congress. The year after that George Pataki took office as the first Republican governor of New York State in two decades.

Any group of politicians elected at this time would have had to make spending cuts, since the city, state, and federal governments all had sizable deficits; but the new leaders' agendas went far beyond the fiscal requirements of the moment. They were ideologically committed to reducing the size and cost of public programs. As Governor Pataki explained in his inaugural address: "Less government means lower taxes and more jobs." The new Republican officials argued that the existing programs were ineffective, while their excessive costs soaked up resources that could otherwise remain in the private sector, fostering economic growth. Accordingly, they sought to scale back public spending and return the money to the private sector by cutting taxes. When this approach proved successful at the polls, many Democrats jumped on the bandwagon. After the 1994 U.S. congressional elections, one observer commented: "The climate is so profoundly different since November that people in public life no longer defend things that they once thought were absolute necessities."[43]

As funding cuts proceeded, the impact fell disproportionately on programs for the poor, since they had the fewest effective defenders. Sociologist Herbert Gans suggested that the War on Poverty had turned into the War against the Poor. In the area of health care, the cuts in funding for direct services were exacerbated by initiatives like welfare reform, which reduced the number of people on public assistance, and therefore the number of people eligible for Medicaid. Medicare was not as affected as Medicaid, because it had an active political constituency, but it too faced new limits—particularly in its supplements for medical education and for hospitals that served disproportionate numbers of the uninsured. Thus, while managed care was putting new limits on the income that hospitals received from private sources, their public funding was also being eroded.

The onslaught of changes in health-care funding presented particularly daunting problems for New York's municipal hospitals. Every assessment of New York City's future prospects stressed that some facilities would have to be closed, and that the closings would not occur randomly. Hospitals that specialized in serving the poor—municipal facilities and "distressed" private hospitals in the city's poorest neighborhoods—would be disproportionately affected. The changes, warned one report, "may create gaping holes in the City's safety net for uninsured and medically indigent patients."[44] And even as these words were being written, the experience of the New York City Health & Hospitals Corporation made clear that the predictions were starting to come true.

In 1991, Medicaid patients constituted more than 70 percent of the municipal hospitals' paying patients. That year, believing that Medicaid costs could be reduced by using managed care, New York State established a new system of incentives and penalties that led private HMOs to recruit Medicaid patients actively for the first time. HHC tried to counter by establishing its own HMO, but it was slow in starting and made little headway. Within months, thousands of Medicaid patients had enrolled in private HMOs, thus committing themselves to using the affiliated private hospitals when they needed inpatient care. As HHC's only remaining pool of paying patients began to melt away, the agency experienced a sharp drop in revenue. In one year, Bellevue alone lost $74 million in Medicaid payments, forcing it both to cut its staff by 680 and to close seven wards.[45]

This was the situation in 1994, when Rudolph Giuliani took office as mayor. Like many other Republicans, Giuliani had campaigned on a platform of reducing the role of government. His political preferences were reinforced by the city's problematic fiscal situation; he inherited a $2.3 billion deficit and, although he reduced the city payroll by 14,000 jobs, the gap between spending and revenues remained wide throughout most of the his first term in office. Yet, to some extent, this situation suited Giuliani's purposes. As he explained to a reporter, if the city had no deficit, "the Mayor would have no defense against a City Council that wanted to spend ten billion dollars more. This is a valuable thing to have, to restrain the desire of any legislative body to spend more money."[46] And indeed in 1996 and 1997, when an upturn in the stock market produced enough taxes to put the city budget back in balance—just in time for Giuliani's reelection—few of the new-found dollars went to social programs.

For the public hospitals, Giuliani's policies meant a steady decline in the city's annual cash contribution to the HHC operating budget. Throughout the 1980s, this payment had never fallen below $350 million per year; by 1997, it had sunk to $14 million. The city's contribution had been written into the legislation establishing HHC in 1970, to reimburse the agency for its costs in serving city prisoners, uniformed city employees, and the uninsured; but by the mid-1990s, the total contribution had fallen well below that level. A 1995 survey of eight American cities showed that, while the citizens of Boston, Los Angeles, Phoenix, Dallas, Memphis, and Indianapolis were paying between $24 and $50 per person in taxes to support their public hospital systems, the contribution in New York was only $6 per person.[47]

As the Health & Hospitals Corporation struggled to meet its budget, staff members who resigned or accepted the city's various buyout offers were not replaced; in just two years, 1994 and 1995, New York hospitals lost 5,000 employees. Many talented administrators joined the exodus. In 1992, Bellevue had given a guarded welcome to Pamela Brier, its tenth director in a decade, the seventh in less than five years. Brier set energetically to work, building up the hospital's primary-care services and reversing the downward slide in admissions. Bellevue's problems continued to mount, however, while the political atmosphere seemed to promise a future of declining revenues and increasingly needy patients. "What will I do with them?" Brier asked a visitor in 1994. "Say 'Oh, I'm so sorry; go see the Governor, go see the President?' It's going to be a problem and I haven't figured it out, frankly, I just haven't." A few months later, after less than three years on the job, Brier—like most of her predecessors—left Bellevue for the private sector.[48]

Whether to Stay in the Hospital Business

By the time of Brier's departure, HHC's loss of Medicaid patients and the prevailing political climate had reopened a familiar question: should New York City be running public hospitals? To those who favored privatization, the sad state of the municipal system was proof of governmental incompetence. Back in 1987, urban analyst Peter Salins had accused HHC of "inefficiency, bad management, corruption, and a record of bad care," and he concluded: "It's about time that the municipal government got out of the hospital business." Rudolph Giuliani had taken a similar position during his first run for mayor in 1989, observing that under city management the municipal hospitals had become "hell centers."[49]

New York had always had more municipal hospitals than any other American city, but by the 1990s, the numbers had become even more lopsided, as many communities turned their public hospitals over to private management. San Diego, Seattle, Cleveland, St. Louis, Kansas City, Toledo, Newark, Philadelphia, Memphis, Detroit, and a number of California counties had all "got out of the hospital business." Should New York do the same?

The Privatization Debate

Those who favored privatization pointed to the many administrative flaws of the city's public hospitals and insisted that private management could provide better care at lower cost. The HHC Central Office staff had been sharply reduced, but it was still widely regarded as a cumbersome administrative superstructure. Individual hospitals were generally thought to be doing their best, but city regulations, union agreements, and political considerations made it difficult for them to borrow money, to pay their top executives well, to complete needed construction promptly, or to readjust their staffing arrangements to meet changing service demands. Their obligation to make their records public also put them at a disadvantage in negotiating with third-party payers; and the backlog of unaddressed capital needs promised either huge expenses or worse physical deterioration in the future.

The problems of the public system were expected to worsen in the years ahead. Most experts were predicting that thousands of beds and many New York hospitals would close. Already the city's leading private hospitals were maneuvering for position, absorbing smaller facilities and merging with their strongest rivals. The most notable of the hospital mergers occurred in 1996, when New York Hospital and Presbyterian Hospital announced their decision to join forces. An observer called the combination "inevitable and obvious," but it had not seemed so until recently. Only after managed care had transformed their world did these two institutional giants make up their minds to sacrifice the autonomy they had cherished for so many years.[50]

The decisiveness of the step taken by New York Hospital and Presbyterian only emphasized the intensity of the competition that every hospital in the city was facing. In such a Darwinian environment, the cumbersome decision-making and procedural inefficiencies of government—always a drawback—could be disastrous. Jeremiah Barondess, president of the New York Academy of Medicine, expressed a widely held view when he maintained that municipal government could not run hospitals effectively in the emerging world of managed care. For New York to have maintained its public system for so many years was a "nice thing, a good thing, a proper thing," he said, but "a city cannot run a system this complex in a world this complex, politically, socially, or medically."[51]

As discussed above, most private hospitals had shown little enthusiasm in the past for taking over the public system. Although they had not said so explicitly, they appeared to find the municipal hospitals a convenient backup and had expressed little interest in assuming their burdens. Even Medicaid patients, whose care was funded but whose social characteristics or race sometimes made them less welcome in private hospitals, had been allocated disproportionately to the public system. But by the 1990s, changes in the larger world of health care had begun to alter this pattern. As managed care reduced the voluntary hospitals' income from private insurance, they found themselves treating fewer inpatients and earning less for each one served. Under such circumstances, Medicaid recipients had new appeal, since (at least for the present) there were funds to cover their care.

The trends of the early 1990s had important implications for the public system. In a world of cut-throat competition among hospitals, the hard-pressed public facilities could be expected to fare the worst, especially if their only significant group of paying patients—those covered by Medicaid—was now departing for private care. Whatever the public system had cost the city in the past, it seemed reasonable to predict that it might cost more in the future. In addition, the debate over privatization occurred at a moment when the private institutions were particularly active in serving the poor. Pointing to the voluntaries' rising Medicaid rolls, supporters of privatization could argue that the municipal hospitals no longer had any distinctive role to play.

Despite those arguments, many of those concerned with the hospital system continued to have doubts about depending on private institutions to meet public responsibilities. In opposing privatization they drew on three kinds of evidence: information from other communities, the current pattern of public and private care in New York City, and the likely direction of future changes in health care.

Various national studies gave reason for concern about the private sector's capacity to ensure universal access to health services. One report indicated that in an eighteen-month period, eighty-six hospitals in twenty-two states had been cited by the government for rejecting emergency patients for non-medical reasons—usually because they could not pay for their care. The role of public hospitals as a safety net for such patients was highlighted by a California study, which found that after one community closed its public hospital, the proportion of uninsured patients denied health care more than doubled.[52]

Another study, one surveying the nation's 100 largest cities, reported that the average rate of care for the uninsured was 40 percent higher in cities that had public hospitals than in those without any. The authors found that private institutions tended to provide more care to the uninsured if they were in communities with no public services. But even with this increase, the total volume of care provided to the uninsured was lower than the level achieved in cities that had public hospitals.[53]

Insurance coverage was not the only issue that affected people's access to health services; a growing literature documented the numerous other factors involved. Patients who were black or Latino, those with AIDS, those who were drug addicted, chronically disabled, homeless, violent, mentally ill—all these groups were shown to have encountered barriers to care. Access was also affected by service location; the hospital closings of previous decades had occurred disproportionately in poor urban neighborhoods, raising new obstacles for people with little time or money to travel to more distant hospitals.[54]

The doubts about privatization raised by the national data were confirmed by the pattern of public and private care in New York City. For example, although by the early 1990s, public hospitals had only 20 percent of the general care beds in New York, they accounted for about 33 percent of the hospital beds in the Bronx and in Harlem. Furthermore, they treated 40 percent of the city's tuberculosis and AIDS patients and 50 percent of its mental patients. They also averaged twice as many emergency room visits per facility as private hospitals. Homeless patients and prisoners were treated primarily in the public hospitals, as were most of the city's several hundred thousand undocumented immigrants. As for people of color, even though non-whites represented only about 50 percent of the city's population by 1995, they accounted for about 80 percent of the public hospitals' patient population. Many of the public system's patients were, as Brier had observed, "people who are not valued in the outside world."[55] If the municipal government laid down the responsibility for their care, would someone else pick it up?

One who expressed growing concern over this question was Bruce Siegel, head of the Health & Hospitals Corporation from 1994 to 1996. Although appointed by a mayor who seemed to have little regard for the public system, Siegel grew steadily cooler to privatization, largely because of his experience with HHC's affiliation program. This initiative, which cost the city more than $500 million per year, had represented the city's first effort to bring the excellence of private medicine to municipal health care. But Siegel complained that instead of providing the services that were needed, many of the private affiliates were wasting public money on arcane specialty departments, "a luxurious maze of clinics with very few patients in them." Siegel questioned whether these same institutions would be more responsive to community needs if they had full control of the hospitals. "Would they take care of every undocumented immigrant we now take care of? Would they take care of the city's AIDS patients? Could they do it? Theoretically. Would they do it? I don't know."[56]

Siegel's questions were echoed by others, including Martin Begun, a vice-president of Bellevue's private affiliate, the New York University Medical Center. "I don't buy the attitude at all that in a crunch New York City can do without public hospitals," he said. "There is absolutely no evidence for this. Will private hospitals take care of prisoners? Will they take care of the homeless mentally ill? Will they take care of uninsured immigrants? If an epidemic were to break out in this city, do you think for one minute the private hospitals are equipped to deal with this?" Public hospitals were originally founded, he said, to deal with the very poor and with epidemics. New York still had plenty of both, if one thought of contemporary epidemics like AIDS and drug abuse, and most private institutions were glad to have the public hospitals deal with them. "Listen to that," he said as an ambulance screamed past his office window on the way to Bellevue. "Do you think our hospital would want those ambulances to roll in with what we see out there?"[57]

Besides raising questions based on past experiences around the country and on present practices in New York City, the opponents of privatization urged decision makers to consider the likely direction of future changes in health care. Given the economic pressures faced by all hospital managers, it seemed probable that privatization might draw off only the healthier municipal facilities—those with the best reimbursement patterns and newest buildings—leaving the rest in public hands. Even Barondess, who ultimately came to favor privatization, had predicted this danger, warning the City Council: "Only the pretty girls are going to get asked to dance." Under such circumstances, he warned, privatization might leave New York "with a residual, shrunken municipal hospital system characterized by the most antiquated physical facilities and a patient mix characterized to a disproportionate degree by patients with mental illness, substance abuse, AIDS and drug-resistant tuberculosis."[58]

Some municipal hospitals would probably find private takers, but what would happen if they became unprofitable in the future? It seemed likely, given the predictions of widespread downsizing, that some of their beds—and perhaps entire facilities—might have to be closed. Would private managers do so in a way that ensured adequate services for poor neighborhoods throughout the city, or would they simply close the facilities that cost the most to run?[59]

What about New Yorkers without health insurance—a group approaching 1.5 million in the mid-1990s and clearly on the rise? State funds currently reimbursed hospitals for inpatient services to the uninsured; but if state funds were reduced, would the private hospitals continue to treat the uninsured? A clue existed in the statistics for outpatient care, where reimbursement was much less generous and uninsured patients much more numerous; in this area, private hospitals served a far lower proportion of the city's patients.[60] Cuts in Medicaid could throw many more people into the ranks of the uninsured or push reimbursement rates far below costs. When that happened, would the private hospitals still compete to serve them? If not, who would care for them?

To some extent, the two sides in this debate were talking past each other. While the supporters of privatization pointed to HHC's undeniable handicaps for competing in the emerging world of managed care, the opponents focused on the private sector's undeniable lapses in providing universal access. Ideally, an approach might emerge that would take both these issues into account. If the system was to be privatized, the new managers would have to be monitored much more rigorously than had ever been done in the past. If the system was to flourish as a public institution, it would require more resources and more creativity than the city had given it for years.

Going All the Way

Even as the two sides debated, Mayor Giuliani made clear his own position on the subject. One year into his first term, in 1995, he announced that he had decided to sell three of New York's eleven public general hospitals—a transaction that would represent the largest sale of city assets in history. The facilities selected tended to confirm the fears of those who believed that even partial privatization might weaken the public system. Coney Island Hospital was among the most prosperous institutions in the HHC network, while Queens Hospital and Elmhurst Hospital appeared to have made the list primarily because their private affiliate, Mount Sinai Hospital, was likely to be interested in bidding on them. Overall, the selection process seemed to have been shaped more by what private institutions might be interested in buying than by a long-term vision for the public system.[61]

Six months after Mayor Giuliani made his announcement, an even more ambitious plan was proposed by the Blue Ribbon Panel that he had appointed to study the public hospitals. The committee made clear its agenda when it explained that one of the three objectives that had guided its work was as follows: "To take New York City out of the role of owning and operating a hospital system." As one observer commented: "The Blue Ribbon panel did not *conclude* that the system ought to be privatized; it *assumed* that the system ought to be privatized." The final report held to that line, recommending that all eleven acute-care municipal hospitals should be sold, leased, set up as freestanding private institutions, or closed.[62]

The Blue Ribbon Panel report evoked considerable criticism, particularly for its rather vague treatment of how care for the uninsured would be sustained under the new plan. In addition, several law suits were filed by community groups and by the City Council, arguing that neither the mayor nor HHC had the legal right to close down the public system. Mayor Giuliani refrained from explicitly endorsing the panel's report, but he continued to move in the direction of privatization by pursuing his search for private institutions to manage—either by purchase or by ninety-nine-year lease—the three hospitals he had initially targeted. However, the lack of interest shown by the various facilities that been expected to jump at the opportunity suggested that there had been some merit in the opponents' questions.[63]

Undaunted, Mayor Giuliani soon announced that Coney Island Hospital would be taken over by Primary Health Systems (PHS), a for-profit health-management company from Delaware. Calling the forty-nine-year lease "a model for things we're going to have to do throughout the rest of the city," Giuliani assured community residents that the new managers would maintain the hospital's present level of services for the poor at no cost to the city. A PHS official explained that free care would be subsidized by new private patients whom the hospital would attract from the surrounding community. Yet the difficulties that other hospitals were facing in maintaining cross-subsidies of this kind left many observers skeptical.[64] The Mayor's deal with PHS evoked immediate opposition, and the proposal met a series of defeats in court, where two levels of the judiciary ruled that the city had committed itself to providing public hospital care when HHC was established in 1969; it could not abandon that commitment without permission from the State Legislature. Nevertheless, the Mayor vowed to appeal again, and plans for the lease went forward.

New York City's consideration of the PHS deal emphasized another emerging pattern in American health care: the growing significance of for-profit corporations. By the mid-1990s, about 20 percent of the 6,500 hospitals in the United States were owned by publicly traded companies, many of them controlling huge chains of medical institutions and other health-care services. New York State was unusual in having a law written specifically to discourage hospital ownership by such corporations; at the time the bill was passed, its supporters argued that these firms' large scale, absentee ownership, and financial orientation ill equipped them to run responsive community institutions. By the mid-1990s, however, the profound changes under way in hospital care had already eroded many of the traditions that had made for-profit management seem so distasteful. As profitmaking HMOs and insurance companies exerted growing influence over all branches of health care, as private hospi-

tals' decision making became more and more money driven, as hospital mergers created ever larger corporate entities, it became increasingly difficult to
make a moral distinction between for-profit and not-for-profit management.

"I know it's sacrilegious to say," admitted the head of one New York hospital, "but when I look at all the red ink in my books I can't help but wonder,
would it be so terrible if one of the chains came in here, bailed us out and ran
a tighter ship?" The entry of for-profits into New York State was still opposed
by powerful vested interests—most notably the Roman Catholic church,
which had its own vast commitment to providing hospital care. Yet the very
fact that for-profit management was being favorably discussed—and that
it was being considered for Coney Island Hospital—emphasized how profoundly the world had changed for both public and private hospitals in just a
few years.[65]

"No Elsewhere"

No matter whether privatization of the public system turned out to mean for-
profit or nonprofit management, sale or long-term lease, the central question
remained: could private managers be counted on to shoulder the tasks that
public hospitals had performed for New York City for more than two hundred
years? Even as this debate raged, an incident occurred to suggest that the answer might be no.

One morning in November 1995, an eleven-year-old Dominican girl named
Yiomaris Sanchez was brought to the New York Hospital emergency room by
her mother and an English-speaking friend. Suffering from advanced
leukemia, Sanchez had entered the United States on a special visa to seek
medical care. New York Hospital's initial examination and laboratory tests
confirmed that she had a fever, as well as dangerously high levels of white
blood cells and uric acid. She was also found to have no insurance. Sanchez
remained in the emergency room for the next sixteen hours, during which
she was examined once more and given various medications to lower her
fever and uric acid level. Meanwhile, one of the emergency room physicians,
Sabina Bizzoco, was on the telephone, trying to arrange a transfer. Two of the
calls went to Bellevue. In the first, at 10 P.M., Dr. Bizzoco indicated that the
transfer was being recommended for medical reasons: Sanchez needed a
bone-marrow transplant, a procedure that New York Hospital did not perform. Bellevue staff pointed out that since their facility did not perform such
transplants either, there was nothing they could do for the patient that could
not be done at New York Hospital. Two hours later, Bellevue was called again,
a transfer was again requested, and this time it was mentioned that the girl
had no insurance. The Bellevue staff reiterated that New York Hospital could
care for the girl at least as well as they—and probably better, because of New
York Hospital's excellent pediatric oncology department.[66]

Not long after this conversation, Sanchez's mother was told that her
daughter was being discharged. Accounts differ as to what else the physicians said. According to New York Hospital staff, they indicated that the girl

was clinically stable and that the operation she needed was not available at their hospital, after which the mother declined an offer to have the patient spend the rest of the night in the emergency room. Sanchez's mother and her friend recall being told there were no rooms available and that no other hospital would accept Yiomaris because of her insurance status. They also say that when they requested ambulance transport because of the driving rain, the hospital refused, but a nurse gave them $10 for a taxi. The only available documentation of the exchange is the discharge slip the mother was handed, which read: "Diagnosis/Condition on Discharge—Leukemia; Discharge Instructions—Allopurinol, 100 mg; Referral to NYC HHC hospital as soon as possible."[67]

The next morning, Sanchez was brought by her mother to Bellevue, where she was admitted immediately to the intensive care unit. Judged too fragile to undergo a bone-marrow transplant, she was treated with massive chemotherapy—an intervention that New York Hospital could have provided. She died after four months at Bellevue, having received care that cost about $150,000. Meanwhile, press coverage brought the case to the attention of the federal Health Care Financing Administration (HCFA), which launched its own investigation into whether New York Hospital had violated the conditions of its Medicare funding, then totaling about $150 million per year. After a four-month review, HCFA concluded that New York Hospital had not fulfilled its legal obligations, since it had discharged Sanchez in an unstable condition after "only minimal treatment."[68]

As required by the review procedure, New York Hospital developed a remediation plan (among other things, it hired the deputy director of Bellevue's Emergency Department to run its emergency room), and little was heard of the case thereafter. Nevertheless, Yiomaris Sanchez's experience at New York Hospital and at Bellevue is important, because it is only the latest chapter in a history that we have traced back more than a hundred years—the story of the vital role that public hospitals have played in the life of the city. New York's private hospitals have their own charitable tradition, and it is a distinguished one; but the record explored in this volume makes clear that no matter how strong that tradition, and no matter how generously it has been supplemented by public funds, it has always been subject to certain limits.

Yiomaris Sanchez had a number of the characteristics that, over the years, have caused ailing New Yorkers to be excluded from private care. At various times in history and at various facilities, she might have faced rejection because of her immigrant status, her ethnicity, or her poor medical prognosis. She might have been referred elsewhere because her case did not seem useful for medical training, did not fit a hospital's research priorities, or simply because there were no available beds. Or she might have been excluded because of one other characteristic—perhaps the most damaging in the health-care environment of the 1990s—a lack of health insurance.

The essential fact of New York's health-care history is that for more than a century, every patient like Yiomaris Sanchez who has failed to find a place in private care has had somewhere to turn: the public hospital system. Year in, year out, it has been the public system's unique responsibility to ensure that everyone in New York was included in the city's circle of care, that continuity of service was sustained; that health care was provided in a way that was responsive to the multiple voices of the city; and that the health needs of the city's least valued citizens were kept visible.

In 1996, Bellevue's medical director summed up the unique expectations under which the public system operates when he observed that staff at private facilities could always refer less desirable cases elsewhere, but that at Bellevue such referrals were not an option. Here was the difference, he said: "When you're at Bellevue there is no elsewhere."[69] This distinctive mission—reinforced by law and tradition—has always set public hospitals apart from private ones. In the final decades of the twentieth century, when cost considerations are assuming growing dominance in medical discourse, the public hospitals' visible commitment to universal service remains more important than ever.

Conclusion

S. S. Goldwater, who served as Commissioner of Hospitals during the 1930s, once described the hospital as "the response of prudence and sympathy to man's hatred of suffering and his fear of death."[1] One way that the people of New York City have expressed their prudence and sympathy during the past two centuries is by maintaining the largest public hospital system in the United States. In a city renowned for its array of urban services, perhaps no facilities have more consistently provided urgently needed services than New York's public hospitals.

The creation of this health-care network owed much to the city's wealth and to its tradition of expansive social welfare. It was shaped, too, by the strong left/liberal coalition in the city's politics and labor movement, which for many years provided working-class New Yorkers with an unusually influential voice in city affairs. More mundane factors also played a role: each hospital built, each service established, generated a new set of constituents—recipients and providers—to encourage further expansion. Politicians wanted patronage, builders wanted contracts, workers wanted jobs, unions wanted members, neighborhoods wanted services, private hospitals wanted a place to refer the patients they were not serving, and medical schools wanted teaching and research opportunities. Even private employers benefited, since the city's array of free and low-cost health care constituted an indirect subsidy of workers' salaries. Thus, besides caring for the medical needs of its citizens, the public hospitals have served the social, economic, and political interests of the city in numerous ways. Even after the hard times of the 1970s and 1980s, even in the privatizing atmosphere of the 1990s, the intensity of the debate over the fate of New York's public hospitals makes clear that they still occupy a significant place in the life of the city.

A Public-Private Network

The debate in the 1990s over whether to turn the municipal hospitals over to private management is only the most recent development in the long and complicated relationship between the city's public and private hospitals. Together the two systems have provided a high level of care for local residents. As the commissioner of hospitals observed in 1965: "New York has always been a generous city, and no person who needs medical and hospital care is denied such service, whether it be in municipal or voluntary hospitals."[2]

The commissioner's statement was accurate, but it left out a crucial part of the story: the way that responsibility has been divided between municipal and voluntary hospitals. There have always been social distinctions between the two systems. Private hospitals have long provided the majority of care in the city, while the public system has functioned as the provider of last resort, taking in the people who had nowhere else to go. Yet this distinction was eased throughout the nineteenth century by one crucial factor: the majority of patients in every hospital, public or private, were members of the same vast urban class, the working poor. After the 1920s, the growing tendency of private hospitals to charge for their services gave free municipal care greater stigma—so did the increasing use of private hospitals by the city's middle and upper classes. Even so, case records, memoirs, and newspaper accounts all make clear that at least until World War II, receiving free care in a public hospital was still perceived as a common experience for working-class New Yorkers. And as long as so many ordinary New Yorkers depended on public medical care, the facilities that provided it held a certain position in the mainstream of civic life.

Starting in the 1940s, one initiative after another—each actively supported by public policy—narrowed the circle of New Yorkers who depended on the public hospital system. Hospital insurance provided a passport to private care for some, Medicare and Medicaid for still more. As each new patient group departed, the municipal hospitals found themselves serving a higher proportion of fundless, untreatable, or stigmatized patients. And the more marginalized their patients, the more marginalized became the institutions that treated them.

The affiliation program launched during the 1960s, despite its sponsors' optimistic intentions, did little to correct the municipal hospitals' second-class status, and in some ways it reaffirmed it. Each private affiliate, whether medical school or hospital, was expected to lift its municipal partner to its own higher level, but as a mayoral commission observed in 1992: "Affiliated institutions have not always approached their responsibilities for their associated HHC [Health & Hospitals Corporation] facilities with the same level of concern about quality that they show in their own institutions."[3] Several generations of auditors and investigators have confirmed this conclusion. Established on the assumption that private medicine could rectify many of the deficiencies of public hospitals, the affiliation program brought important benefits, but it never came close to contributing all that was promised or all that was needed.

The limitations of the affiliation program can be attributed, at least in part, to the leaders of private medical institutions; many were less responsive than they might have been to the needs of the community whose tax dollars they were receiving. Yet this question cannot be raised without acknowledging, as well, the public officials who acquiesced in and rewarded the choices made by the affiliates. Despite reports that might have inspired more rigorous questions, city leaders for many years tended to accept at face value the affiliates' claims to excellence, without taking sufficient cognizance of the benefits that those institutions gained from their association with the city and without questioning the applicability of their services to public needs. Not until the late 1990s did the city begin insisting on contractual terms that would hold the affiliates strictly accountable for the millions of public dollars they were receiving.

The city's tendency to defer to leaders of the private medical establishment extended far beyond the affiliation program. Throughout the twentieth century, men whose primary associations lay in private medical institutions played important roles in every major decision about the municipal hospitals, from planning the separate board for Bellevue & Allied Hospitals in 1902 through the establishment of the Department of Hospitals in 1928 to the design of the Health & Hospitals Corporation in 1970. Several of the most influential commissioners, too—men like S. S. Goldwater in the 1930s and Joseph Terenzio in the 1960s—spent most of their professional lives associated with private medical institutions.

It is understandable that such individuals came to be chosen repeatedly to make or recommend city policy. The very impoverishment that made municipal hospitals an object of study also made them a less fertile career ground for top medical talent, particularly when the hegemonic power of academic medicine defined the standard of excellence against which individuals and careers were to be measured. Seeking the best professionals to define the course of public medicine, the city turned again and again to the private sector. These men in turn, working from their own experience and perspective, helped ensure that the public system would continue to function primarily as a supplement to the city's private medical institutions. The performance of private affiliates was only sporadically questioned, proposals for broadening the municipal system's base by accepting private patients were discouraged, and the private facilities' time-honored practice of sending unwanted patients to the public hospitals was never systematically challenged.

Hospital Commissioner Marcus Kogel explained in 1952 to a meeting of municipal system doctors: "We are the last resort. We are the sanctuary for the voluntary hospitals' overflow. We are thus the instrument which makes it possible for the great voluntaries to be what they are—magnificent models of hospital practice."[4] Functioning under this philosophy, the public hospitals consistently accepted responsibility for serving the network's least wanted patients and performing its least wanted tasks; the physical surroundings they provided were often less than ideal, and their quality of care sometimes fell well below the best private standards. Nevertheless, the municipal hospitals lived on, serving their unique function within the city's public-private network.

The Value of the Public Hospitals

Given the public hospitals' many flaws and their unequal status within the city's network of hospitals, was New York justified in maintaining them for more than two centuries? The answer is yes. One way of assessing their contribution is by reviewing the qualities that ideally should characterize a public institution and by considering how those qualities relate to the role that municipal hospitals have played in New York City.

Inclusiveness is the first important quality of a public institution, and in this respect the municipal hospitals have established a compelling tradition. The years between 1910 and 1930 were especially important in this regard, because during those years the leading private hospitals redefined their mission. Instead of concentrating on caring for the poor as they had done in the past, they began to offer themselves as centers of scientific treatment, research, and education. Middle- and upper-class patients assumed a growing place in the private hospital population, while the provision of charity services was reduced, except for patients whose cases were of value for teaching or research. Generations earlier, when Samuel Bard presented the first call to establish New York Hospital in 1769, he articulated a mission that would guide the founding of nearly every private hospital in the city: "Let those who are at once the unhappy Victims, both of Poverty and Disease, claim your particular Attention."[5] By the end of the 1920s, only the public hospitals were still living by Bard's words.

Over the years that followed, a variety of programs—city subsidies, health insurance, Medicare, Medicaid, and state pools—all helped ensure that private hospitals continued to serve some low-income people without great financial loss. In service areas for which external funding was minimal, however, such as outpatient clinics, the private hospitals were much less active; here, once again, the public hospitals carried a disproportionate share of the burden, serving large numbers of people who had neither the insurance nor the personal means to pay for care in the private sector.

The poor are not the only New Yorkers who have had reason to be grateful for the inclusiveness of the public system. From their earliest days, private hospitals made a practice of excluding certain patients because of their types of disease, social characteristics, moral "unworthiness," poor prognoses, or simply because of bed shortages. The municipal facilities, by contrast, made it a policy to admit all patients in need, whatever their medical, social, or behavioral characteristics. Patients with tuberculosis, AIDS, mental illness, or syphilis, patients who were drunk and disorderly, homeless and dirty, illegal immigrants, unwed mothers, drug addicts, the uninsured, or the chronically ill—all such patients have at one time or another found a welcome in the public system when they were acceptable nowhere else.

Public hospitals have also been inclusive in a geographical sense, helping to draw poorer neighborhoods into the wider circle of city services and economic opportunities. In parts of New York where few doctors remain in private practice, these hospitals have provided a vital source of medical treatment, social support, and preventive care. At the same time, because of their geographical dispersal, they have often represented economic outposts in neighborhoods with few other job opportunities.

The municipal hospitals have also practiced inclusiveness as employers. They were the first in the city to hire female doctors, black doctors, black nurses, and male nurses. In many cases, the doors of the public hospitals were opened belatedly and reluctantly to these groups, but they opened, and well before similar opportunities were made available elsewhere in the city. Employees, like patients, have benefited from the inclusiveness of the public system.

Continuity is the second characteristic shared by public institutions in general and by the municipal hospitals in particular. Private medical institutions have often altered their services in accordance with changes in funding patterns, research priorities, donor interest, or program eligibility. The city's public hospitals have functioned with much greater consistency, ensuring that care has always been available, no matter what the economic, political, or institutional climate.

The 1930s represented one of the most dramatic examples of the public hospitals' capacity to sustain continuity under adverse circumstances. During the Great Depression, while demands for free health care escalated, many of the city's private hospitals actually closed ward beds because of their own financial problems. City subsidies helped see these facilities through, but the the public hospitals also played a major role. During the 1930s the public system served historic numbers of needy New Yorkers—not only the people who had been poor for generations but also thousands of middle-class citizens who until the Depression had been able to pay for private care. Would the same effect have been achieved if the entire public hospital budget had been divided up as subsidies to the private facilities? Probably not. The public hospitals played the vital role they did, not only because they had access to municipal funds but because their tradition of serving all needy citizens, no matter how many and no matter what the circumstances, was uniquely suited to those difficult times. Indeed, it is hard to imagine how adequate levels of care could have been sustained in the city during the Depression without the contribution of the public hospitals.

If the Depression was the most dramatic example of the public hospitals' commitment to continuity of service, there have been many others, before and since: the influenza epidemic of 1918–1919; the inflationary period just after World War II when many private hospitals increased their rates; the sharp cutback in Medicaid eligibility during the late 1960s; and the sudden increase in homelessness in the 1980s. On each of these occasions, the public hospitals' consistent availability sustained the level of available care although external conditions changed dramatically. Year in, year out, in good times and bad, through economic crises and city-wide epidemics, the municipal hospitals have provided New York City with a vital feature of urban life: a medical safety-net.

Since the 1980s, for-profit organizations have assumed growing importance in American health care. Many critics of this trend have warned that such organizations could not be depended upon to provide consistent community service, and their likely performance is often compared unfavorably with the record of voluntary institutions. For instance, it is suggested that because of their corporate orientation and their financial obligations to their stockholders, for-profit hospital managers would be more likely to close programs—or even entire institutions—if financial problems developed. In particular, care for the uninsured might be subordinated to the business obligations of a for-profit organization.

These are serious issues, worthy of genuine concern. Yet, as this book makes clear, private non-profit hospitals have had their own problems with sustaining continuity of care. These facilities also have budgets to balance, donors to please, and institutional priorities beyond charitable care. Those who wonder how medical care might be sustained by private for-profit corporations might look closely at the performance of private nonprofit hospitals during the twentieth century. At times, it has exemplified the very best in public service, but there have been serious fluctuations when funding problems or other considerations have caused them to curtail services to the community's neediest residents. Under the right conditions, with the right combination of financing and institutional commitment, the best private facilities have often outperformed the public system. But when their financial basis has changed, their institutional commitment has also sometimes been known to waver. For nearly two centuries, the public system has accepted all patients, picking up whomever the private sector let fall, and providing the continuity necessary to guarantee a minimum level of care for all New Yorkers.

Responsiveness is the third fundamental obligation of a public institution—the duty to accommodate the needs, demands, and criticisms of the city's many diverse groups. This characteristic has influenced the public hospitals' approach to administration, patient care, and labor relations. Private hospitals have their own tradition of community service, but in general they have been left quite free to define how that service should be provided, selecting from among the various needs of the community the ones whose fulfillment will best fit with their own institutional goals and priorities. It is sometimes said that private hospitals have become more or less public institutions, because so much of their financial support now comes from public sources. But public hospitals are truly different from private ones: they are more open to public scrutiny and they function under far stricter checks and balances.

In reviewing Bellevue's experience of the 1950s and 1960s one gains a sense of how the obligation to respond can shape the life of a public hospital. During those twenty years, Bellevue found itself responding not only to the needs of its hundreds of thousands of patients but also to an expansionist medical school affiliate, an increasingly militant work force, a coalition of public and private interests intent on upgrading the neighborhood, an increasingly intrusive bureaucracy, the fluctuations of New York City politics, the dramatic arrival of Medicare and Medicaid, a parade of investigations, and a major reorganization of the municipal hospital system. Some of these events (like the hospital investigations) left New York Hospital quite untouched, and even the events that affected it had much less impact there than at Bellevue. The medical school affiliate of New York Hospital, for example, remained less powerful in relation to the hospital; one union after another retreated from the scene; the development of the neighborhood accorded well with the hospital's own plans; and Medicare/Medicaid brought generous new public funding without significantly limiting the hospital's freedom to choose its patients or its priorities.

The special responsiveness required of public institutions is clear when one considers the role of labor in the municipal hospitals. Decades before Local 1199's breakthrough in the private hospitals, labor unions had become an accepted part of the municipal hospital scene. Although the formal structures of collective bargaining emerged only gradually, city employees played an indirect part in city policymaking from the 1930s onward, through their leaders' influence at City Hall. Not every union leader was a visionary, nor was every union a democracy, but the existence and power of these organizations gave workers a place within the city structure that they rarely achieved in the private sector.

Labor, of course, has been only one of many voices demanding a say in public hospital affairs, and this is part of what has always made managing public hospitals so difficult. Some demands have been destructive, like the pressure to staff Bellevue with the dregs of Tammany Hall in the 1890s; the heavy hand of Mayor John Hylan during the 1920s; or the turmoil that dogged the Health & Hospitals Corporation in the 1970s. Yet responding to public pressure has also led to important achievements, like the early hiring of female and black doctors; the decision that public hospitals must continue to accept all applicants even during the depths of the Depression; the worker-training programs established under the union's prodding in the 1960s; and Bellevue's important work with homeless patients suffering from drug-resistant tuberculosis in the 1990s. Public hospitals were and are instruments of their community, and if they have suffered the conflicts of the city that surrounded them, they have also reflected its diverse vitality.

Visibility, the fourth characteristic, may be the most important for a public institution. The municipal hospitals have met this standard in two senses.

First, they have made certain that the needs of the city's least influential citizens have remained visible to the rest of the community. Second, they have themselves operated as visible expressions of what the community can do for its members.

The capacity to make visible the community's shared needs and achievements became particularly important during the final decades of the twentieth century, when so many other tendencies in national life were working in the opposite direction. To take just a few examples, those were years characterized by city campaigns to rid their downtown districts of undesirable characters, like the homeless; by the suburban growth of climate-controlled shopping malls and gated residential communities; and by a national plan for welfare reform that reduced enrollment numbers whether or not the former recipients actually found work. Whatever the motives of these various initiatives, each one had the effect of making social problems less visible and, therefore, more forgettable. At the same time, public institutions were themselves becoming less visible, with little attention being paid to their past accomplishments, their current value, or what they might contribute in the future.

In this social and political climate, New York's municipal hospitals continued to play a crucial role. Their very existence made it impossible for the poor to disappear from sight when they failed to find a place in the system of private medical care. The outcry in 1995, when Mayor Giuliani's Blue Ribbon Panel seemed to be ignoring the health-care needs of the poor, bore eloquent witness to the importance of this contribution. Thanks to the public hospitals, community advocates did not have to estimate or hypothesize how many poor New Yorkers *might* need care; the evidence of their need was clearly visible in municipal facilities all over the city. Providing this validation had importance beyond the field of health care. In a society increasingly inclined to overlook the poor and move them out of sight, the mere presence of the busy public hospitals confirmed the fact that the poor remained part of the community, that they had needs, and that their needs merited attention.

At a deeper level, the public hospitals continued to give visibility to the whole process of social citizenship. Each facility was a demonstration, a concrete example of the community caring for its members. In this sense the public hospitals not only provided health care but also presented an affirmation of the fact that the basic services necessary to preserve life are rights, not privileges, and that part of a community's job is to ensure that those rights are available to all its members. To enter Bellevue's doors one did not need to be financially solvent, employed, or even an American citizen. "What is the basis of allotment?" asks a visitor to a utopian community in Edward Bellamy's classic novel, *Looking Backward*. "His title . . . is his humanity," his host explains. "The basis of his claim is the fact that he is a man."[6] The municipal hospitals applied this principle to health care—extending it, of course, beyond the gendered limitations of Bellamy's statement. And in so doing they provided New York City with a visible demonstration of community membership in action.

A Reminder of the Possible

Commentators across the political spectrum have often inveighed against "two-track" medicine, warning that if separate facilities are maintained for the poor, they will inevitably be inferior. In 1968, Martin Cherkasky pointed to this danger as a reason to close down the municipal hospitals; about the same time, the city Health Services administrator used the same argument as a reason for expanding those hospitals to serve private patients. Neither proposal was carried out, and by the end of the twentieth century, New York's system of private and public hospital care exemplified all the flaws of two-track medicine.

Yet there is something worse than a two-track system of medicine, and that is a one-track system from which many persons are excluded. The performance of New York's private hospitals over the years—and of other private hospitals in cities across the country—suggests that fiscal, academic, and administrative pressures have often led them to avoid treating certain types of patients. In the years since World War II, growing numbers of patients have been enabled to pay for private care. But policies can change, as recent trends make very clear. And if funding is reduced for any of these patients, they may well find themselves excluded from the private system again. Furthermore, not all exclusions are based on finances, so even universal health insurance might not ensure universal access to private facilities. Nor is government's record of monitoring the performance of private medical institutions sufficiently strong to believe that public oversight could effectively enforce universal access if the private institutions were disinclined to provide it. Given these circumstances, a marginalized system of public care for the patients excluded from private institutions is far preferable to a system in which some of them get no care at all.

Ideally, one might envision an expansive public hospital system that served most city residents, with perhaps only the very wealthy using private services. Such a system could link public funding and public priorities, bring New Yorkers of various classes and races together, and create a broader constituency for the city hospitals' maintenance and improvement. But current trends hardly support such a vision. Public medicine is shrinking, not expanding, and even urban institutions like the schools and subways, which used to serve a relatively broad spectrum of the New York population, have lost many of their middle-class consumers.

Despite these changes, the municipal hospitals remain a vital element of the New York scene, a testament to the continuing liberality of the city and also to the limitations of the private system. Private hospitals have never fulfilled all the city's needs, nor are they likely to in the future. For more than two hundred years the public hospitals—beleaguered though they were—picked up the tasks left undone, and made sure that all city residents had access to the care they needed.

On the occasion of Bellevue's 250th birthday, a young medical student wrote this about the hospital:

> The scum and salt of the earth pass through these wards, often in the same person. Bellevue is a neutral territory, a demilitarized zone between the classes: we come together here. . . . The glue that binds is a principle always understood if rarely stated: *No one who is sick is sent away.* No one is too dirty, too drugged, too drunken, or too different, none too poor nor too hopeless. . . . Bellevue is a city on a hill, an ideal that, though abused and insufficient in its reality, stands for the things a caring society might some day achieve.[7]

By continuously struggling to put this ideal into practice, the municipal hospitals have played an essential part in humanizing the life of New York City. As important as this contribution was in the nineteenth and twentieth centuries, it is likely to become even more important in the twenty-first.

Notes

Abbreviations used in the notes

B&AH	Bellevue & Allied Hospitals
BH	Bellevue Hospital
BHC	Bellevue Hospital Center
HHC	NYC Health & Hospitals Corporation
NYAM	New York Academy of Medicine
NYC	New York City
NYH	New York Hospital
NYS	New York State
NYU	New York University
UHF	United Hospital Fund

Collections Cited in the Notes

Barondess Commission Papers: Office of the President, NYAM

B&AH Annual Reports, Board of Trustees Correspondence, Minutes of Board of Trustees and Medical Executive Committee: BH Archives

BH Annual Reports: BH Archives

BH Nursing School Annual Reports, Board of Managers Minutes: BH Archives

Bellush Collection: Tamiment Collection, Robert F. Wagner Labor Archives, NYU Library

Citizens Union Papers: Manuscript Division, Butler Library, Columbia University

Columbia University Oral History Collection
Hospital Council of Greater New York, Annual Reports: NYAM Library
Hospital Council of Greater New York, Papers: Rare Books Collection, NYAM Library
Isaacs, Stanley, Papers: Manuscript Division, New York Public Library
NYAM Public Health Committee Papers: Rare Books Collection, NYAM
NYC Dept. of Hospitals Annual Reports: NYC Municipal Library
NYC HHC Annual Reports: NYC Municipal Library
NYC Mayors' Papers: NYC Municipal Archives
NYH Annual Reports, Minutes of Board of Governors and Medical Board: NYH
    Archives
NYH Secretary-Treasurer's Papers (NYH STP) and Secretary-Treasurer's Papers (NYH
    STP BTF): NYH Archives
NYU Chancellors' Papers: NYU Archives
Rockefeller Family and Rockefeller University Collections: Rockefeller Archives
Society of The NYH, Papers of the President: NYH Archives
Thompson, David D., Papers: NYH Archives
UHF Annual Reports and other UHF publications: UHF Library

Introduction

1. This point is explored in Dan E. Beauchamp, *The Health of the Republic: Epidemics, Medicine, and Moralism as Challenges to Democracy*. Philadelphia: Temple University Press, 1988.

2. *The Washington Post*/Kaiser Family Foundation/Harvard University Survey Project, *Why Don't Americans Trust the Government?* (Menlo Park, Calif.: Henry J. Kaiser Family Foundation, 1996), 5, 6.

3. See, for instance, Sheila B. Kamerman and Alfred J. Kahn, eds., *Privatization and the Welfare State* (Princeton: Princeton University Press, 1989); Florencio López-de-Silanes, Andrei Shleifer, and Robert W. Vishny, *Privatization in the United States*, Working Paper No. 5113 (Cambridge, Mass.: National Bureau of Economic Research, May 1995); Steve H. Hanke, ed., *Prospects for Privatization* (New York: Academy of Political Science, 1987); Martin Rein and Lee Rainwater, eds., *The Public-Private Interplay in Social Protection: A Comparative Study* (Armonk, N.Y.: M. E. Sharpe, 1986).

4. Cited in Charles E. Rosenberg, *The Care of Strangers: The Rise of America's Hospital System* (New York: Basic Books, 1987), 243.

5. Ray E. Brown, "The Hospital as an Obligated Enterprise,: *Trustee* 17 (Aug. 1964), 1.

6. Seth Low, "An American View of Municipal Government in the United States," in James Bryce, *The American Commonwealth* (New York: MacMillan, 1912), 451.

Chapter 1

1. *New York Times*, 22 April 1904.

2. NYH Annual Report 1909, 16.

3. The dispute for precedence between NYH and Bellevue essentially turns on when Bellevue's ancestor, the Almshouse infirmary is considered to have become a hospital. Although the infirmary opened inside the Almshouse in 1736, it was not formally given the title of Hospital until 1826.

4. Part of the Bellevue site had been leased by the city since 1794 for a fever hospital. In 1811, the city bought more land along the East River and began constructing

the new Almshouse. This structure, which opened in 1816, served as Bellevue's central building for more than a century; the last section was demolished in 1938.

5. The first building constructed to house the hospital burned down in 1775 before it could be occupied. The second, erected in 1776, was diverted to other uses during the Revolutionary War, serving for part of the time as American and, later, British barracks. The building's use as a hospital began in 1791.

6. Cited in Robert H. Bremner, *From the Depths: The Discovery of Poverty in the United States* (New York: NYU Press, 1972), 3.

7. *Nichols' Illustrated New York* (New York: W. Wellstood, 1847), 51.

8. Ibid., 50.

9. Cited in David Rosner, "Health Care for the 'Truly Needy': Nineteenth Century Origins of the Concept," *Milbank Memorial Fund Quarterly* 60 (1982), 376.

10. The hospital opened a new Private Patients' Building in 1900, but the average daily census during its early years rarely exceeded five or ten patients. NYH Annual Reports, 1900–1910.

11. Cited in David Ward, *Poverty, Ethnicity, and the American City, 1840–1925: Changing Conceptions of the Slum and the Ghetto* (Cambridge: Cambridge University Press, 1989), 46.

12. William H. Van Buren, "Address," in Society of the New York Hospital, *Report of the Building Committee* (New York: Society of The New York Hospital, 1877), 22. The best overviews of American hospital care during this period are provided in Charles E. Rosenberg, *The Care of Strangers: The Rise of America's Hospital System* (New York: Basic Books, 1987) and Morris Vogel, *The Invention of the Modern Hospital: Boston, 1870–1930* (Chicago: University of Chicago Press, 1980). For public hospitals, see Harry F. Dowling, *City Hospitals: The Undercare of the Underprivileged* (Cambridge: Harvard University Press, 1982).

13. UHF, *Medical Care for a Million People: A Report of Clinics in New York City and of The Six Years' Work of the Committee, 1920–1926* (New York: UHF Committee on Dispensary Development, 1927), 2.

14. E. H. Lewinski-Corwin, *The Hospital Situation in Greater New York: Report of a Survey of Hospitals in New York City by the Public Health Committee of the New York Academy of Medicine* (New York: Putnam, 1924), 20–23.

15. Hospital statistics for the period are inconsistent, and terms like "private hospital" and "general hospital" tend to be used differently by different authorities. For slightly different figures, see the State Charities Aid Association, *New Hospitals Needed in Greater New York* (New York: State Charities Aid Association, 1908), 43, which appears to include proprietary hospitals.

16. State Charities Aid Association, *New Hospitals Needed*, 56. See also NYC Commission on Hospitals, *Report of the New York City Commission on Hospitals* (New York: Martin B. Brown Press, 1909), 628.

17. See, for instance, Susan Reverby and David Rosner, "Beyond 'The Great Doctors'," in *Health Care in America: Essays in Social History*, ed. Susan Reverby and David Rosner (Philadelphia: Temple University Press, 1979), 3–16.

18. See, for instance, Paul Starr, *Social Transformation of American Medicine* (New York: Basic Books, 1982), 79–144.

19. Robert P. Hudson, "Abraham Flexner in Perspective: American Medical Education, 1865–1910," in *Sickness and Health in America: Readings in the History of Medicine and Public Health*, 2d ed., ed. Judith Walzer Leavitt and Ronald L. Numbers (Madison: University of Wisconsin Press, 1985), 148–158.

20. Rosenberg, *Care of Strangers*, 154–161.

21. Bellevue: NYC Dept. of Hospitals Annual Report 1929, 110; Brannan to Mayor George B. McClellan, B&AH Trustees' Letters, 15 August 1906. NYH: Joel D. Howell, *Technology in the Hospital: Transforming Patient Care in the Early Twentieth Century* (Baltimore: Johns Hopkins University Press, 1995), 113, 120.

22. Barr, Oral History, 39, Columbia Oral History Collection; Eric Larrabee, *The Benevolent and Necessary Institution: The New York Hospital, 1771–1991* (New York: Doubleday, 1971), 287.

23. George Stewart to Brannan (B&AH Trustees), 20 March 1902, B&AH Trustees Minutes; B&AH Annual Report 1910, 1; President, BH Medical Board to Out-Patient Dept. doctors, 2 February, 1911, B&AH Trustees' Letters; BH Casebooks, 1904–1909, Special Collections, Health Sciences Library, Columbia University.

24. Testimony to NYC Commission on Hospitals, *Report*, 519; NYH Annual Report 1905, 14.

25. "Hospital Life in New York," *Harper's New Monthly Magazine*, 57 (1878), 175.

26. Michael Gold, *Jews without Money* (New York: Avon, 1930), 15.

27. Miriam Cohen, *Workshop to Office: Two Generations of Italian Women in New York City, 1900–1950* (Ithaca: Cornell University Press, 1992), 66–68. Deborah Dwork, "Health Conditions of Immigrant Jews on the Lower East Side of New York: 1880–1914," *Medical History 25* (1981), 1–40.

28. Clifton Hood, *722 Miles: The Building of the Subways and How They Transformed New York* (New York: Simon & Schuster, 1993), 84–90.

29. "Hospital Life in New York," 178–179.

30. *New York Times*, 1 February 1901.

31. Cited in Henry C. Wright, "Proper Distribution of Duties among the Departments of Health, Public Charities and Bellevue and Allied Hospitals," *Proceedings of the New York State Conference of Charities and Corrections* (1914), 155. The plan had already been discussed by the Charter Revision Commission (*New York Times*, 30 December 1900), but the revelations about Bellevue helped to ensure its adoption.

32. Brannan's account, cited in Wright, "Proper Distribution of Duties," 152.

33. Mayor Seth Low to B&AH Trustees, [January 1902], Dept. of Public Charities Folder, Box 38, LS-5, NYC Mayors' Papers.

34. Brannan to Peter Scully, 7 October 1904, to Bronx Borough President, 30 June 1905, to Chair, Finance Committee, 7 October 1905. All in B&AH Trustees Letters. Brannan to Mayor George McClellan, 4 January 1909, Item 8, MGB-56, NYC Mayors' Papers. Brannan testimony to NYC Commission on Hospitals, *Report*, 58.

35. Emily [Dunning] Barringer, *Bowery to Bellevue: The Story of New York's First Woman Ambulance Surgeon* (New York: Norton, 1950), 143–144.

36. Leland M. Roth, *McKim, Mead & White, Architects* (New York: Harper & Row, 1983), 294–295.

37. Cited in Larrabee, *Benevolent and Necessary Institution*, 300.

38. NYH Board of Governors Minutes, 31 January 1910.

39. Rev. J. F. Richmond, *New York and Its Institutions, 1609–1871* (New York: E. B. Treat, 1871), 373.

40. NYH Special Committee to NYH Board of Governors, 24 February 1909, Folder 8, Box 42, NYH STP; Henry W. Crane, "History of the New York Hospital," 5 (1920), 672c.

41. George Ludlam to George Rives, 21 June 1909 and 22 June 1909, Folder 8, Box 42, NYH STP.

42. Mrs. Helen Campbell, *Darkness and Daylight, or Lights and Shadows of New York Life* (Hartford Publishing Company, 1897), 280.

43. Barringer, *Bowery to Bellevue*, 144.

44. B&AH Trustees Minutes, 23 April 1907; Kenneth Ludmerer, *Learning to Heal: The Development of American Medical Education* (New York: Basic Books, 1985), 159.

45. BH Case-Books, 1st Division, 1907–1909, lobar pneumonia, Special Collections. "New Management for Bellevue and Allied Hospitals," *Charities* 8 (8 February 1902), 139. C. Irving Fisher, "The Need of an Intermediate Single Room Service in Hospitals," *Transactions of the American Hospital Association*, 12th Annual Conference, 1910 (Toronto: AHA, 1911), 170.

46. State Charities Aid Association, *New Hospitals Needed*, 43; David Rosner, *A Once Charitable Enterprise: Hospitals and Health Care in Brooklyn and New York, 1885–1915* (Cambridge: Cambridge University Press, 1982), 62–81.

47. Campbell, *Darkness and Daylight*, 294. *New York Times*, 8 June 1906, 8 June 1906. Supervising Nurse's Memorandum, Harlem Hospital, 5 September 1905, B&AH Trustees Letters.

48. Larrabee, *Benevolent and Necessary Institution*, 301. Rosemary Stevens, *In Sickness and in Wealth: American Hospitals in the Twentieth Century* (New York: Basic Books, 1989), 72.

49. See, for instance: Starr, *Social Transformation of American Medicine*, 154–177.

50. Brannan to Marcus Stine, 7 June 1905, B&AH Trustees Letters.

51. Cited in Stevens, *In Sickness and In Wealth*, 65. Petition from NYH house staff to Board of Governors, 25 December 1904, Folder 4, Box 36, NYH STP; "Bellevue Doctor Snared by Cupid" [undated newspaper clipping, author's files].

52. Cited in Susan Reverby, *Ordered to Care: The Dilemma of American Nursing, 1850–1945* (Cambridge: Cambridge University Press, 1987), 22.

53. Reverby, *Ordered to Care*, 63–65; Rosenberg, *Care of Strangers, 219–220*.

54. Barbara Melosh, *The Physician's Hand: World, Culture and Conflict in American Nursing* (Philadelphia: Temple University Press, 1982), 66. Jane E. Mottus, *New York Nightingales: The Emergence of the Nursing Profession at Bellevue and New York Hospital, 1850–1920* (Ann Arbor, Mich.: UMI Research Press, 1981), 79, 89.

55. George Ludlam, "The Organization and Control of Training Schools," *New York Medical Journal 83* (28 April 1906), 850.

56. William H. Smith, Report to B&AH Board, 7 December 1909, B&AH Trustees Minutes, 305, BH Archives.

57. *New York Times*, 17 December 1909; Minutes of 1909–1910 for: Bellevue Training School Board of Managers, BH Medical Board, and B&AH Trustees; B&AH Folder, GWJ-2, NYC Mayors' Papers. Mills School reopened in the 1920s and remained open until the 1970s, except for a hiatus during World War II.

58. Barringer, *Bowery to Bellevue*, 144, Barr, Oral History, 35; President, Ambulance Drivers, to Mayor George McClellan, 1 February 1904, Item 7, MGB-3, NYC Mayors' Papers.

59. NYH employees' petition to NYH Visiting Committee, 16 January 1903, Folder 4, Box 35, and L. Heptonstall to George Ludlam, 29 December 1905, Folder 5, Box 37. Both in NYH STP.

60. George O'Hanlon to John O'Keeffe, 3 June 1910, B&AH Folder, Item 9, GWJ-2, NYC Mayors' Papers.

61. NYH Board of Governors, Special Committee on Finance and Retrenchment, 6 January 1903, Folder 5, Box 35, NYH STP. Regarding salary comparisons, see author's database on salaries at BH and NYH.

62. J. L. Tindale to NYH Board of Governors, 5 October 1907, Folder 7, Box 39, NYH STP.

Chapter 2

1. See, for instance, Charles E. Rosenberg, *The Care of Strangers: The Rise of America's Hospital System* (New York: Basic Books, 1987), 159–161; Paul Starr, *The Social Transformation of American Medicine* (New York: Basic Books, 1982), 134–140.

2. J. W. Pugh, "Some Impressions of American Hospitals," *University College Hospital Magazine*, 14 February 1929), 22; NYH Annual Report 1926, 41. For general discussion of this topic, see Rosemary Stevens, *American Medicine and the Public Interest* (New Haven: Yale University Press, 1971), 34–174.

3. Connie Guion, Oral History, 42, 76, Columbia University Oral History Collection.

4. B&AH Annual Report 1910, 26.

5. B&AH Annual Report 1928, 34. *New York Times*, 3 October 1924; 7 October 1924; 27 April 1925; 20 February 1926.

6. NYH Annual Report 1914, 23. *New York Times*, 13 March 1924.

7. Stevens, *In Sickness and in Wealth*, 111. For trends in New York, see *New York Times*, 1 January 1928, sec. II.

8. Stevens, *In Sickness and in Wealth*, 113.

9. UHF, *Medical Care for a Million People: A Report on Clinics in New York City* (New York: UHF Committee on Dispensary Development, 1927), 3. Odin Anderson and Norman Gevitz, "The General Hospital: A Social and Historical Perspective," in *Handbook of Health, Health Care and the Health Professions*, ed. David Mechanic (New York: Free Press, 1983), 26.

10. Guion, Oral History, 177. Clarence de la Chapelle, Oral History, 83, Columbia University Oral History Collection. *New York Tribune*, 27 February 1920.

11. NYH Annual Report 1922, 37. De la Chapelle, Oral History, 105.

12. Cited in Stevens, *In Sickness and in Wealth*, 49.

13. Case 59, July 1927–January 1928, Valvular Heart Disease, 1st Division, NYH Case-Records, NYH Archives. A picture of the statuette appears in Albert W. Snoke, *Hospitals, Health, and People* (New Haven: Yale University Press, 1987), xii.

14. NYH Annual Report 1921, 66.

15. UHF, *Medical Care for One Million People* 65. NYH Annual Report 1929, 34, 39.

16. BH: B&AH Annual Report 1910 and *New York Times*, 15 February 1929; NYH: NYH Annual Reports 1910 and 1929.

17. *New York Times*, 29 January 1912. See also NYC Board of Estimate, *Report of the Committee of Inquiry*, 49.

18. *New York Times*, 20 March 1922.

19. Inflation data based on "Consumer Price Indexes (BLS)," *Statistical History of the United States* (New York: Basic Books), 211.

20. Includes all hospital staff except physicians. B&AH Annual Report 1922, and E.H. Lewinski-Corwin, *The Hospital Situation in Greater New York: Report of a Survey of Hospitals in New York City by the Public Health Committee of the New York Academy of Medicine* (New York: Putnam, 1924), 132.

21. Henry Bruere, "Administrative Reorganization and Constructive Work in the Government of the City of New York: 1914." (NYC Chamberlain's Office, May 1915).

22. Citizens Union, "Hylan and the City Employees" (1921). Folder: Hylan, Memoranda, Box A-20, Citizens Union Papers. John W. Brannan to Grover Whalen, 6 June 1918, Folder 1, Box 6, Hylan Correspondence, NYC Mayors' Papers. *Brooklyn Eagle*, 23 June 1924. Hylan reappointed only two former members—both Irish Catholics in their seventies. Both died soon after taking office and were replaced by Hylan loyalists.

23. George David Stewart, M.D., to Mayor Walker, 18 July 1927, File: B&AH, Box

354, Walker Correspondence, NYC Mayors' Papers. S.S. Goldwater, *On Hospitals* (New York: Macmillan, 1947), 6.

24. Lewinsky-Corwin, *Hospital Situation in Greater New York*, 65.

25. Mount Sinai Annual Report 1910, 21.

26. NYH Annual Report 1924, 32.

27. David Rosner, *A Once Charitable Enterprise: Hospitals and Health Care in Brooklyn and New York, 1885–1915*. Cambridge: Cambridge University Press, 1982, 36–93. *New York Times*, 11 January 1920, sec. II; 14 November 1923.

28. NYH Annual Report 1921, 29. NYAM Public Health Committee, Dispensary Subcommittee Minutes, 24 August 1918, File: Dispensaries–Letters, NYAM Public Health Committee Papers.

29. NYH Board of Governors Minutes, 2 September 1919.

30. *New York Times*, 19 October 1919.

31. Joel Howell, "Machines and Medicine: Technology Transforms the American Hospital," in *The American General Hospital: Communities and Social Contexts*, ed. Diana Elizabeth Long and Janet Golden (Ithaca: Cornell University Press, 1989), 131. William Elser to George Rives, 24 June 1910, Folder 2, Box 44, NYH STP.

32. NYC Board of Estimate, *Report of the Committee on Inquiry*, 43; *New York Times*, 28 March 1914. Thomas Howell to NYH Executive Committee, 11 February 1919, Folder 6, Box 50, NYH STP. Brannan to Mayor John Purroy Mitchel, 6 February 1917, Folder: B&AH, Item 8, MJP–79, NYC Mayors' Papers.

33. Cited in Kenneth Ludmerer, *Learning to Heal: The Development of American Medical Education* (New York: Basic Books, Inc., Publishers, 1985), 159.

34. David Barr, Oral History, 28, Columbia University Oral History Collection. The First Division was assigned to Columbia. Until 1898, University Medical College and Bellevue Hospital Medical College each had one division at Bellevue. When they combined, the new University & Bellevue Hospital Medical College (which was renamed the NYU College of Medicine in 1935) took the Third Division, and the recently established Cornell Medical College took the Second.

35. B&AH Annual Reports, 1913–1916; Frank Berry, Oral History, Columbia University Oral History Collection, 34; Ludmerer, *Learning to Heal*, 225.

36. De la Chapelle, Oral History, 111–112. The patient's name is not recorded.

37. Presbyterian Hospital Annual Report 1911, 15.

38. NYH Board of Governors Minutes, 6 November 1912; *New York Times*, 15 November 1912.

39. Albert R. Lamb, *The Presbyterian Hospital and the Columbia–Presbyterian Medical Center, 1868–1943: A History of a Great Medical Adventure* (New York: Columbia University Press, 1955), 92; Place [first name not recorded] to Howard Townsend, 15 June 1917, Folder 2, Box 49, NYH STP. NYH Board of Governors Minutes, 14 June 1927, includes full text of the agreement.

40. NYH Annual Report 1927, 21. G. Canby Robinson, *Adventures in Medical Education: A Personal Narrative of the Great Advance of American Medicine* (Cambridge: Harvard University Press, 1957), 189. NYH Annual Reports. Eric Larrabee, *The Benevolent and Necessary Institution: The New York Hospital, 1771–1991* (New York: Doubleday, 1971), 311, says that all together, Whitney gave the hospital a total of $45 million, but I have been unable to confirm this higher figure.

41. Guion, Oral History, 206.

42. G. Canby Robinson, "An Account of My Experience as Director of New York Hospital–Cornell Medical College Association," 16 July 1934, Folder 5, Box 9, NYH STP (BTF).

43. Includes funds for land, buildings, and endowments. *New York Times*, 18 June 1929 and 16 August 1929.

44. See, for instance, Morris Vogel, *The Invention of the Modern Hospital: Boston, 1870–1930* (Chicago: University of Chicago Press, 1980), 113–116, 120; Rosenberg, *Care of Strangers*, 190–211; Stevens, *In Sickness and in Wealth*, 105–114.

45. *New York Times*, 18 April 1926.

46. Robert W. Hebberd, "The Hospital Situation in New York City," in *Proceedings of the New York State Conference on Charities and Corrections* (1912), 133; NYC Dept. of Hospitals, "The Department of Hospitals" [no date but context indicates Fall 1932], 32, Hospital History File, NYC Municipal Archives.

47. B&AH Board Secretary to Secretary, BH Medical Board, 10 April 1915, B&AH Trustees Letters.

48. John Starr, *Hospital City: The Story of the Men and Women of Bellevue* (New York: Crown, 1957), 203.

49. Alfred W. Crosby, *America's Forgotten Pandemic: The Influenza of 1918* (Cambridge: Cambridge University Press, 1976), 60–61. Guion, Oral History, 96, 101; Starr, *Hospital City*, 215; B&AH Annuals, 1918 and 1919, passim; Bellevue Training School for Nurses, Annual Reports, 1918 and 1919, passim; Salvatore Cutolo with Arthur and Barbara Gelb, *Bellevue Is My Home* (Garden City: Doubleday, 1956), 85; John O'Keeffe to Mayor John F. Hylan, 30 November 1918, Folder 1, Box 6, Hylan Correspondence, NYC Mayors' Papers.

50. B&AH Annual 1918, 41. Bellevue Training School, Annual Report, 1919, 19.

51. *New York Times*, 26 February 1923.

52. *New York Times*, 9 December 1923, sec. I. Stevens, *American Medicine and the Public Interest*, 116. Guion, Oral History, 173.

53. Emily [Dunning] Barringer, *Bowery to Bellevue: The Story of New York's First Woman Ambulance Surgeon* (New York: W.W. Norton & Company, Inc., 1950), 88. *New York Times*, 30 June 1903. A woman served briefly as resident physician at Mount Sinai in 1884, but this predated the development of the formal internship system. Regina Morantz-Sanchez, *Sympathy and Science: Women Physicians in American Medicine* (New York: Oxford University Press, 1985), 165.

54. Starr, *Hospital City*, 194; B&AH Annual 1914, 31.

55. Edith Lincoln, biographical file, BH Archives; Guion, Oral History, 99; Eunice Trowbridge and April Radbill, *Dr. Josephine Evarts: A Tribute* (Privately printed, 1981), 32.

56. W. Gilman Thompson to Samuel Sachs, 10 March 1915, Folder: Roscoe Conkling Giles, BH Archives.

57. John O'Keeffe to Mayor John F. Hylan, 18 July 1918, Folder 1, Box 6, Hylan Correspondence, NYC Mayors' Papers; *New York Times*, 2 January 1919. BH Medical Executive Committee to Chair, Bellevue House-Staff Committee, 19 December 1921, B&AH Trustees Letters 1911–1931, v. 5. Gilbert Osofsky, *Harlem: The Making of a Ghetto: Negro New York, 1890–1930*, 2d ed. (New York: Harper & Row, 1971), 170.

58. *New York Times*, 2 July 1927. Adah B. Thoms, *Pathfindfers: A History of the Progress of Colored Graduate Nurses* (New York: Garland, 1985), 238; Mabel Keaton Staupers, *No Time for Prejudice:A Story of the Integration of Negroes in Nursing in the United States* (New York: Macmillan, 1961), 69.

59. Lewinski-Corwin, *Hospital Situation in Greater New York*, 64. Morantz-Sanchez, *Sympathy and Science*, 297. Judith Barrett Litoff, *The American Midwife Debate: A Sourcebook on its Modern Origins* (New York: Greenwood Press, 1986), 134.

60. B&AH Annual Report, 1912, 31; B&AH Trustees Minutes, 4 October, 1921. Morantz-Sanchez, *Sympathy and Science*, 297.

61. George O'Hanlon memorandum, 16 September 1918, Folder 1, Box 6, Hylan Correspondence, NYC Mayors' Papers.

Chapter 3

1. Mayor LaGuardia, press release, 14 March 1938, Folder: Dept. of Hospitals, Box 3209, LaGuardia Correspondence, NYC Mayors' Papers.

2. Bayrd Still, *Mirror for Gotham* (New York: New York University Press, 1956), 317. Robert P. Ingalls, *Herbert H. Lehman and New York's Little New Deal* (New York: New York University Press, 1975), 31. David A. Shannon, *The Great Depression* (Englewood Cliffs: Prentice-Hall, 1960), 10. William W. Bremer, *Depression Winters: New York Social Workers and the New Deal* (Philadelphia: Temple University Press, 1984), 66. Mauritz A. Hallgren, *Seeds of Revolt: A Study of American Life and the Temper of the American People during the Depression* (New York: Alfred A. Knopf, 1933), 113, 191. Roy Rosenzweig and Elizabeth Blackmar, *The Park and the People: A History of Central Park* (Ithaca: Cornell University Press, 1992), 435.

3. John F. Bauman and Thomas H. Coode, *In the Eye of the Great Depression: New Deal Reporters and the Agony of the American People* (DeKalb: Northern Illinois University Press, 1988), 39. Richard Lowitt and Maurine Beasley, eds., *One-Third of a Nation: Lorena Hickok Reports on the Great Depression* (Urbana: University of Illinois Press, 1981), 44.

4. Ingalls, *Herbert H. Lehman*, 38. Anthony J. Badger, *The New Deal: The Depression Years, 1933–1940* (London: Macmillan, 1989), 209.

5. George Baehr, Oral History, 28, Columbia University Oral History Collection.

6. Robert S. McIlvaine, *Down and Out in the Great Depression: Letters from the "Forgotten Man"* (Chapel Hill: University of North Carolina Press, 1983), 151. *New York Times*, 7 March 1941.

7. Hallgren, *Seeds of Revolt*, 4. Milton Jonathan Slocum, *Manhattan Country Doctor* (New York: Ballantine, 1986), 46.

8. Joseph Hirsh and Beka Doherty, *The First Hundred Years of the Mount Sinai Hospital of New York, 1852–1892* (New York: Random House, 1952), 230. Gwendolyn Berry, *Idleness and the Health of a Neighborhood: A Social Study of the Mulberry District* (New York: New York Association for the Improvement of the Condition of the Poor, 1933), 36.

9. Lowitt and Beasley, *One-Third of a Nation*, 141. Haven Emerson. *The Hospital Survey for New York*, 1 (New York: UHF, 1937), 14, 247. Rosemary Stevens, *In Sickness and in Wealth: American Hospitals in the Twentieth Century* (New York: Basic Books, 1989), 147.

10. David McAlpin Pyle, "The Critical Situation of the Hospitals in New York City: A Confidential Statement to the Trustees of the Voluntary Hospitals of New York City" (UHF, June 1935), 3. Ryllis Alexander Goslin and Omar Pancoast Goslin, *You and Your Hospitals: A Digest of the Hospital Survey for New York* (New York: UHF, 1938), 14.

11. E.H.L. Corwin, *The American Hospital* (New York: The Commonwealth Fund, 1946), 194. Stevens, *In Sickness and in Wealth*, 145.

12. G. Canby Robinson, *Adventures in Medical Education: A Personal Narrative of the Great Advance of American Medicine* (Cambridge: Harvard University Press, 1957), 220. NYH Annual Report 1932, 4. Henry E. Sigerist, *American Medicine* (New York: Norton, Inc., 1934), 142.

13. NYH Annual Report 1937, 23. Free patients averaged about 8 percent of the ward census, 5 percent of the entire hospital census. NYH Annuals 1937–1939.

14. See, for instance, *The New York Hospital: A City of Healing—A Report on Progress by the Society of The New York Hospital* (New York: Society of The New York Hospital, 1935) and *So Near the Gods* (New York: Society of The New York Hospital, 1938). Helen Worden, *Society Circus* (New York: Covici Friede, 1936), 33, 110.

15. Society of The New York Hospital, *So Near the Gods*, Preface.

16. S. S. Goldwater to Mayor LaGuardia, 3 May 1940, Folder: Dept. of Hospitals, Box 3272, LaGuardia Correspondence, NYC Mayors' Papers.

17. Mary Ross, "Crisis in the Hospitals," *Survey Graphic* 22 (July 1933), 364. New York *Evening Post*, 8 February 1937.

18. "The Grateful Patient Speaks," *Chicago Jewish Daily* (Feb. 1941) [translated from the Yiddish].

19. Hurlbert Footner, *New York: City of Cities* (Philadelphia: Lippincott, 1937), 247. Jack Lewis, "Inside Stories of Bellevue Hospital," Radio Broadcast, Station WNYC, 7:55–8:15 P.M., 19 July 1932, Folder: Dept. of Hospitals, Box 375, Walker Correspondence, NYC Mayors' Papers. David Margolis, interview.

20. Director, Dept. of Hospitals' Bureau of Investigation, to Epstein [first name not listed], Mayor LaGuardia's office, 15 January 1940, Folder: Mayor's Office: Epstein, Dept. of Hospitals, Box 3255, LaGuardia Correspondence, NYC Mayors' Papers. NYC Dept. of Hospitals Annual Reports. BH Medical Board Executive Minutes, 22 October 1930.

21. "List of Higher Salaried Positions as Reduced" [no date, but context indicates 1938], Folder II (4), Box 9, Earle Papers; NYH Board of Governors Minutes, 1 October 1935. S.S. Goldwater to Charles G. Hill, 29 March 1939. Box 3251, Folder: Dept. of Hospitals, NYC Mayors' Papers. The Society of the NYH also maintained a psychiatric facility in Westchester County, but the NYH Administrator had relatively few responsibilities for this institution.

22. In 1931, there were 1.76 staff per patient in UHF hospitals, compared to 0.80 per patient in the municipal institutions; NYC Dept. of Hospitals memorandum: "The Dept. of Hospitals" [undated, but context indicates Fall 1932], 3, Hospital History File, Municipal Archives. BH Annual Report 1936, 57. New York *Evening Journal*, 8 February 1937. NYC Dept. of Hospitals Annual Report 1940, 29.

23. *New York Times*, 18 April 1940.

24. UHF Annual Reports.

25. Still, *Mirror for Gotham*, 326. Harry Woodburn Chase to Currier McEwen, 28 June 1944, File 12, Box 50, RG 3.0.5, Chase Papers II, NYU Chancellors' Papers.

26. Still, *Mirror for Gotham*, 326. Lingeman, *Don't You Know There's a War on?* 29, 46.

27. *New York Times*, 9 April 1942, 15 November 1942. Clarence de la Chapelle, Oral History, 245, Columbia University Oral History Collection. Mayor LaGuardia to Medical Director, New Jersey State Hospital, 27 August 1942, Folder: Dept. of Hospitals, Box 3332, LaGuardia Correspondence, NYC Mayors' Papers.

28. *New York Times*, 15 May 1943. BH Annual Reports. NYH Annual Report 1944, 22.

29. UHF Annual Report 1941, 9.

30. *New York Times*, 21 June 1942.

31. NYC Dept. of Hospitals, "Negro Employees–Division of Nursing, Dept. of Hospitals," 11 December 1942, File: Negroes, Admissions of Nurses to Training Schools; Box 8, Stanley Isaacs Papers.

32. Mabel Keaton Staupers, *No Time for Prejudice: A Story of the Integration of Negroes in Nursing in the United States* (New York: Macmillan, 1961), 61–76; *New York Times*, 3 January 1945.

33. *New York Times*, 6 October 1943, 10 October 1943, 19 November 1947. *Bellevue Bulletin*, 1945.

34. Langdon Marvin, "New York Hospital, 1942–5, Some Developments," Folder 12, Box 9, NYH STP (BTF).

35. *New York Times*, 25 October 1941.

36. Commissioner Bernecker to Mayor O'Dwyer, 12 November 1947. See also *New York Times*, 28 October 1947.

37. *New York Times*, 6 January 1947. Alan Gregg, "Memorandum of Interviews, December 20 and December 21, 1937," File 45, Box 4, Series 235A, RG 1.1, Rockefeller Family Collection.

38. Rosenzweig and Blackmar, *Park and the People*, 458.

39. NYC Dept. of Hospitals, "Hospital Care Data for the Year 1950," File 1, Box 17, Impelliterri Correspondence, NYC Mayors' Papers; *New York Times*, 11 February 1950; NYH Annual Report 1950.

40. Clifton Hood, "Subways, Transit Politics, and Metropolitan Spatial Expansion," in *The Landscape of Modernity: Essays on New York City, 1900–1940*, ed. David Ward and Oliver Zunz (New York: Russell Sage Foundation, 1992), 191. *New York Times*, 7 November 1947, 14 March 1948, 28 April 1949.

41. William Harding Jackson, "The Society of New York Hospital: Its History, Its Purpose and Its Program for Public Service," *Hospitals* (August 1940), 47–48. NYH Annual Report 1947, 5.

42. UHF Annual Report 1948, 5.

43. C. Irving Fisher, "The Need of an Intermediate Single Room Service in Hospitals," *Transactions of the American Hospital Association*, 12th Annual Conference, 1910 (Toronto: AHA, 1911), 170. *New York Times*, 24 March 1926, 11 January 1920.

44. See, for instance, Ronald L. Numbers, "The Third Party: Health Insurance in America," in *Sickness and Health in America: Readings in the History of Medicine and Public Health*, 2d ed., ed. Judith Walzer and Ronald L. Numbers (Madison: University of Wisconsin Press, 1985), 233.

45. UHF Annual Reports 1933, 1934, and 1935 describe the establishment of AHS.

46. David J. Rothman, "The Public Presentation of Blue Cross, 1935–65," *Journal of Health Politics, Policy and Law*, 16 (Winter 1991), 678.

47. UHF Annual Report 1940. Blue Cross was an association of autonomous plans throughout the country.

48. UHF Annual Report 1935, 6. NYH Annual Report 1934, 19. Emerson, *Hospital Survey*, 224.

49. See, for instance, Numbers, "Third Party" 233–238; Stevens, *In Sickness and in Wealth*, 198–199.

50. Rothman, "Public Presentation of Blue Cross," 680; Gerald Markowitz and Davis Rosner, "Seeking Common Ground: A History of Labor and Blue Cross," *Journal of Health Politics, Policy and Law* 16 (December 1991), 704, 707.

51. *New York Times*, 2 March 1946.

52. Robert Cunningham, *Hospitals, Doctors and Dollars* (New York: F.W. Dodge Corporation, 1946, 1961), 44.

53. John Gambs, "Hospitals and the Unions," *Survey Graphic* 26 (August 1937), 435–438.

54. Stevens, *In Sickness and in Wealth,* 179.

55. *Brooklyn Jewish Hospital v. John Doe*, 300 NYS 1112, 1114.

56. *New York Evening Journal*, 31 January 1937 to 8 February 1937. Laguardia announcement, 4 February 1937, Folder: Dept. of Hospitals, Box 3189, Laguardia Correspondence, NYC Mayors' Papers; NYC Dept. of Hospitals General Orders, 1 July 1937; NYC Dept. of Hospitals Annual Report 1938, 17.

57. *22 Years, Local 240, Hospital Division of District Council 37* (New York: American Federation of State, County, and Municipal Employees, 1976) [pages unnumbered].

58. *New York Times*, 19 September 1943.

59. Mark H. Maier, *City Unions: Managing Discontent in New York City* (New Brunswick, N.J.: Rutgers University Press, 1987), 57.

60. Ibid., 11. *New York Times*, 25 April 1946, 25 December 1946.

61. *New York Times*, 27 October 1945, 21 November 1945; New York *Sun*, 19 November 1945; New York *Post*, 19 November 1945.

62. *Society of The New York Hospital v. Hanson et al.*, 185 Misc. 936, 937. (The defendant in the case was Charles Hanson, chair of the BCTC Maintenance Organization.) *New York Times*, 20 December 1945, 23 December 1945.

63. *New York Times*, 26 September 1940.

Chapter 4

1. They shared the prize with a German scientist, Werner Forsstman, who had done earlier work in the same field.

2. Philip Brickner, interview, expanded with information about typical rounds procedure.

3. E. B. White, *Here is New York* (New York: Harper & Brothers, 1949), 22.

4. Theodore White, *In Search of History: A Personal Adventure* (New York: Harper & Row, 1978), 370.

5. White, *Here is New York*, 19, 21.

6. For a fuller discussion of this question, see Kenneth Jackson, *The Crabgrass Frontier: The Suburbanization of the United States* (New York: Oxford University Press, 1985), 231–245.

7. Ira Rosenwaike, *Population History of New York City* (Syracuse: Syracuse University Press, 1972), 141.

8. Dan Wakefield, *New York in the Fifties* (Boston: Houghton Mifflin, 1992), 98.

9. William A. Nolen, "Bellevue: No One Was Ever Turned Away." *American Heritage* 38 (February 1987), 36–43.

10. Robert Boris, Philip Brickner, interviews.

11. BH Annual Reports 1934, 1963; Salvatore R. Cutolo, with Arthur Gelb and Barbara Gelb, *Bellevue Is My Home* (Garden City, N.Y.: Doubleday, 1956), 130; Nancy Dallett, "NYU/Bellevue Pediatric Department, Oral History Project: Interim Report" (24 September 1991), 2, BH Archives; Marjorie Lewisohn, interview.

12. White, *Here Is New York*, 39. Marcus Kogel to Deputy Mayor, Monthly Reports, 1951, Folder 2, Box 5, Impelliterri Correspondence, NYC Mayors' Papers; New York *Post*, 24 January 1967.

13. Rebecca Morris, "Bellevue Circus" [unlabeled newspaper clipping in BH Archives].

14. Ibid.

15. Boris, Interview. Nolen, "Bellevue," 40.

16. Cutolo, *Bellevue Is My Home*, 30.

17. *Bellevuer* (March 1966).

18. Hospital Council of Greater New York Annual Report 1959, 22; NYH Annual Report, 48.

19. Callman [first name unlisted] to Dr. John Pastore, 26 June 1945; NYH Executive Committee Minutes, 19 March 1946. Both in Folder 8, Box 1, NYH STP (BTF).

20. *New York Hospital: City of Healing–A Report on Progress by the Society of The New York Hospital* (New York: Society of The New York Hospital, 1935), 17.

21. NYH Annual Report 1952, 39.

22. Jeremiah Barondess, interview.

23. Claire Meyerowitz, Madeline Sugimoto, George Reader, interviews.

24. NYH Annual Report 1951, 8.

25. Martin Begun, interview.

26. Dallett, "NYU/Bellevue Pediatric Department."

27. NYH Board of Governors, Committee on Financial Problems, Report, 5 June 1950, Folder 4, Box 15, NYH STP (BTF).

28. Claude Edwin Heaton and Alan E. Dumont, *The First 125 Years of the New York University School of Medicine, 1841–1966* (NYU School of Medicine, 1966), 34.

29. Harry Woodburn Chase to Percy S. Straus, 21 July 1937, Folder 3, Box 51, RG 3.0.5, Chase Papers 2, NYU Chancellors' Papers.

30. Ray Trussell, "The Municipal Hospital System in Transition." *Bulletin of the NYAM* 2d ser., 38, no. 4 (April 1962): 221–236.

31. Women's City Club of New York, "A Summary of the Report on the NYC Dept. of Hospitals by Booz, Allen & Hamilton, made to the Mayor's Committee on Management Survey," 13 November 1952, Folder: Dept. of Hospitals, Box 17, Impellitteri Correspondence, NYC Mayors' Papers. UHF City Hospital Visiting Committee, *State of the Municipal Hospitals 1966*, 53.

32. Louise Lander, Constance Bloomfield, and Jonathan Morley, "Bellevue Hospital: Growing Up Absurd," *Health-PAC Bulletin* (15 November 1973), 4. Commission on the Delivery of Personal Health Services [Piel Commission], *Community Health Services for New York City* (New York: Praeger, 1969), 211–213.

33. Lewis Thomas, "Public Hospitals Face Life–Death Issues in Changing Times," *Modern Hospital* 109 (October 1976), 95, and Statement presented at meeting of NYU administrative officers with Mayor John Lindsay and his Cabinet, 27 October 1967, Folder 3, Box 60, NYU Chancellors' Papers.

34. "Health Care for the Bellevue Communities: A Policy Proposal," 24, File: same name, BH Archives.

35. BH Medical Board Executive Committee Minutes, 13 March 1968.

36. *Bellevuer*, October 1966.

37. Robert Boris, interview; Commission on the Delivery, *Community Health Services*, 118.

38. Robert Caro, *The Power-Broker: Robert Moses and the Fall of New York* (New York: Vintage, 1975), 793, 795; Mayor Impellitteri to Winthrop Rockefeller, 24 February 1953, Folder 1010, Box 91, Impellitteri Correspondence, NYC Mayors' Papers; Richard Plunz, *A History of Housing in New York City: Dwelling Type and Social Change in the American Metropolis* (New York: Columbia University Press, 1990), 288; NYC Planning Commission, *Plan for New York City 1969*, 87; Edwin Salmon, "Report on Planning and Building Center," 12 November 1962, Folder 3, Box 10, Office of the President I (1951–65), NYU Archives; Bellevue South Advisory Council, "Bellevue South" [no date, but context indicates 1961], Folder: Bellevue South Urban Renewal Program, BH Archives.

39. Edwin Salmon to Robert Moses, 5 December 1952; Salmon to Winthrop Rocke-

feller, 10 November 1952. Both in Folder 007.b1.30, Office of the Planning Consultant Files, NYU Medical Center Archives. Bellevue South Advisory Council. "Bellevue South"; NYC Planning Commission, *Plan for New York City 1969*, 87.

40. Herman Glaser to Robert Moses, 8 September 1959; Robert Moses to Mrs. John J. McCloy, 10 September 1959. Both in Folder: Bellevue South Urban Renewal Program, BH Archives.

41. Bellevue South Advisory Council, "Bellevue South"; Plunz, *History of Housing in New York City*, 289; New York *Herald–Tribune*, 27 May 1964; New York *Herald–Tribune*, *New York City in Crisis*, (New York: McKay, 1965), 109.

42. NYC Planning Commission, *Plan for New York City 1969*, 87, 93. Kips Bay displaced 1,400 families and an unrecorded number of businesses. Bellevue South displaced 2,100 families and 300 businesses. Estimating each household and business conservatively as involving 2.5 people, the total dislocated was 9,500.

43. Mayor O'Dwyer press release, 14 January 1949, Folder: 1273, Box 122, O'Dwyer Correspondence, NYC Mayors' Papers.

44. Robert Boris, interview.

45. Paul B. Gillen, *A Social Survey of Health and Idleness in Urban Families: A Pilot Study* (Kips Bay–Yorkville District Health Committee and Cornell University Medical College, Dept. of Public Health and Preventive Medicine, June 1945).

46. George Reader, interview; White, *In Search of History*, 371.

47. NYH Board of Governors Minutes, 10 November 1970.

48. Laurence Payson to Felt et al., 20 December 1950, Folder: Neighborhood Development, RG 210.3, Business Manager, Rockefeller University Collection.

49. E. J. Kahn, Jr., *Jock: The Life and Times of John Hay Whitney* (Garden City, N.Y.: Doubleday, 1981), 176.

50. Jane Jacobs, *Death and Life of Great American Cities* (New York: Vintage, 1963), 14, 29–54, 143–240.

51. Ibid., 257–269.

52. Henry Pratt to Maurice Iserman, 16 December 1958, Folder 6, Box 15, NYH Secretary-Treasurer's Papers (NYH STP), BTF.

53. Dan Wakefield, "Victims of Charity," *Nation* 188 (14 March 1959), 228.

54. Pratt to all supervisors, 26 February 1959, Folder 6, Box 15, NYH STP BTF.

55. *New York Times*, 26 March 1959; Pratt to NYC Police Commissioner, 27 March 1959, Folder 6, Box 15, NYH STP BTF; Pratt to Iserman, 2 December 1959, 9 December 1959, Folder: Unions, Box 1, NYH Personnel.

56. Pratt to Iserman, 2 December 1959, Folder: Unions, Box 1, NYH Personnel.

57. NYH Annual 1960, 48.

58. Teamsters leaflets, in Pratt to Iserman, 12 February 1959, 7 July 1959; Folders 5 and 6, Box 15, NYH STP BTF.

59. Leon Fink and Brian Greenberg, *Upheaval in the Quiet Zone: A History of Hospital Workers' Union, Local 1199* (Urbana: University of Illinois Press, 1989), 82. The struck hospitals were Mount Sinai, Beth David, Jewish Hospital, Bronx Hospital, Lenox Hill, Flower-Fifth Avenue, and Beth Israel.

60. Dan Wakefield, "Hospital Workers Knock at the Door," *Dissent* 6 (Autumn 1959), 412.

61. Pratt to all employees, 16 October 1964, Folder: Unions (1964), NYH Personnel. *New York Times*, 13 November 1964. Another nineteen workers chose the Building & Construction Trades Council, but the great majority went against any union representation. The total turnout represented about 70 percent of the hospital's approximately 2,000 nonprofessional workers.

62. Barry Feinstein, interview. *22 Years, Local 420, Hospital Division of District Council 37* (New York: American Federation of State, County, and Municipal Employees, 1976) [pages unnumbered]. The most comprehensive account of DC 37's activities in the city hospitals is Jewel and Bernard Bellush, *Union Power and New York: Victor Gotbaum and DC 37* (New York: Praeger, 1984).

63. *22 Years, Local 420*. Austin to Felix, 26 May 1959, Folder: Strikes (1/59–12/59, Pt. 1), Box 298, Wagner Correspondence, NYC Mayors' Papers; Teamsters leaflet, 15 July 1959, Folder 5, Box 15, NYH STP BTF.

64. Barry Feinstein, interview.

65. Victor Gotbaum, interview.

66. Maier, *City Unions*, 54. According to other accounts, the key intermediary was Paul Hall of the Seafarers' Union.

67. Victor Gotbaum and Ella Woodley, interviews; Susan Reverby, "From Aide to Organizer: The Oral History of Lillian Roberts," in *Women of America: A History*, ed. Carol Ruth Berkin and Mary Beth Norton (Boston: Houghton Mifflin, 1979), 289–317.

68. Ella Woodley and Lillian Roberts, interviews; Bellush and Bellush, *Union Power*, 154.

69. Lillian Roberts, interview.

70. DC 37 received 5,903 of the 11,130 votes counted in the aides' category, 191 of the 287 messengers' votes, and 1,523 of the 2,162 clericals'. In the cooks' unit, the Teamsters took 168 of the 324 votes. Seventy-two percent of those eligible to vote did so. "Election Returns," 3 December 1965, Folder: Hospital Affiliations 1968, Bellush Collection. Bellush and Bellush, *Union Power*, 156, 176; David Denton, "The Union Movement in American Hospitals" (Ph.D. diss., Boston University, 1976), 226.

71. A. H. Raskin, "Politics Up-Ends the Bargaining Table," in *Public Workers and Public Unions*, ed. The American Assembly, Columbia University (Englewood Cliffs, N.J.: Prentice-Hall, 1972), 130, 132.

72. New York *Daily News*, 5 August, 1944.

Chapter 5

1. New York *Herald–Tribune*, 25 January 1965.

2. "Does New York City Have a Future?" *US News and World Report* (24 January 1966), 44–46.

3. Bellevue & Mills School Annual Report, 1966–67, 14; New York *Post*, 24 December 1966. For a summary of the major investigations between 1966 and 1971, see Robert Alford, *Health Care Politics: Ideological and Interest Group Barriers to Reform* (Chicago: University of Chicago Press, 1975), 23–101.

4. Blue Ribbon Panel, *Report to Governor Nelson A. Rockefeller on Municipal Hospitals of New York City* (April 1967), 8; Carl Berntsen, Philip Brickner, Gloria Bailey, interviews.

5. Commission of the Delivery of Personal Health Services [Piel Commission], *Community Health Services for New York City* (New York: Praeger, 1969), 499.

6. NYS Legislature, *Annual Report of the Joint Legislative Committee on the Problems of Public Health and Medicare* (31 March 1967), 12, 102; Clarence de la Chapelle, Oral History, 6, Columbia University Oral History Collection; William Nolen, "Bellevue: No One Was Ever Turned Away," *American Heritage* 38, no. 2 (February 1987), 40; Howard Rusk, "A Critically Ill Hospital," *New York Times*, 9 October 1966.

7. In 1966, the NYS Health Department assumed jurisdiction over all voluntary and proprietary hospitals in the state (previously the responsibility of the State Wel-

fare Department) and jurisdiction also over all municipal hospitals (which had previously been exempted from state oversight). *New York Times*, 22 January 1967; New York *Daily News* [undated clipping in BH Archives, but context indicates November 1966].

8. New York *Daily News*, 11 January 1967; *New York Times*, 11 January 1967; 16 January 1967; 23 January 1967.

9. Dickinson Richards, "Report to the Medical Research Planning Conference" (NYC Dept. of Health, 25 April 1957), Folder 139, Box 130, Wagner Correspondence, NYC Mayors' Papers.

10. Institute for Policy Studies, "Payments to Voluntary Hospitals as Percentage of Total City Payments for Hospital Care" [in unlabeled folder] Box 4, Bellush Collection.

11. New York *Daily News*, 7 January 1967, 19 January 1967. See also: New York *Times*, 14 December 1966, 16 December 1966; New York *Post*, 13 January 1967.

12. Bellevue and Mills Schools of Nursing, Annual Report 1966–67, 14; NYS Legislature, *Annual Report of the Joint Legislative Committee*, 24.

13. ". . . And An Attendant's View," *Fact* [month unclear] 1966, in Folder 11, Box 203, Hospital Council Papers; New York *World–Journal Tribune*, 14 October 1966.

14. E. Hugh Luckey to Arthur H. Dean and Dr. James A. Perkins, 14 December 1966, Folder 4, Box 7, Thompson Papers.

15. Arthur Zitrin, interview.

16. *New York Times*, 7 September, 1966.

17. Nora K. Piore, "Metropolitan Medical Economics," *Scientific American* 212, no. 1 (January 1965), 21. This article provides an excellent analysis of New York City's pre-Medicare health-care financing.

18. Barbara and John Ehrenreich, *American Health Empire: Power, Profits, and Politics—A Report from the Health Policy Advisory Center* (New York: Vintage, 1970), 166.

19. Howard Lewis, "Buffer Corporation Offers Hope to New York City Hospitals," *Modern Hospital* 114 (February 1970), 84.

20. Director's Report, BHC Annual Report 1966 [pages unnumbered].

21. Luckey to Dean and Perkins, 14 December 1966, Folder 4, Box 7, Thompson Papers. See also *New York Times*, 1 November 1966, 1 December 1966. During the same period, the Bellevue School of Nursing was converted from a two-year diploma school controlled by the hospital to a four-year baccalaureate program under Hunter College of the City University of New York. Bellevue's own nursing school graduated its last class in 1969.

22. Eli Ginzberg and the Conservation of Human Resources Staff, *From Health Dollars to Health Services: New York City, 1965–1985* (Totowa, N.J: Rowman & Allenheld, 1986), 24; *New York Times*, 8 December 1967; Rosemary Stevens, *Welfare Medicine in America: A Case Study of Medicaid* (New York: Free Press, 1974), 109.

23. Epilogue, *Medicaid: A Definition and a Hope*, Proceedings of a symposium conducted 12 December 1967 by the NYC Depts. of Health and Social Services (NYAM, 1968).

24. Stevens, *Welfare Medicine*, 162, 164; Barbara Ehrenreich, "New York City Medicaid: Five Steps Backward, One Forward," *Health/PAC Bulletin* (May 1969), 4; *New York Times*, 21 November 1967; New York *Daily News*, 27 November 1967; Edith M. Davis, Michael L. Millman, and Associates, *Health Care for the Urban Poor: Directions for Policy* (Totowa, N.J.: Rowman & Allanheld, 1983), 17; NYC Dept. of Health, *Materia Medicaid New York City: A Compendium of Selected Medicaid Data* (30 December 1970), 46.

25. Ehrenreich, "New York City Medicaid," 4; UHF City Hospital Visiting Committee, *Report on the Municipal Hospitals, 1967–68* (New York: UHF, 1968), 12.

26. Westermann-Miller Associates, *Bellevue Comprehensive Plan* (December 1972), 58; BH Annual; NYC Dept. of Hospitals Annual.

27. Nora Piore, Purlaine Lieberman, and James Linnane, *Health Expenditures in New York City: A Decade of Change* (Center for Community Health Systems, 1976), 7.

28. The city policy was upheld by the State Supreme Court in a suit brought by hospital community boards in 1980. *New York Times*, 16 April 1996. Budget: NYC Dept. of Hospitals, "Cost Analysis: Year Ended Dec. 31, 1967," and NYC HHC, "Cost Analysis, Year Ending Dec. 31, 1970;" both in NYC Municipal Library. Tax-levy contribution: Ehrenreich, "New York City Medicaid," 6–7. Real dollars calculated according to GDP implicit price-deflator (1992 = 100), *Economic Report of the President 1997* (Washington, D.C.: U.S. Government Printing Office, 1997), 306.

29. NYH Annual Report 1965, 26; 1966, 5.

30. Hospital records make clear that the board attributed most of the 1967 surplus to Medicaid and to Medicare. See, for instance, NYH Board of Governors Minutes, 11 November 1969. NYH Annual Report 1968, 6; 1969, 2. Barbara Ehrenreich, "HSA: On the Job Training," *Health/PAC Bulletin* (January 1970), 11.

31. *New York Times*, 5 December 1967; Rosemary Stevens, *In Sickness and in Wealth: American Hospitals in the Twentieth Century* (New York: Basic Books, 1989) 296–297.

32. John Ehrenreich, "Hospital Unions: A Long Time Coming," in *Prognosis Negative: Crisis in the Health Care System*, ed. David Kotelchuck (New York: Vintage, 1976), 261; Ehrenreich, "New York City Medicaid," 7; UHF, *Analysis of In-Patient and Out-Patient Department Income and Cost Based on Reports Submitted by UHF Voluntary General and Special Hospital Members* (1965, 1969); Piore, Lieberman, and Linnane, *Health Care Expenditures*, 9.

33. Gilbert Millstein, *New York: True North* (Garden City, N.Y.: Doubleday, 1964), 20, 23.

34. Arthur H. Dean to E. Hugh Luckey, 22 March 1968, Folder 4, Box 7, Thompson Papers.

35. *New York Times*, 29 April 1966. See also Martin Cherkasky, "Medicaid: Implications for Quality of Care," in *Medicaid: A Definition and a Hope*, 56.

36. Robb K. Burlage, *New York City's Municipal Hospitals: A Policy Review* (Washington, D.C.: Institute for Policy Studies, 1967), 51; Marcus Kogel to Lincoln Hospital Medical Board Annual Dinner, 8 October 1952, Folder 3, Box 17, Impellitteri Correspondence, NYC Mayors' Papers.

37. *New York Times*, 7 July 1966.

38. Howard J. Brown, *Familiar Faces, Hidden Lives: The Story of Homosexual Men in America Today* (New York: Harcourt Brace Jovanovich, 1976), 4, 14, 45; *New York Times*, 3 February 1975; "The Job Nobody Wanted: New York City's Chief of Health Services," *Medical World News 9* (24 May 1968), 45; Irving Leveson and Jeffrey Weiss, *Analysis of Urban Health Problems* (New York: Spectrum, 1976), 21; *New York Times*, 28 May 1968, 4 January 1970.

39. Davis, Millman, and Associates, *Health Care for the Urban Poor*, 17; NYS Legislature, *Annual Report of the Joint Legislative Committee*, 76.

40. New York *Post*, 24 December 1966.

41. *New York Times*, 4 October 1966.

42. Fitzhugh Mullan, *White Coat, Clenched Fist: The Political Education of an American Physician* (New York: Macmillan, 1976).

43. *New York Times*, 21 December 1966; Commission on the Delivery, *Community Health Services*, viii.

44. Institute for Policy Studies, *New York City's Municipal Hospitals: A Policy Review* [Burlage Report](May 1967).

45. Commission on the Delivery, *Community Health Services*; also Gerard Piel, interview.

46. Gerard Piel, interview.

47. *New York Times*, 16 December 1967, 23 December 1967; Gerard Piel, Robb Burlage, and Victor Gotbaum, interviews.

48. *New York Times*, 29 June 1966.

49. *New York Times*, 26 September 1967.

50. *New York Times*, 27 September 1967, 7 October 1967, 9 October 1967. Jewel and Bernard Bellush, *Union Power and New York: Victor Gotbaum and DC 37* (New York: Praeger, 1984), 200.

51. A. H. Raskin, "Politics Up-Ends the Bargaining Table," in *Public Workers and Public Unions*, ed. The American Assembly, Columbia University (Englewood Cliffs, N.J.: Prentice-Hall, 1972), 132; *New York Times*, 24 October 1967; Bellush and Bellush, *Union Power and New York*, 200.

52. *New York Times*, 3 April 1968, 15 April 1968; NYS Commission of Investigation, *Investigation Concerning New York City's Municipal Hospitals and the Affiliation Program*, 68; Bellush and Bellush, *Union Power and New York*, 201.

53. Gerard Piel and others have suggested that Victor Gotbaum almost single-handedly persuaded Mayor Lindsay to go ahead with the corporation proposal. Gotbaum acknowledges that he played an important role. But in any case, a review of the evidence and chronology suggests that by the spring of 1968, it was the only remaining idea that appeared politically feasible. Gerald Piel and Victor Gotbaum, interviews.

54. Rajewshar Prasad, "Health and Hospitals Corporation: A Halting Start at Change," in *The Politics of Health Care: Nine Case Studies of Innovative Planning in New York City*, ed. Herbert Harvey Hyman (New York: Praeger, 1973), 111; Barbara Ehrenreich, "New York City Tries a New Model" *Social Policy* 1 (January 1971), 30–34; Victor Gotbaum to Julie Topol, 29 July 1968, Folder: Hospital Affiliations 1968, Box 3, and Jewel Bellush's interview with union attorney Murray Gordon, who participated in these sessions, Folder: NYC Politics, 1961–1981, Box 4. Both in Bellush Collection.

55. Victor Gotbaum, interview.

56. Kramer, *New York City Health and Hospitals Corporation*, 65.

57. Ibid., 69–70.

58. *New York Times*, 7 March 1995.

59. NYS Legislature, *Annual Report of the Joint Legislative Committee*, 73, 75.

60. *New York Times*, 8 May 1967.

Chapter 6

1. Lewis R. Goldfrank, with Edward Ziegler, *Emergency Doctor* (New York: Harper & Row, 1987), 97.

2. Dick Netzer, "The Economy and the Governing of the City," in *Urban Politics New York Style*, ed. Jewel Bellush and Dick Netzer (Armonk, N.Y.: M. E. Sharpe, 1990), 62.

3. Mark H. Maier, *City Unions: Managing Discontent in New York City* (New Brunswick, N.J.: Rutgers University Press, 1987), 170–192.

4. Eric Lichten, *Class, Power, and Austerity: The New York City Fiscal Crisis* (South Hadley, Mass: Bergin & Garvey, 1986), 64, 186.

5. *Statistical Abstract of the United States 1985* (Washington D.C.: U.S. Government Printing Office, 1984), 96.

6. Bruce Vladeck, "A History of the New York Prospective Hospital Reimbursement Methodology," and Louis Caligiuri, "Bad Debt and Charity Care in New York State: Past, Present, and Future," both in UHF, *Health Care Financing in New York State: A Blueprint for Change* (1993), 7–13, 15–27; Kenneth E. Thorpe and Charles E. Phelps, "The Social Role of Not-For-Profit Organizations: Hospital Provision of Charity Care," *Economic Inquiry* 29 (July 1991), 472–484.

7. Vladeck, "History of the New York Prospective Hospital Reimbursement," 7–9.

8. Lyndon B. Johnson, "Annual Message to the Congress on the State of the Union," 8 January 1964, in *Public Papers of the Presidents of the United States: Lyndon B. Johnson, 1963–1964*, v. 1 (Washington, D.C.: U.S. Government Printing Office, 1965), 113.

9. Pascal J. Imperato, "Current Problems of Some New York City Health Agencies," *Bulletin of the NYAM*, 2d ser., 55 (May 1979), 471; Rosemary Stevens, *In Sickness and in Wealth: American Hospitals in the Twentieth Century* (New York: Basic Books, 1989), 312.

10. Victor Gotbaum, interview; *New York Times*, 16 August 1987.

11. *New York Times*, 24 December 1978.

12. Arthur Browne, Dan Collins, and Michael Goodwin, *I, Koch* (New York: Dodd, Mead, 1985), 195; Edward Koch, *Mayor* (New York: Simon & Schuster, 1984), 62, 146, 206.

13. Koch, *Mayor*, 144; Charles Brecher and Sheila Spiezio, *Privatization and Public Hospitals: Choosing Wisely for New York City* (New York: Twentieth Century Fund Press, 1995), 79; *New York Times*, 30 August 1989.

14. UHF City Hospital Visiting Committee, *State of New York City's Municipal Hospital System* (1992), 5; HHC Annual Report 1992; *New York Times*, 18 July 1992, 16 April 1996.

15. *New York Times*, 22 October 1991.

16. Bernard Weinstein, Speech, 15 November 1973, BH Archives.

17. William A. Nolen, "Happy Days at Bellevue," *Esquire* 72 (November 1969), 329.

18. Arleen Wilcox, "A View from the Municipal Hospital," presented at NYAM Annual Health Conference, *Cost Containment and Resource Allocation in Health Care*. Published in *Bulletin of the NYAM*, 2d ser., 56 (January 1980), 59; Victor Gotbaum, interview.

19. Lorinda Klein, interview.

20. Arthur D. Little, "Bellevue Hospital Center: Space and Long-Range Planning Issues. Report to the Bellevue Hospital Site Planning Task Force" (December 1985), 3; *New York Times*, 23 December 1985.

21. *New York Times,* 9 January 1989, 10 January 1989; New York *Post,* 11 January 1989, 15 January 1989.

22. Smith was convicted of the murder; his plea of insanity was rejected. After a wrongful death suit brought by Hinnant's family, Bellevue was found not guilty of having contributed to the physician's death through negligence in dealing with Smith. *New York Times*, 10 January 1989, 15 January 1989, 21 November 1989, 15 February 1996, 27 February 1996.

23. *New York Times* 15 January 1989.

24. Robert Frost, "The Death of the Hired Man," in *Robert Frost's Poems*, ed. Louis Untermeyer (New York: Washington Square Press, 1971), 65.

25. Nora Piore, Purlaine Lieberman, and James Linnane, *Health Care Expenditures in New York City: A Decade of Change* (New York: Center for Community Health Systems, 1976), 5.

26. NYH Annual Report, 1977, 7, 10; 1973, 8; 1974, 4.

27. NYH Annual Report 1975, 5.

28. Starting in 1979, the hospital began to include "essential capital improvements" in its reported annual operating deficit. Based on the first few years, during which deficits calculated under both methods were reported, it appears that the effect of the new system was to increase the reported deficit by between $1 and $3 million per year.

29. Vladeck, "History of the New York Prospective Hospital Reimbursement," 9–10.

30. The fullest account of the Zion case appears in Natalie Robins, *The Girl Who Died Twice: Every Patient's Nightmare—The Libby Zion Case and the Hidden Hazards of Hospitals* (New York: Delacorte, 1995).

31. After several levels of review, all professional charges against the house staff involved were dismissed. In Zion's negligence suit against the physicians and NYH, three of Ms. Zion's four physicians were ultimately found to have contributed to her death; NYH was described as negligent for not having provided closer supervision, but it was found not to have contributed to the young woman's death. *New York Times,* 13 January 1987; 24 March 1987; November 1994–Febuary 1995 passim; Robins, *Girl Who Died Twice*, 285 ff.

32. The Warhol case was settled in December 1991, when the hospital agreed to pay his estate an undisclosed sum. *New York Times*, 11 December 1987, 6 December 1991, 23 December 1991. *New York Times Magazine*, 24 January 1988, 16.

33. NYH Annual Report 1983. *New York Times*, 4 April 1994.

34. Robb Kendrick Burlage, "From Campus to Corporation: New York City Medical Empires, 1960–1985: Urban Planning, Regional Policy, and the Structure of Health Care" (Ph.D. diss., Cornell University, 1994), 182, 190–91.

35. This law, which applied to every hospital that operated an emergency room and received federal Medicare funding, was part of the Federal Consolidated Omnibus Reconciliation Act of 1986; its popular name was COBRA.

36. *New York Observer*, 6 May 1996.

37. BH Community Board, "Statement of Need for Bellevue Hospital's Patients, Staff and Community" (April 1989), 3, BH Archives; Walter Klein and George Reader, "Epidemic Diseases at the New York Hospital," *Bulletin of the NYAM*, 2d ser., 67 (September 1991), 450–451; *New York Times*, 22 February 1994.

38. *New York Times*, 6 December 1995; 8 July 1996.

39. *New York Times*, 29 November 1994.

40. *New York Times*, 29 November 1994.

41. *New York Times*, 26 March 1996.

42. *New York Times*, 14 April 1996.

43. *New York Times*, 8 May 1995; 19 February 1995.

44. John Billings, Sue Kaplan, and Tod Mijanovich, *Projecting Hospital Utilization and Bed Need in New York City for the Year 2000* (New York: Robert F. Wagner Graduate School of Public Service, New York University, April 1996), ii; Health Systems Agency of NYC, Inc., *New York City's Health Care System Faces Traumatic Changes* (March 1996).

45. See, for instance, UHF, *The State of New York City's Municipal Hospital System* (1994); Katherine Eban Finkelstein, "Bellevue Emergency," *New York Times Magazine* (11 February 1996), 47.

46. *New York Times*, 1 November 1997.

47. HHC, "Funds Appropriated by the City of New York for Operations" (12 January 1998). Raymond J. Baxter and Robert E. Mechanic, "The Status of Local Health Care Safety Nets," *Health Affairs* 16 no. 4 (July–August 1997), 18; Baxter and Mechanic's figure for the amount of the 1995 subsidy is somewhat lower than HHC's.

48. *New York Times*, 3 November 1995; Pamela Brier, interview.

49. Peter D. Salins, "New York Ought to Quit the Hospital Business," *New York Times*, 31 January 1987; *New York Times*, 29 August 1989. For other arguments in favor of privatization, see William B. Eimicke and Anne Lenhard Reisinger, "Privatizing HHC," *City* (Spring 1993), 69–75; Privatization Task Force, New York City Partnership, Inc., New York Chamber of Commerce and Industry, Inc., *Putting the Public First: Making New York Work through Privatization and Competition* (1993), 133–156.

50. *New York Times*, 8 July 1995; 25 July 1996.

51. Jeremiah Barondess, interview.

52. *New York Times*, 30 October 1994; Andrew Bindman, "A Public Hospital Closes," *Journal of the American Medical Association* 264 (12 December 1990), 2899–2904.

53. Kenneth Thorpe and Charles Brecher, "Improving Access to Care for the Uninsured Poor in Large Cities: Do Public Hospitals Make a Difference?" *Journal of Health Politics, Policy and Law* 12 (Summer 1987), 313–324. For further discussion, see "The Closing of Philadelphia General Hospital," *Urban Health* 7 (November 1978), 40–47; William Shonick and Walter Price, "Reorganizations of Health Agencies by Local Government in American Urban Centers: What Do They Portend for 'Public Health'?" *Milbank Memorial Fund Quarterly* 55 (March 1977), 233–271; Dwayne Banks, "Cost and Access Among Non-Profit Hospitals in Jurisdictions with and without Public Hospitals," *Applied Economics* 28 (July 1996), 875–883; Brecher and Spiezio, *Privatization and Public Hospitals*.

54. For a useful summary of these studies, see Emily Friedman, "Money Isn't Everything: Nonfinancial Barriers to Access," *Journal of the American Medical Association* 271 (18 May 1994), 1535–1538.

55. Pamela Brier, personal interview. HHC Annual Report 1993, 7–9; UHF, *Health Care Annual* (New York, 1995), 15, 39; Alan G. Hevesi, NYC Comptroller, "Unresolved Questions about Plans for Privatizing New York City Health and Hospitals Corporation Facilities" (11 December 1995), 3; *American Hospital Association Guide to the Health Care Field*, 1996–97 ed. (Chicago: American Hospital Association, 1997); HHC, "Bellevue Hospital Discharges—Demographics, Fiscal Year 95" (12 January 1998).

56. Siegel resigned in August 1995. *New York Times*, 5 March 1995; 8 May 1995.

57. Finkelstein, "Bellevue Emergency," 60; Martin Begun, interview.

58. Jeremiah Barondess, Testimony to the Committee on Health of the City Council, 26 April 1994, Barondess Commission Papers; Barondess, interview; Jeremiah Barondess, "Municipal Hospitals in New York City—A Review of the Report of the Commission to Review the Health and Hospitals Corporation." *Bulletin of the NYAM* (June 1993).

59. Billings, Kaplan, and Mijanovich, *Projecting Hospital Utilization*, 20.

60. UHF, *Health Care Annual* (New York: UHF, 1997), 46; Hevesi, "Unresolved Questions about Plans for Privatizing." 2.

61. *New York Times*, 24 February 1995.

62. James Tallon, interview; Mayoral Advisory Panel for the Health and Hospitals Corporation, *Report of the Advisory Panel on the Future of the Health and Hospitals Corporation* (August 1995).

63. *New York Times*, 29 September 1995, 27 October 1995, 29 October 1995; Denise Soffel, interview.

64. *New York Times*, 27 June 1996.

65. *New York Times*, 5 July 1996.

66. *New York Observer* (25 December 1995–1 January 1996); *New York Post*, 21 December 1995, 23 December 1995.

67. *New York Observer* (25 December 1995–1 January 1996); Paul Macielak and Lewis Goldfrank, interviews.

68. *New York Observer* (8 April 1996); U.S. Health Care Financing Administration, "Summary Statement of Deficiencies" (19 December 1995).

69. Finkelstein, "Bellevue Emergency," 52.

Conclusion

1. S. S. Goldwater, "The Hospital and the Dollar," *Modern Hospital* (July 1930), reprinted in S. S. Goldwater, *On Hospitals* (New York: Macmillan, 1947), 60.

2. NYC Dept. of Hospitals, "Department of Hospitals, City of New York, Historical Report, with Emphasis on Last Decade" [undated, but context indicates 1965], 12, Hospitals Dept. History File, NYC Municipal Library.

3. *Report of the Mayoral Commission to Review the Health and Hospitals Corporation* [Barondess Commission] (Nov. 1992), 66.

4. Marcus D. Kogel, Speech, 8 October 1952, Folder: Dept. of Hospitals, Box 17, File 3, O'Dwyer Correspondence, NYC Mayors' Papers.

5. Cited in Eric Larrabee, *The Benevolent and Necessary Institution: The New York Hospital*, 1771–1991 (New York: Doubleday, 1971), 6.

6. Edward Bellamy, *Looking Backward* (Boston: Houghton Mifflin, 1966), 56.

7. Michael Pillinger, "The Bellevue Experience," *NYU Physician* 42, no. 1 (Spring 1986), 35.

Bibliography

Oral Histories (from the Columbia University Oral
History Collection)

James Armsey
George Baehr, M.D.
David Barr, M.D.
Frank Berry, M.D.
Frederic René Coudert
B. B. Crohn, M.D.
Michael M. Davis
Miguel de Capriles
Clarence de la Chapelle, M.D.

Haven Emerson, M.D.
Homer Folks
Connie Guion, M.D.
James Hester
Louis Pink
Dickinson Richards, M.D.
Martin Steinberg, M.D.
Isabel Stewart, R.N.

Interviews

Gloria Bailey, former ward aide at BH
Jeremiah Barondess, M.D., President, New York Academy of Medicine
Martin Begun, former Vice President for External Affairs, NYU School of Medicine
Carl Berntsen, M.D., interned at NYH, served at BH
Robert Boris, D.D.S., trained at NYU Dental School
Philip Brickner, M.D., interned at BH
Pamela Brier, former Executive Director, BH
Robb K. Burlage, directed a study of the municipal hospitals, 1967
James Butler, President, Hospital Workers' Local 420, DC 37, AFSCME

E. William Davis, Jr., M.D., Vice President for Medical Affairs and Quality Assurance, NYH

Jay Dopkin, M.D., active in Council of Interns and Residents, 1970s

Saul Farber, M.D., former Dean of NYU School of Medicine; Chief of Medical Services, BH

Barry Feinstein, former Teamsters organizer at BH

Moe Foner, helped lead Local 1199's campaign in the voluntary hospitals

Lewis R. Goldfrank, M.D., Director of Emergency Department, BH

Victor Gotbaum, former head of DC 37, AFSCME

Gregory Kaladjian, former Executive Director, BH

Peter Klemperer, Assistant Vice President, Corporate Reimbursement Services, HHC

Frances Kraljic, former patient at NYH

Seth Lederman, M.D., former medical student, intern, and resident at NYH

Marjorie Lewisohn, M.D., former resident at NYH and BH, attending physician at BH

Paul F. Macielak, Vice President and Vice Provost for Public Affairs, NYH–Cornell Medical Center

David Margolis, former WPA worker at BH

Claire Meyerowitz, R.N., trained and worked at NYH

Emilio Morante, former Executive Director, North Central Bronx Hospital

Elena Padilla, health activist; former member of HHC board

Gerard Piel, headed study of the municipal hospitals in 1967

George Reader, M.D., entire medical career at NYH; rotated through BH as student

Lillian Roberts, former DC 37 organizer

John Sarno, M.D., NYU School of Medicine faculty member, rotated through BH

Haran T. Schlamm, M.D., Medical Director, BH AIDS Clinic

Denise Soffel, Health Policy Analyst, Community Service Society

Madeline Sugimoto, R.N., trained and worked at NYH

James Tallon, President, United Hospital Fund

Timothy Tempel, former Acting Executive Director, BH

Brenda Verbeck, former neighborhood resident

Aaron Wells, M.D., attending physician at NYH

Judy Wessler, Policy Coordinator, Commission on the Public's Health System

Ella Woodley, former organizer at BH for DC 37, AFSCME

Arthur Zitrin, M.D., former Director of BH Psychiatric Division

Books, Articles, and Reports

Adcock, Joe, and Cynthia Adcock. "Houston's Hospitals: The Smell of Charity." *Nation* 200, no. 1 (4 January 1965): 5–8.

Alford, Robert. *Health Care Politics: Ideological and Interest Group Barriers to Reform.* Chicago: University of Chicago Press, 1975.

Allison, Fred, Jr. "Public Hospitals—Past, Present, and Future." *Perspectives in Biology and Medicine* 36, no. 4 (Summer 1993): 596–611.

Altman, Drew. "Health Care for the Poor." *Annals of the American Academy of Political Science: Health Care Policy in America* 468 (July 1983): 103–121.

Alumnae Association of Bellevue. *Bellevue: A Short History of Bellevue Hospital and of the Training Schools.* New York: Alumnae Association of Bellevue Pension Fund Committee, 1915.

Anderson, Odin W. *Uneasy Equilibrium: Private and Public Financing of Health Services in the United States, 1875–1895.* New Haven: College & University Press, 1968.

Andrulis, Dennis P., et al., "Public Hospitals and Health Care Reform: Choices and Challenges." *American Journal of Public Health* 86, no. 2 (February 1996): 162–165.

Banks, Dwayne, "Cost and Access among Non-Profit Hospitals in Jurisdictions with and without Public Hospitals." *Applied Economics* 28 (July 1996): 875–883.

Barondess, Jeremiah. "The Academic Health Center and the Public Agenda: Whose Three-Legged Stool?" *Annals of Internal Medicine* 115, no. 12 (15 December 1991): 962–967.

————. "Municipal Hospitals in New York City—A Review of the Report of the Commission to Review the Health and Hospitals Corporation." *Bulletin of the New York Academy of Medicine* (June 1993).

Barringer, Emily. *Bowery to Bellevue: The Story of New York's First Woman Ambulance Surgeon.* New York: Norton, 1950.

Baxter, Raymond J., and Robert E. Mechanic. "The Status of Local Health Care Safety Nets." *Health Affairs* 16 (July–August 1997): 7–23.

Beauchamp, Dan E. *The Health of the Republic: Epidemics, Medicine, and Moralism as Challenges to Democracy.* Philadelphia: Temple University Press, 1988.

Bellush, Jewel. "A Municipal Hospital System: Myths and Realities." *National Civic Review* 69, no. 6 (June 1980): 313–320.

Bellush, Jewel, and Bernard Bellush. *Union Power and New York: Victor Gotbaum and DC 37.* New York: Praeger, 1984.

Bellush, Jewel, and Stephen M. David. *Race and Politics in New York City: Five Studies in Policy-Making.* New York: Praeger, 1971.

Bellush, Jewel, and Dick Netzer, eds. *Urban Politics New York Style.* Armonk: M. E. Sharpe, 1990.

Better Bellevue Association. *This Is Bellevue.* New York: Better Bellevue Association, 1965.

Billings, John, Sue Kaplan, and Tod Mijanovich. *Projecting Hospital Utilization and Bed Need in New York City for the Year 2000.* New York: Robert F. Wagner Graduate School of Public Service, New York University, April 1996.

Blue Ribbon Panel to Governor Nelson A. Rockefeller on Municipal Hospitals of New York City. *Report.* Albany, April 1967.

Brecher, Charles, and Sheila Spiezio. *Privatization and Public Hospitals: Choosing Wisely for New York City.* New York: Twentieth Century Fund Press, 1985.

Brown, E. Richard. *Rockefeller Medicine Men: Medicine and Capitalism in America.* Berkeley: University of California Press, 1979.

Brown, Howard J. "Municipal Hospitals." *Bulletin of the New York Academy of Medicine* 2d ser., 43, no. 6 (June 1967): 450–455.

Bunker, Charles Stephen. "A Study to Determine the Impact of Unionization and the Threat Thereof on New York City's Voluntary, Nonprofit Hospitals: 1959 to 1966." Ph.D. diss., George Washington University, 1968.

Burlage, Robb Kendrick. "From Campus to Corporation: New York City Medical Empires, 1960–1985: Urban Planning, Regional Policy, and the Structure of Health Care." Ph.D. diss., Cornell University, 1994.

Campion, Nardi Reeder, and Rosamond Wilfley Stanton. *Look to this Day! The Lively Education of a Great Woman Doctor: Connie Guion, M.D.* Boston: Little, Brown, 1965.

Cannings, Kathleen, and William Lazenick. "The Development of the Nursing Labor Force in the United States: A Basic Analysis." *International Journal of Health Services* 5, no. 2 (1975): 185–216.

Cherkasky, Martin. "New York City Medical Care—Some Problems and Prospects." *Bulletin of the New York Academy of Medicine* 2d ser., 39, no. 6 (June 1963): 343–348.

Commission on the Delivery of Personal Health Services [Piel Commission Report]. *Community Health Services for New York City.* New York: Praeger, 1969.

Conley, Walter H. "The Unification and Control of Public Hospitals." *1919 Proceedings of the New York State Conference on Charities and Corrections* (1920): 76–90.

Cooney James P., Jr. "Public Hospitals: We Must Love Them or Leave Them, Study Says." *Modern Hospital* 118, no. 5 (May 1972): 87–92.

Cooper, Page. *The Bellevue Story.* New York: Crowell, 1948.

Corwin, E. H. L. *The American Hospital.* New York: The Commonwealth Fund, 1946.

Coser, Rose Laub. *Life in the Ward.* East Lansing: Michigan State University Press, 1962.

Craig, John, and Michael Koleda. "The Urban Fiscal Crisis in the United States, National Health Insurance, and Municipal Hospitals." *International Journal of Health Services* 8, no. 2 (1978): 329–349.

Crane, Henry W. "History of The New York Hospital." Unpublished manuscript, 1920, New York Hospital Archives.

Cutolo, Salvatore R., M.D., with Arthur and Barbara Gelb. *Bellevue Is My Home.* Garden City: Doubleday & Company, Inc. 1956.

Damrau, William F. "The Rise of Municipal Hospital Expenditures in New York City, 1914–1954." Ph.D. diss., New York University, 1957.

Davis, Edith M., and Michael L. Millman. *Health Care for the Urban Poor: Directions for Policy.* Totowa, NJ: Rowman & Allanheld, 1983.

Davis, Leon J., and Moe Foner. "Organization and Unionization of Health Workers in the United States: The Trade Union Perspective." *International Journal of Health Services* 5, no. 1 (1975): 19–26.

Davis, Michael M. *Immigrant Health and the Community.* New York: Harper & Brothers, 1921.

———. *Clinics, Hospitals and Health Centers.* New York: Harper & Brothers, 1927.

———. *Public Medical Services: A Survey of Tax-Supported Medical Care in the United States.* Chicago: University of Chicago Press, 1937.

Davis, Michael M., and Mary C. Jarrett. *A Health Inventory of New York City: A Study of the Volume and Distribution of Health Services in the Five Boroughs.* New York: Welfare Council of New York City, 1929.

Deardorff, Neva R., and Marta Fraenkel. *Hospital Discharge Study.* Welfare Council of New York City, 1942.

de Hartog, Jan. *The Hospital.* New York: Atheneum, 1964.

Denton, David. "The Union Movement in American Hospitals." Ph.D. diss., Boston University, 1976.

de Terra, Joyce, Alan Craig Leslie, and Elsa Marshall. "A Study of Long-Stay Patients Unnecessarily Hospitalized in Municipal Hospitals." New York City Health Services Administration, March 1971.

Dicker, Albert. "An Analysis of Labor-Management Relations in Voluntary Hospitals in New York City." Ph.D. diss., City University of New York, 1964.

Doing Better and Feeling Worse, special edition of *Daedalus,* ed. John Knowles. (December 1977).

Dowling, Harry F. *City Hospitals: The Undercare of the Underprivileged.* Cambridge: Harvard University Press, 1982.

Duffy, John. *A History of Public Health in New York City, 1866–1966*. New York: Russell Sage Foundation, 1974.

Ehrenreich, Barbara. "New York City Medicaid: Five Steps Backward, One Forward." *Health/PAC Bulletin* (May 1969): 3–7.

———. "New York City Tries a New Model." *Social Policy* 1 (January 1971): 25–34.

———. "Giving Power to the People: The Early Days of Health/PAC." *Health/PAC Bulletin* 18 (December 1988): 4–8.

Ehrenreich, Barbara, and John Ehrenreich. *The American Health Empire: Power, Profits and Politics—A Report from the Health Policy Advisory Center*. New York: Vintage, 1970.

———. "Hospital Workers: Class Conflicts in the Making." *International Journal of Health Services* 5, no. 1 (1975): 43–51.

Eimicke, William B., and Anne Lenhard Reisinger. "Privatizing HHC." *City* (March 1993): 69–75.

Emerson, Haven. *Hospital Survey for New York*. New York: United Hospital Fund, 1937.

Farber, M. A., and Lawrence K. Altman. "A Great Hospital in Crisis." *New York Times Magazine* (24 January 1988), 16 ff.

Farber, Saul J. "NYU Medical Center Salutes Bellevue at 250." *NYU Physician* (March 1986): 2–23.

Faxon, N. W. "Half-Empty Hospitals." *Survey Graphic* 23, no. 12 (December 1934): 604–605.

Fink, Leon, and Brian Greenberg. *Upheaval in the Quiet Zone: A History of Hospital Workers' Union, Local 1199*. Urbana: University of Illinois Press, 1989.

Finkelstein, Katherine. "Bellevue Emergency." *New York Times Magazine* (11 February 1996), 47 ff.

Fishman, Linda E., and James D. Bentley. "The Evolution of Support for Safety-Net Hospitals." *Health Affairs* 16 (July–August 1997): 30–45.

Flexner, Abraham. *Medical Education in the United States and Canada: A Report to the Carnegie Foundation for the Advancement of Teaching*. New York: Arno Press and The New York Times, 1972.

Folks, Homer. "The City's Health—Public Hospitals: With Special Reference to New York City." *Municipal Affairs: A Quarterly Magazine* 2 (1898): 271–285.

Fossett, James W. "Medicaid and Health Reform: The Case of New York." *Health Affairs* 12, no. 3 (September 1993): 81–94.

Fraenkel, Marta, and Carl L. Erhardt. *Morbidity in the Municipal Hospitals of the City of New York: Report of an Exploratory Study in Hospital Morbidity Reporting*. New York: Russell Sage Foundation, 1955.

Freidson, Eliot, ed. *The Hospital in Modern Society*. London: The Free Press of Glencoe, 1963.

Friedman, Emily. "The End of the Line: When a Hospital Closes." *Hospitals* 52, no. 23 (1 December 1978): 69–75.

———. "Problems Plaguing Public Hospitals: Uninsured Patient Transfers, Tight Funds, Mismanagement, and Misperception." *Journal of the American Medical Association* 257, no. 15 (10 April 1987): 1850–1857.

———. "Money Isn't Everything: Nonfinancial Barriers to Access." *Journal of the American Medical Association* 271, no. 19 (18 May 1994): 1535–1538.

———. "California Public Hospitals: The Buck Has Stopped." *Journal of the American Medical Association* 277 (19 February 1997): 577–581.

Gage, Larry, et al. *America's Urban Health Safety Net: Preserving Access in the Era of Reform*. Washington, D.C.: National Association of Public Hospitals, 1994.

Gambs, John. "Hospitals and the Unions." *Survey Graphic* 26, no. 8 (August 1937): 435–439.

Gamm, Sara. "Toward Collective Bargaining in Non-Profit Hospitals: Impact of New York Law." *New York State School of Industrial and Labor Relations at Cornell Bulletin* 60 (October 1968).

Gelb, Arthur, and Barbara Gelb. "The Plus Side of the Bellevue Story." *New York Times Magazine* (2 June 1957).

Gerdes, John W. "Anticipated Directions for the Future of Public General Hospitals." *American Journal of Public Health* 59, no. 4 (April 1969): 680–688.

Gibson, Count D. Jr. "Will the Urban University Medical Center Join the Community?" *Journal of Medical Education* 45, no. 3 (March 1970): 144–148.

Giles, Dorothy. *A Candle in Her Hand*. New York: Putnam, 1949.

Gilpatrick, Eleanor G., and Paul K. Corliss. *The Occupational Structure of New York City Municipal Hospitals*. New York: Praeger, 1970.

Ginzberg, Eli. *A Pattern for Hospital Care: Final Report of the New York State Hospital Study*. New York: Columbia University Press, 1949.

Ginzberg, Eli, and the Conservation of Human Resources Staff. *From Health Dollars to Health Services: New York City, 1965–1985*. Totowa, N.J.: Rowman & Allanheld, 1986.

———, eds. *Urban Health Services: The Case of New York*. New York: Columbia University Press, 1971.

Gold, Don. *Bellevue: A Documentary of a Large Metropolitan Hospital*. New York: Harper & Row, 1975.

Goldberg, Joel H. "The Cook County Lesson: How to Cripple a Great Hospital." *Hospital Physician* (May 1972): 23–35.

Goldfrank, Lewis R. *Emergency Doctor*, with Edward Ziegler. New York: Harper & Row, 1987.

Goldstein, Nathan. "Surgery in the Past at Bellevue." *Medical Violet* (1935): 100–106.

Goldwater, S. S. "Proper Distribution of Duties among the Departments of Health, Public Charities and Bellevue & Allied Hospitals." *Proceedings of the New York State Conference on Charities and Corrections* (1914): 160–166.

———. *On Hospitals*. New York: Macmillan, 1947.

Goodrich, Charles H., Margaret Olendzki, and George G. Reader. *Welfare Medical Care: An Experiment*. Cambridge, Mass.: Harvard University Press, 1970.

Goslin, Ryllis Alexander, and Omar Pancoast Goslin. *You and Your Hospitals: A Digest of the Hospital Survey for New York*. New York: United Hospital Fund, 1938.

Health and Hospital Planning Council of Southern New York. *Hospital Closures and Mergers, New York City, 1960–1975*. New York: Health and Hospital Planning Council of Southern New York, May 1976.

Health Systems Agency of New York City, Inc. *Report on the Acute Care Hospital System in New York City*. New York, 1979.

———. *New York City's Health Care System Faces Traumatic Changes*. New York, March 1996.

Heaton, Claude Edwin. "The Origins and Growth of Bellevue Hospital." *The Academy Bookman* 12, no. 1 (1959): 3–10.

Heaton, Claude Edwin, and Alan E. Dumont. *The First 125 Years of the New York University School of Medicine, 1841–1966*. New York: New York University, 1966.

Hebberd, Robert W. "The Hospital Situation in New York City." In *Proceedings of the New York State Conference on Charities and Corrections* (1912): 133–143.

Henry, J. Norman. "The Relations of the Philadelphia General Hospital to the Private Hospitals of Philadelphia." *Medical Life* 150 (March 1933): 104–108.

Hepton, Estelle. "Battle for the Hospitals: A Study of Unionization in Non-Profit Hospitals." *New York State School of Industrial and Labor Relations at Cornell Bulletin* 49 (March 1963).

Holloman, John L. "Plans and Policies for the Operation of the Health and Hospitals Corporation." *Bulletin of the New York Academy of Medicine* 51, no. 8 (September 1975): 967–973.

Horton, Raymond D. *Municipal Labor Relations in New York City: Lessons of the Lindsay-Wagner Years.* New York: Praeger, 1973.

Hospital Council of Greater New York. *The Master Plan for Hospitals and Related Facilities for New York City.* Hospital Council of Greater New York, 1947.

"Hospital Life in New York." *Harper's New Monthly Magazine* 57 (1878): 171–189.

Howell, Joel D. *Technology in the Hospital: Transforming Patient Care in the Early Twentieth Century.* Baltimore: Johns Hopkins University Press, 1995.

Hyman, Herbert H. "Are Public Hospitals in New York City Inferior to Voluntary Nonprofit Hospitals? A Study of JCAH Hospital Surveys." *American Journal of Public Health* 76, no. 1 (January 1986): 18–22.

Hyman, Herbert Harvey, ed. *The Politics of Health Care: Nine Case Studies of Innovative Planning in New York City.* New York: Praeger, 1973.

Imperato, Pascal J. "Current Problems of Some New York City Health Agencies." *Bulletin of the New York Academy of Medicine* 2d ser., 55, no. 5 (May 1979): 463–476.

Institute for Policy Studies. *New York City's Municipal Hospitals: A Policy Review* [Burlage Report]. May 1967.

Kamerman, Sheila B., and Alfred J. Kahn, eds. *Privatization and the Welfare State.* Princeton: Princeton University Press, 1989.

Kingsdale, Jon Michael. "The Growth of Hospitals: An Economic History in Baltimore." Ph.D. diss., University of Michigan, 1981.

Klarman, Herbert. *New York City and Its Hospitals: The Roles of the Municipal and Voluntary Hospitals Serving New York City.* New York: Columbia University Press, 1963.

Klein, Walter, and George Reader. "Epidemic Diseases at The New York Hospital." *Bulletin of the New York Academy of Medicine* 2d ser., 67, no. 5 (September 1991): 439–459.

Kramer, Elizabeth Jane. *The New York City Health and Hospitals Corporation: Issues, Problems, and Prospects.* Chicago: Hospital Research and Educational Trust, 1977.

Krasner, Melvin I., ed. *Poverty and Health in New York City.* New York: United Hospital Fund, 1989.

Langner, Elinor. "Inside the Hospital Workers' Union." *New York Review of Books* 17, no. 9 (20 May 1971): 25–33.

Larrabee, Eric. *The Benevolent and Necessary Institution: The New York Hospital, 1771–1971.* New York: Doubleday, 1971.

Leavitt, Judith Walzer, and Ronald L. Numbers, eds. *Sickness and Health in America: Readings in the History of Medicine and Public Health,* 2d ed. Madison: University of Wisconsin Press, 1985.

Leveson, Irving, and Jeffrey Weiss. *Analysis of Urban Health Problems.* New York: Spectrum, 1976.

Lewinski-Corwin, E. H. *The Hospital Situation in Greater New York: Report of a Survey of Hospitals in New York City by the Public Health Committee of the New York Academy of Medicine.* New York: Putnam, 1924.

Lewis, Howard L. "'Buffer' Corporation Offers Hope to New York City Hospitals." *Modern Hospital* 114, no. 12 (February 1970): 84–89.

Local 420, Hospital Division, District Council 37. *22 Years, Local 420, Hospital Division of District Council 37.* New York: American Federation of State, County and Municipal Employees, 1976.

Lopez, Frank W. "The Bellevue Connection." *NYU Physician* (March 1983).

Ludmerer, Kenneth. *Learning to Heal: The Development of American Medical Education.* New York: Basic Books, 1985.

Maier, Mark H. *City Unions: Managing Discontent in New York City.* New Brunswick: Rutgers University Press, 1987.

Manning, Henry. "The Future Governance of Public Hospitals." *Bulletin of the New York Academy of Medicine* 2d ser., 45, no. 7 (July 1969): 702–712.

Markowitz, Gerald, and David Rosner. "Seeking Common Ground: A History of Labor and Blue Cross." *Journal of Health Politics, Policy and Law* 16, no. 4 (December 1991): 695–718.

Maynard, Aubré de L. *Surgeons to the Poor: The Harlem Hospital Story.* New York: Appleton-Century-Crofts, 1978.

Maynard, Lorraine. *Bellevue.* New York: Julian Messner, 1940.

Mayoral Advisory Panel for the Health and Hospitals Corporation. *Report of the Advisory Panel on the Future of the Health and Hospitals Corporation.* New York, August 1995.

McDermott, Walsh. "Social Ramifications of Control of Microbial Disease." *Johns Hopkins Medical Journal* 151 (1982): 302–312.

Melosh, Barbara. *"The Physician's Hand": Work Culture and Conflict in American Nursing.* Philadelphia: Temple University Press, 1982.

Milliken, Ralph, and Dennis D. Pointer. "Organization and Delivery of Public Medical Services in New York City." *New York State Journal of Medicine* 74, no. 1, pt. 1 (January 1974): 98–104.

Mottus, Jane E. *New York Nightingales: The Emergence of the Nursing Profession at Bellevue and New York Hospital, 1850–1920.* Ann Arbor, Mich.: UMI Research Press, 1981.

Nesbitt, Susan, and Melvin Krasner. *The Financial Condition of New York City Voluntary Hospitals: The First Year of NYPHRM.* New York: United Hospital Fund, December 1985.

"New Management for Bellevue and Allied Hospitals." *Charities* 8, no. 6 (8 February 1902): 137–139.

New York Academy of Medicine, Committee on Public Health Relations. "The Municipal Hospitals of New York City." *Bulletin of the New York Academy of Medicine* 2d ser., 43, no. 5 (May 1967): 435–442.

New York City Board of Estimate, *Report of the Committee on Inquiry into the Departments of Health, Charities and Bellevue & Allied Hospitals.* New York, 1913.

New York City Board of Estimate and Apportionment, Committee on Hospitals. *Report on the Program for the Improvement and Construction of Hospitals and Additions Thereto.* New York, 19 June 1925.

New York City Commission on Hospitals. *Report.* New York: Martin B. Brown Press, 1909.

New York City Department of Hospitals. *Report by the Mayor's Committee on the Needs of the Department of Hospitals.* New York, 17 February 1950.

New York City Partnership, Inc., and New York Chamber of Commerce and Industry, Inc. *Putting the Public First: Making New York Work Through Privatization and Competition.* New York, 1993.

New York City Planning Commission. *Plan for New York City: A Proposal.* New York: Department of City Planning, 1969.

"New York City's Troubled Hospital System." *Urban Health* 6, no. 1 (February 1977): 16–17, 38–43.

New York Herald-Tribune, *New York City in Crisis.* New York: McKay, 1965.

New York State Commission of Investigation. *An Investigation Concerning New York City's Municipal Hospitals and the Affiliation Program.* Albany, March 1969.

New York State Legislature, Joint Committee on the Problems of Public Health and Medicare. *Annual Report: Legislative Document #40.* Albany, 31 March 1967.

New York State Study Commission for New York City. *Health Care Needs and the New York City Health & Hospitals Corporation.* Albany, April 1973.

Nolen, William A. "Happy Days at Bellevue," *Esquire* 72, no. 11 (November 1969), 270, 329.

———. "Bellevue: No One Was Ever Turned Away." *American Heritage* 38 (February 1987): 36–43.

Norton, Rupert. "Municipal Hospitals and Their Relation to the Community." *Modern Hospital* 1, no. 1 (September 1913): 43–44.

Perrott, G. St J., Edgar Sydenstricker, and Selwyn Collins. "Medical Care during the Depression: A Preliminary Report upon a Survey of Wage-Earning Families in Seven Large Cities." *Milbank Memorial Fund Quarterly* 12, no. 2 (April 1934): 99–114.

Piore, Nora K. "Metropolitan Medical Economics." *Scientific American* 212, no. 1 (January 1965): 19–27.

Piore, Nora, Purlaine Lieberman, and James Linnane. *Health Expenditures in New York City: A Decade of Change.* New York: Center for Community Health Systems, 1976.

———. "Public Expenditures and Private Control? Health Care Dilemmas in New York City." *Milbank Memorial Fund Quarterly* 55, no. 1 (December 1977): 79–116.

Pomrinse, S. David. "Hospital Beds in New York City—'The Numbers Game'." *Bulletin of the New York Academy of Medicine* 2d ser., 55, no. 9 (October 1979): 875–885.

Pugh, J. W. "Some Impressions of American Hospitals." *University College Hospital Magazine* 14, no. 1 (February 1929): 20–23.

Queen, Robert I. *History of the Municipal Hospitals and Institutions.* New York Health & Hospitals Corporation, 18 February 1971.

Rein, Martin, and Lee Rainwater, eds. *The Public-Private Interplay in Social Protection: A Comparative Study.* Armonk, N.Y.: M. E. Sharpe, 1986.

Report of the Mayoral Commission to Review the Health and Hospitals Corporation [Barondess Commission]. November 1992.

Reverby, Susan. "From Aide to Organizer: The Oral History of Lillian Roberts." In *Women of Americas: A History,* 289–317, ed. Carol Ruth Berkin and Mary Beth Norton. Boston: Houghton Mifflin, 1979.

———. *Ordered to Care: The Dilemma of American Nursing, 1850–1945.* Cambridge: Cambridge University Press, 1987.

Reverby, Susan, and David Rosner, eds. *Health Care in America: Essays in Social History.* Philadelphia: Temple University Press, 1979.

Reznikoff, Paul. "Salute to The New York Hospital, 1927–1971." *New York State Journal of Medicine* 72 (15 Sept. 1972): 2351–2358.

Rice, Frederick. "Obstetrics at Bellevue Hospital." *Bellevue Violet* (1929): 93–95.

Rice, Louis. "The 'Productive' Years." *NYU Physician* (March 1986): 28–31.

Riesman, David. "How the New Blockley Came into Being." *Medical Life* 150 (March 1933): 137–148.

Robins, Natalie. *The Girl Who Died Twice: Every Patient's Nightmare—The Libby Zion Case and the Hidden Hazards of Hospitals.* New York: Delacorte, 1995.

Robinson, G. Canby. *Adventures in Medical Education: A Personal Narrative of the Great Advance of American Medicine.* Cambridge, Mass.: Harvard University Press, 1957.

Roper, Elmo, and Associates. *The Public's Attitudes toward Hospitals in New York City and Their Financing.* New York: United Hospital Fund, 1958.

Rosenberg, Charles E. "From Almshouse to Hospital: The Shaping of Philadelphia General Hospital." *Milbank Memorial Fund Quarterly* 60, no. 1 (1982): 108–154.

———. *The Care of Strangers: The Rise of America's Hospital System.* New York: Basic Books, 1987.

Rosner, David. "Health Care for the 'Truly Needy': Nineteenth Century Origins of the Concept." *Milbank Memorial Fund Quarterly* 60, no. 3 (1982): 355–385.

———. *A Once Charitable Enterprise: Hospitals and Health Care in Brooklyn and New York, 1885–1915.* Cambridge: Cambridge University Press, 1982.

Ross, Mary. "Crisis in the Hospitals." *Survey Graphic* (July 1933): 346–366.

Rossman, John C., and S. David Pomrinse. "New York City." In *Health Care in Big Cities,* 50–79, ed. Leslie H. W. Paine, New York: St. Martin's, 1978.

Rothman, David J. "The Public Presentation of Blue Cross, 1935–65." *Journal of Health Politics, Policy and Law* 16 (Winter 1991): 671–693.

Rowland, Diane, "Medicaid at 30: New Challenges for the Nation's Health Safety Net." *Journal of the American Medical Association* 274 (19 July 1995): 271–273.

Russell, William Logie. *The New York Hospital: A History of the Psychiatric Service, 1771–1936.* New York: Columbia University Press, 1945.

Schneider, David M., and Albert Deutsch. *History of Public Welfare in New York State, 1867–1940.* Chicago: University of Chicago Press, 1941.

Shonick, William, and Walter Price. "Reorganizations of Health Agencies by Local Government in American Urban Centers; What Do They Portend for 'Public Health'?" *Milbank Memorial Fund Quarterly* 55, no. 2 (March 1977): 233–271.

Society of The New York Hospital. "Condensed History of the Society of The New York Hospital Compiled from Its Records, 1769–1921." [no date].

———. *The New York Hospital: A City of Healing—A Report on Progress by the Society of The New York Hospital.* New York: Society of The New York Hospital, 1935.

———. *So Near the Gods.* New York: Society of The New York Hospital,1938.

Starr, John. *Hospital City: The Story of the Men and Women of Bellevue.* New York: Crown, 1957.

Starr, Paul. *The Social Transformation of American Medicine.* New York: Basic Books, 1982.

State Charities Aid Association, Standing Committee on Hospitals. *New Hospitals Needed in Greater New York.* New York: State Charities Aid Association, 1908.

Staupers, Mabel Keaton. *No Time for Prejudice: A Story of the Integration of Negroes in Nursing in the United States.* New York: Macmillan, 1961.

Stevens, Robert, and Rosemary Stevens. *Welfare Medicine in America: A Case Study of Medicaid.* New York: Free Press, 1974.

Stevens, Rosemary. *American Medicine and the Public Interest.* New Haven: Yale University Press, 1971.

————. *In Sickness and in Wealth: American Hospitals in the Twentieth Century*. New York: Basic Books, 1989.

Thompson, John D., and Grace Goldin. *The Hospital: A Social and Architectural History*. New Haven: Yale University Press, 1975.

"Transfer of Dying Hospital Patients." *Charities* 8, no. 4 (25 January 1902): 83.

Trussell, Ray. "The Municipal Hospital System in Transition." *Bulletin of the New York Academy of Medicine* 2d ser., 38, no. 4 (April 1962): 221–236.

————. "Current Efforts in the Municipal Hospitals." *Bulletin of the New York Academy of Medicine* 2d ser., 43, no. 3 (March 1967): 211–218.

United Hospital Fund, Committee on Dispensary Development. *Medical Care for a Million People: A Report on Clinics in New York City and of the Six Years' Work of the Committee, 1920–1926*. New York: United Hospital Fund, 1927.

Vogel, Morris J. *The Invention of the Modern Hospital: Boston, 1870–1930*. Chicago: University of Chicago Press, 1980.

Vogel, Morris J., and Charles E. Rosenberg, eds. *The Therapeutic Revolution: Essays in the Social History of Medicine*. Philadelphia: University of Pennsylvania Press, 1979.

Wakefield, Dan. "Hospital Workers Knock at the Door." *Dissent* 6, no. 4 (1959): 412–416.

————. "Victims of Charity." *Nation* 188, no.11 (14 March 1959): 226–229.

Weissman, Joel. "Uncompensated Hospital Care: Will It Be There If We Need It?" *Journal of the American Medical Association* 276 (11 September 1996): 823–828.

Weissmann, Gerald. "Holmes and Watson at Bellevue." *NYU Physician* (March 1986): 25–27.

Westermann-Miller Associates. *Bellevue Comprehensive Plan*. New York, December 1972.

Wright, Henry C. "Proper Distribution of Duties among the Departments of Health, Public Charities and Bellevue & Allied Hospitals—Defects of the Present System." *Proceedings of the New York State Conference of Charities and Corrections* (1914): 146–160.

Young, Gary J. et al. "Does the Sale of Nonprofit Hospitals Threaten Health Care for the Poor?" *Health Affairs* 16 (January–February 1997): 137–141.

Zisowitz, Milton L. *One Patient at a Time: A Medical Center at Work*. New York: Random House, 1961.

Index